Peter Weverka

San Francisco ◆ Paris ◆ Düsseldorf ◆ Soest ◆ London

Associate Publisher: Cheryl Applewood
Contracts and Licensing Manager: Kristine O'Callaghan
Acquisitions & Developmental Editor: Sherry Bonelli
Editor: Malka Geffen
Production Editor: Teresa Trego
Technical Editor: JR Jenkins
Book Designer: Maureen Forys, Happenstance Type-O-Rama
Electronic Publishing Specialist: Maureen Forys, Happenstance Type-O-Rama
Proofreaders: Amey Garber, Camera Obscura, Suzanne Stein, Laurie O'Connell
Indexer: Lynnzee Elze
CD Coordinator: Kara Schwartz
Cover Designer: Gorska Design
Cover Illustrator/Photographer: Gorska Design

Library of Congress Card Number: 00-102138

ISBN: 0-7821-2750-9

Manufactured in the United States of America

10 9 8 7 6 5 4 3 2 1

Software License Agreement: Terms and Conditions

The media and/or any online materials accompanying this book that are available now or in the future contain programs and/or text files (the "Software") to be used in connection with the book. SYBEX hereby grants to you a license to use the Software, subject to the terms that follow. Your purchase, acceptance, or use of the Software will constitute your acceptance of such terms.

The Software compilation is the property of SYBEX unless otherwise indicated and is protected by copyright to SYBEX or other copyright owner(s) as indicated in the media files (the "Owner(s)"). You are hereby granted a single-user license to use the Software for your personal, noncommercial use only. You may not reproduce, sell, distribute, publish, circulate, or commercially exploit the Software, or any portion thereof, without the written consent of SYBEX and the specific copyright owner(s) of any component software included on this media.

In the event that the Software or components include specific license requirements or end-user agreements, statements of condition, disclaimers, limitations or warranties ("End-User License"), those End-User Licenses supersede the terms and conditions herein as to that particular Software component. Your purchase, acceptance, or use of the Software will constitute your acceptance of such End-User Licenses.

By purchase, use or acceptance of the Software you further agree to comply with all export laws and regulations of the United States as such laws and regulations may exist from time to time.

Software Support

Components of the supplemental Software and any offers associated with them may be supported by the specific Owner(s) of that material, but they are not supported by SYBEX. Information regarding any available support may be obtained from the Owner(s) using the information provided in the appropriate read.me files or listed elsewhere on the media.

Should the manufacturer(s) or other Owner(s) cease to offer support or decline to honor any offer, SYBEX bears no responsibility. This notice concerning support for the Software is provided for your information only. SYBEX is not the agent or principal of the Owner(s), and SYBEX is in no way responsible for providing any support for the Software, nor is it liable or responsible for any support provided, or not provided, by the Owner(s).

Warranty

SYBEX warrants the enclosed media to be free of physical defects for a period of ninety (90) days after purchase. The Software is not available from SYBEX in any other form or media than that enclosed herein or posted to *www.sybex.com*. If you discover a defect in the media during this warranty period, you may obtain a replacement of identical format at no charge by sending the defective media, postage prepaid, with proof of purchase to:

SYBEX Inc.
Customer Service Department
1151 Marina Village Parkway
Alameda, CA 94501
(510) 523-8233
Fax: (510) 523-2373
e-mail: info@sybex.com
WEB: HTTP://WWW.SYBEX.COM

After the 90-day period, you can obtain replacement media of identical format by sending us the defective disk, proof of purchase, and a check or money order for $10, payable to SYBEX.

Disclaimer

SYBEX makes no warranty or representation, either expressed or implied, with respect to the Software or its contents, quality, performance, merchantability, or fitness for a particular purpose. In no event will SYBEX, its distributors, or dealers be liable to you or any other party for direct, indirect, special, incidental, consequential, or other damages arising out of the use of or inability to use the Software or its contents even if advised of the possibility of such damage. In the event that the Software includes an online update feature, SYBEX further disclaims any obligation to provide this feature for any specific duration other than the initial posting.

The exclusion of implied warranties is not permitted by some states. Therefore, the above exclusion may not apply to you. This warranty provides you with specific legal rights; there may be other rights that you may have that vary from state to state. The pricing of the book with the Software by SYBEX reflects the allocation of risk and limitations on liability contained in this agreement of Terms and Conditions.

Shareware Distribution

This Software may contain various programs that are distributed as shareware. Copyright laws apply to both shareware and ordinary commercial software, and the copyright Owner(s) retains all rights. If you try a shareware program and continue using it, you are expected to register it. Individual programs differ on details of trial periods, registration, and payment. Please observe the requirements stated in appropriate files.

Copy Protection

The Software in whole or in part may or may not be copy-protected or encrypted. However, in all cases, reselling or redistributing these files without authorization is expressly forbidden except as specifically provided for by the Owner(s) therein.

We fully guarantee your satisfaction. If not completely satisfied with *Instant Web Pages!*, just return the book, the CD, and a copy of your receipt within 30 days and Sybex will refund your money.

Acknowledgments

This book owes a lot to many hard-working people at the offices of Sybex in Alameda, California. I would especially like to thank Acquisitions Editor Sherry Bonelli for giving me the opportunity to write this book and for suggesting how to make this book a better one.

Thanks go as well to Cheryl Applewood, who gave my name to Sherry and who showed me, many years ago when we were both editors at Sybex, how to take a pencil and eraser to a manuscript and turn it into a book.

Many thanks to Malka Geffen, this book's copy editor, for wielding the editorial scalpel with such skill, and to Teresa Trego, the production editor, for keeping everything on track.

Technical Editor JR Jenkins dogged me every inch of the way to make sure that all the instructions in this book are correct, and I thank him for his work.

Special thanks to Maureen Forys for her wonderful book design and for laying out this book.

Many thanks also go to the good people at Sierra: Mark Winters, Daryl Joslin, Bob Brennecke, Cherie Lutz, JR Jenkins, Carol Lane, and Elon Gasper.

Finally, thanks to my family—Sofia, Henry, and Addie—for putting up with my vampire-like work schedule and my eerie demeanor at daybreak.

Peter Weverka
San Francisco
March, 2000

For the St. Francis Fountain &
Candy Store, may she rest in peace.

Contents

Introduction *xiii*

Part 1 Getting Ready to Create a Web Site **1**

Chapter 1 Getting Acquainted with Web Studio **3**

Starting Web Studio 4
Introducing the Web Studio Screen 5
A Look at the Different Parts of the Web Studio Screen 6
Changing the Web Studio Screen to Your Liking 7
A Quick Look at the Web Galleries 9

Chapter 2 What You Need to Know before You Begin **11**

Selecting an Internet Service Provider (ISP) to Host Your Web Site 12
Constructing Web Pages One Piece, or Object, at a Time 14
Saving Your Web Site 16
Saving the Work You Do in Web Studio 16
Saving a Backup Copy of Your Work 18
Seeing What Your Web Page Will Look Like to Web Surfers 18
Previewing Your Web Site in the Preview Window 19
Switching between the Preview Window and Web Site Window 21
Ten Tips for Designing an Attractive Web Site with Web Studio 22
1. Ask Yourself, "Who's My Audience?" 22
2. Be Consistent from Page to Page 23
3. Use the Home Page as an Introductory Page to Your Site 23
4. Divide Your Web Site into Distinct Topics, One to a Page 23
5. Hyperlink Your Site to Other Sites on the Internet 24
6. Choose Page Backgrounds Carefully 25
7. Write the Text and Assemble the Graphics Beforehand 26
8. Don't Overload Your Pages with Too Many Gizmos 26
9. Learn the Many Ways to Align Objects 27
10. Use Web Studio's Special FX Tools to Tweak Images 27

Part 2 The Basics: Creating Web Pages **29**

Chapter 3 Constructing Your Web Pages **31**

Creating a Web Site 32
Opening a Web Site You Have Been Working On 34

Adding and Removing Web Pages 34
- Adding a New Page to a Web Site 34
- Deleting a Web Page from a Web Site 37

Changing the Name of a Web Page 37
Choosing Which Page Is the Home Page 39
Establishing the Page Size and Page Margins 39
- Changing the Size of Web Pages 39
- Changing the Size of Page Margins 41

Techniques for Handling Page Windows 41

Chapter 4 Laying Out a Web Page 43

Placing Objects on a Web Page 44
Selecting an Object or Objects 46
Positioning an Object on a Web Page 47
Changing the Size and Shape of Objects 48
- Changing an Object's Size or Shape 49
- Preventing an Object from Changing Size 50
- Making Objects the Same Size 50

Merging Objects So They Are Easier to Work With 51
Quickly Copying an Object 52
Aligning and Spacing Objects on the Page 53
- Aligning Objects with Respect to One Another 53
- Spacing Objects Evenly on the Page 54

When Objects Overlap: Deciding Which Goes Where 55

Chapter 5 Entering the Text for Your Web Site 59

Putting Text on a Web Page 60
- Dragging a Text Object onto the Page 60
- Getting Text from a File You've Already Written 61
- Importing a Paragraph or Two with the Paste Command 62

Editing the Text 63
Spell-Checking a Web Page 63
Formatting Headings and Other Text 65
- Boldfacing, Italicizing, and Underlining Text 65
- Choosing a Font and Font Size for Text 66
- Changing the Color of Text 69
- Choosing a Background Color for Text 70

Laying Out Text on a Web Page 71
- Left-Justifying, Centering, and Right-Justifying Text 71
- Indenting Text 72

Making Text Scroll on the Page 73

Chapter 6 Decorating Your Web Pages 75

Choosing a Background Color, Pattern, or Picture 76
- Using a Solid Color as the Background 76
- Decorating Pages with a Pattern 78

Tweaking a Background in the Special FX Gallery 80
Importing a Graphic for Use as the Background 85
Using Text as the Background 87
Making the Background Scroll 88
Removing the Background 89
Making the Background Show through an Object 89
Dividers for Breaking a Page into Different Parts 91
Placing a Divider across a Web Page 92
Dividing the Sides of a Page 93
Signs for Sprucing Up Web Pages 93

Chapter 7 Putting Hyperlinks on Your Web Pages 95

All about Hyperlinks 96
Managing the Links Gallery 96
A Quick Tour of the Links Gallery 97
Adding Your Own Hyperlinks to the Links Gallery 98
Handling Hyperlinks in the Links Gallery 100
Hyperlinks for Making Your Web Page Jump 100
Turning an Object into a Hyperlink 101
The Quick Way to Turn a Graphic, Button, or Sign into a Hyperlink 102
Turning a Word or Phrase into a Hyperlink 103
Linking One Page on a Site to Another Page 104
Linking Two Different Places on the Same Web Page 105
Removing a Hyperlink 108
Changing the Color of Text Links 108

Part 3 Advanced Techniques for Advanced Web Pages 111

Chapter 8 Handling Graphics, Photos, and Clip Art Images 113

Putting an Image on a Web Page 114
Getting an Image from the Photos or Clipart Gallery 114
Bringing in a Photo or Graphic of Your Own 115
Scanning a Graphic into a Web Page 116
Copying Pictures from the Internet 118
Writing an "Alternate Text Message" for Images 119
Special FX for Altering Images 121
Changing an Image's Orientation 122
Changing an Image's Shading, Tint, or Color Scheme 122
Changing an Image's Contours 123
Changing an Image's Look 124
Putting Buttons on a Page 125
Keeping Your Favorite Images in the My Stuff Gallery 126
Putting an Item in the My Stuff Gallery 127

Rearranging Items in the My Stuff Gallery 129
Removing an Item from the My Stuff Gallery 129

Chapter 9 Doing the Fancy Stuff—Animations, Sounds, and Slides 131

Animations to Make a Web Page Come Alive 132
All About Sounds 134
Getting a Sound from the Sounds Gallery 134
Playing a Sound of Your Own 136
Choosing How Often a Sound Is Played 137
Removing Sounds from Web Pages and Objects 139
Putting a Slide Show on a Web Page 139
Putting Together the Slide Show 140
Revising a Slideshow 144

Chapter 10 Putting "Cool Stuff" on Your Web Pages 147

Placing a Cool Stuff Object on a Web Page 148
Telling Your Visitors the Date and Time 149
Dropping a Calendar on a Page 149
Showing Your Visitors the Date 150
Showing Your Visitors the Time 150
Informing Visitors When You Last Modified Your Site 151
Including a Search Engine with Your Web Site 151
Inviting Others to Send E-Mail Messages 152

Chapter 11 Printing Your Web Pages 155

The Two Ways to Print Web Pages 156
Saving and Printing a Web Page as a Bitmap Graphic 156
Printing Web Pages in Web Studio 158
Choosing a Paper Size and Orientation 159
Printing the Web Page 160

Chapter 12 Entering Your Own HTML in Web Studio 161

The Three Ways to Enter HTML 162
The Basics of Inserting HTML in Web Studio 162
Inserting HTML Items Where You Want Them to Go 164
Inserting HTML Items with Respect to the Page 166
Inserting HTML Items with Respect to an Object 167

Part 4 Launching Your Web Site on the Internet 169

Chapter 13 Putting on the Finishing Touches 171

Describing Your Site So That Others Can Find It on the Internet 172
Choosing Which Kind of HTML to Use on Your Web Pages 174

Chapter 14 **Uploading Your Web Site to Your Internet Service Provider** 177
What You Need to Know Before You Begin 178
Uploading a Web Site for the First Time 179
What to Do if the Upload Fails 182
Uploading a Web Site 184
Uploading Your Web Site to a Place on the Company Network 186

Chapter 15 **Making Sure Your Site Is All It Should Be** 187
Seeing How Long the Pages Take to Download 188
Making Sure the Links Work 189
Viewing Your Web Site through More Than One Browser 189
Viewing Your Web Pages at Different Resolutions 190
Registering a Domain Name for Your Web Site 192
Promoting Your Web Site 194

Appendix A **Installing Web Studio and Internet Explorer 5** 197

Appendix B **Getting the Help You Need** 205

Appendix C **The Ins and Outs of Internet Explorer 5** 211

Appendix D **Speed Techniques for Working with Web Studio** 221

Appendix E **Glossary of Internet and Web Studio Terminology** 229

Index *235*

Introduction

This book is your key to understanding Web Studio 2.0. It looks into every nook and cranny of the program—from creating a Web site to including HTML on a Web page. Along the way, you get design tips and practical instructions for creating a Web site. You learn how to make Web pages that sing. You discover how to put together a Web site that others will find useful and appealing.

At the back of this book is a CD with the Web Studio 2.0 software. As the owner of this book, you can dive in right away. You can load Web Studio on your computer and—no kidding—create a rudimentary Web site in a matter of minutes.

This book presents topics in such a way that you can look up instructions in a hurry. You will find lots of numbered lists and labeled graphics so you know exactly how to complete a task or solve a problem. You will find many cross-references so you know where to turn if one part of the book doesn't completely address your current task. With this book and Web Studio 2.0, you can build a Web site and stake your claim to a part of the Internet.

What's in This Book, Anyway?

To find the information you need in this book, your best bet is to go to the index or table of contents. Other than that, this book is divided into fifteen chapters and four appendices, and you are invited to browse in one place or another until you find what you are looking for.

Chapter 1, "Getting Acquainted with Web Studio," describes the basics of using the program. You learn how to start and close Web Studio and become familiar with the different parts of the screen and the Web Galleries.

Chapter 2, "What You Need to Know Before You Begin," explains how to choose an Internet Service Provider, save your Web site, back up your work, and preview a Web site so you can see what it looks like on the Internet. You will also find ten design tips in this chapter.

Chapter 3, "Constructing Your Web Pages," explains how to build the framework of a Web site. You discover how to add and remove Web pages, choose a home page, and establish the size of pages, among other tasks.

Chapter 4, "Laying Out a Web Page," describes what objects are and how you can use them to position and align the elements on a Web page. You also learn how to change the size of, move, and merge objects.

Chapter 5, "Entering the Text for Your Web Site," explains how to enter, align, indent, and make text scroll on the page. You also learn how to choose fonts and font sizes.

Chapter 6, "Decorating Your Web Pages," looks into techniques for sprucing up a Web page. Topics include choosing a page background, using the Special FX tools on the background, signs, and dividers.

Chapter 7, "Putting Hyperlinks on Your Web Pages," explains how to link your site to others on the Internet. You discover how to create hyperlinks that go from Web site to Web site, from Web page to Web page, and from one place to another place on the same Web page.

Chapter 8, "Handling Graphics, Photos, and Clip Art Images" explains the thousand and one things you can do to graphics, photos, and clip art images with the tools in the Special FX Gallery. You also learn how to put buttons on a page, place your own graphics on a Web page, and scan an item for a Web page.

Chapter 9, "Doing the Fancy Stuff—Animations, Sounds, and Slides," looks into the many different ways to make sound a part of a Web site. It also shows how to present a slide show and a moving image on a Web page.

Chapter 10, "Putting 'Cool Stuff' on Your Web Pages," takes you on a tour of the Cool Stuff Gallery. You find out how to place a calendar and even a search engine on a Web page. You also learn ways to help others contact you by e-mail.

Chapter 11, "Printing Your Web Pages," explains how to render your Web pages on that old-fashioned device, the printer.

Chapter 12, "Entering Your Own HTML in Web Studio," shows how to insert a banner on a Web page and how to code a Web page on your own. You also learn a couple of tricks for importing HTML from other programs.

Chapter 13, "Putting on the Finishing Touches," describes how to increase the chances of your Web site being found in Web searches.

Chapter 14, "Uploading Your Web Site to Your Internet Service Provider," explains how you can upload a Web site to the Internet without leaving Web Studio. You learn how uploading works, what you need to know to upload, and what to do if you can't manage to upload your Web site to an ISP.

Chapter 15, "Making Sure Your Web Site Is All It Should Be," offers advice for fine-tuning your Web site. You also learn how to publicize your Web site and register a domain name.

Appendix A, "Installing Web Studio and Internet Explorer 5," explains how to install the Web Studio 2.0 software on the companion CD. You also learn how to install Internet Explorer 5, which is also found on the CD that comes with this book.

Appendix B, "Getting the Help You Need," demonstrates how to use the Help program that comes with Web Studio 2.0.

Appendix C, "The Ins and Outs of Internet Explorer 5," shows how to surf the Internet, search for information, and bookmark Web sites with Internet Explorer.

Appendix D, "Speed Techniques for Working with Web Studio," briefly describes the techniques that I have found especially useful for getting work done quickly in Web Studio.

The Glossary, which is found at the end of the book, explains Internet and Web Studio terminology.

Conventions Used in This Book

To help you figure things out quickly and get the most out of this book, I've adopted several conventions.

To show you how to give commands, I use the ➢ symbol. For example, you can choose File ➢ Save to save the work you did on a Web site. The ➢ is just a shorthand way of saying, "Choose Save from the File menu."

Margin Definition
Look in the margin to find definitions of Internet and Web Studio terms.

Where you see letters in boldface text in this book, it means that you should type the letters. For example, if you read "Type **www.sybex.com** in the Address bar," do exactly that. Type the letters that appear in boldface.

When a word appears in **this font**, look in the margin for a definition of the word. You will find many word definitions in the margins of this book. You can also turn to the Glossary to find word definitions.

Besides word definitions, you will also find cross-references in the margin. Cross-references tell you where to turn in the book for more information.

Tip

When you see a Tip box like this one, prick up your ears and read attentively, because this is where you will find timesaving tips and techniques that will make you a better user of Web Studio.

Warning

When I describe a task that you might regret doing later or that you should think carefully about doing, I do so in a Warning like this one.

About the Author 

Peter Weverka is the author of 25 computer books, including *Windows 98 for Busy People, Money 2000 for Dummies, The Complete Reference: Word 2000,* and *Word 2000 for Dummies Quick Reference.* His articles and stories—none related to computers, thankfully—have appeared in *Harper's, Spy,* and other magazines for grownups.

Part 1

Getting Ready to Create a Web Site

Before you can create your first Web site, you need to know one or two things about Web Studio. Part 1 introduces the Web Studio screen and shows you how to get around inside it. You'll also find out how Web pages are displayed, the principles of constructing a Web site, and how to create and save a Web site.

Getting Ready to Create a Web Site

Chapter 1 • Getting Acquainted with Web Studio. 3
Chapter 2 • What You Need to Know before You Begin. 11

Chapter 1

Getting Acquainted with Web Studio

This chapter will get you started with Web Studio in a hurry. You'll learn which commands to give and which buttons to click to get around in Web Studio. You'll also find out how to rearrange the screen to your liking so that Web Studio is a comfortable place to create Web pages. Finally, to help you grasp all the wonderful things you can do in Web Studio, this chapter briefly describes the Web Galleries.

- Starting Web Studio
- Getting familiar with the Web Studio screen
- Making the screen work your way
- A quick look at the Web Galleries

Starting Web Studio

Appendix A explains how to install Web Studio on your computer.

Starting Web Studio is as easy as falling off a log. Follow these steps:

1. Click the Start button. You will find it on the left side of the Windows taskbar.
2. Choose Programs.
3. Choose Sierra.
4. Choose Web Studio 2.0.
5. Choose Web Studio.

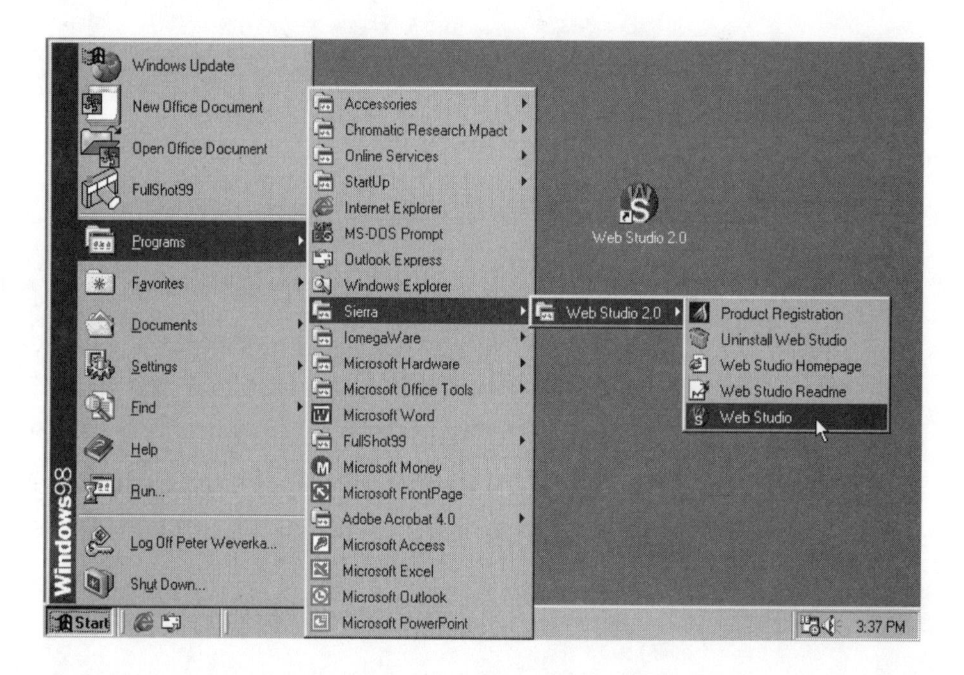

After Web Studio opens, you'll see the Tip of the Day. Read the tip, click the Close button, and wait for the Welcome to Web Studio 2.0 dialog box to show its face.

Note

As long as you created a Web Studio shortcut icon when you installed Web Studio, you can also start the program by double-clicking the Web Studio 2.0 shortcut icon on the Windows desktop.

Tapping into the Tip of the Day

There isn't much to know about the Tip of the Day. Read the tip and then click the Close button. Or click the Next button to read another tip. Here are some tips for handling the Tip of the Day:

- Keeping the tips from appearing: To keep from seeing the Tip of the Day each time you start Web Studio, uncheck the Show Tips on Startup box. If you decide later that you want to see the tips when you start the program, choose Help ➢ Tip of the Day and check the Show Tips on Startup box.
- Reading tips: Besides reading the tips when they appear at startup, you can read tips at leisure by choosing Help ➢ Tip of the Day.

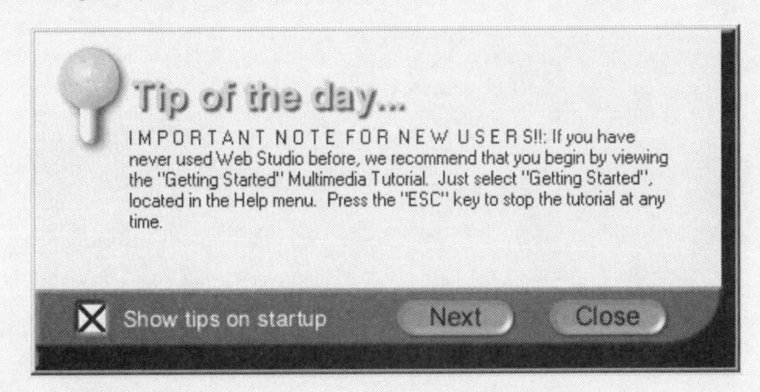

Introducing the Web Studio Screen

The Welcome to Web Studio 2.0 dialog box, which appears whenever you start Web Studio, is the starting point for creating Web sites or opening a Web site you want to work on. For now, don't concern yourself with the buttons in the dialog box. Just click the first button, Create a Web Site from Scratch, to get going.

"Creating a Web Site" at the start of Chapter 3 explains in detail how to create and open Web sites from the Welcome to Web Studio 2.0 dialog box.

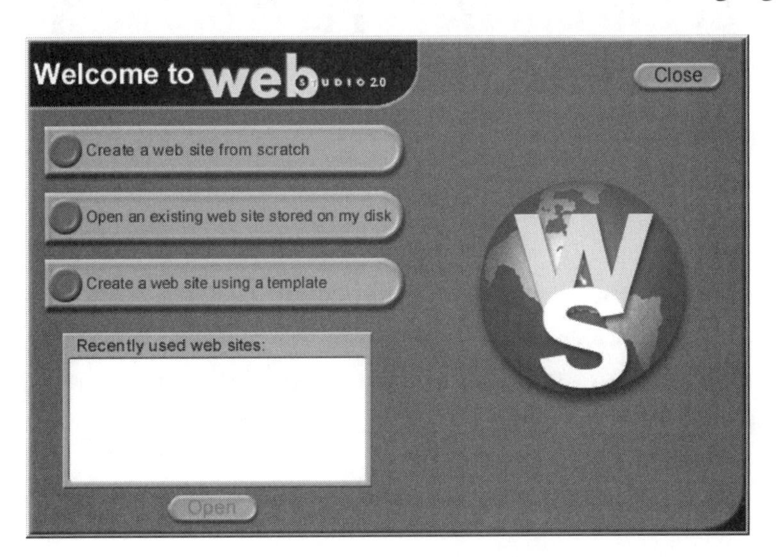

The Web Studio screen, where you do the work of creating **Web pages**, appears and looks something like the following illustration. Read on to learn about the different parts of the Web Studio screen and how you can rearrange the screen so you can work comfortably.

Web Page
One page in a Web site. Usually, a Web site comprises several different Web pages. To get from page to page, you click hyperlinks.

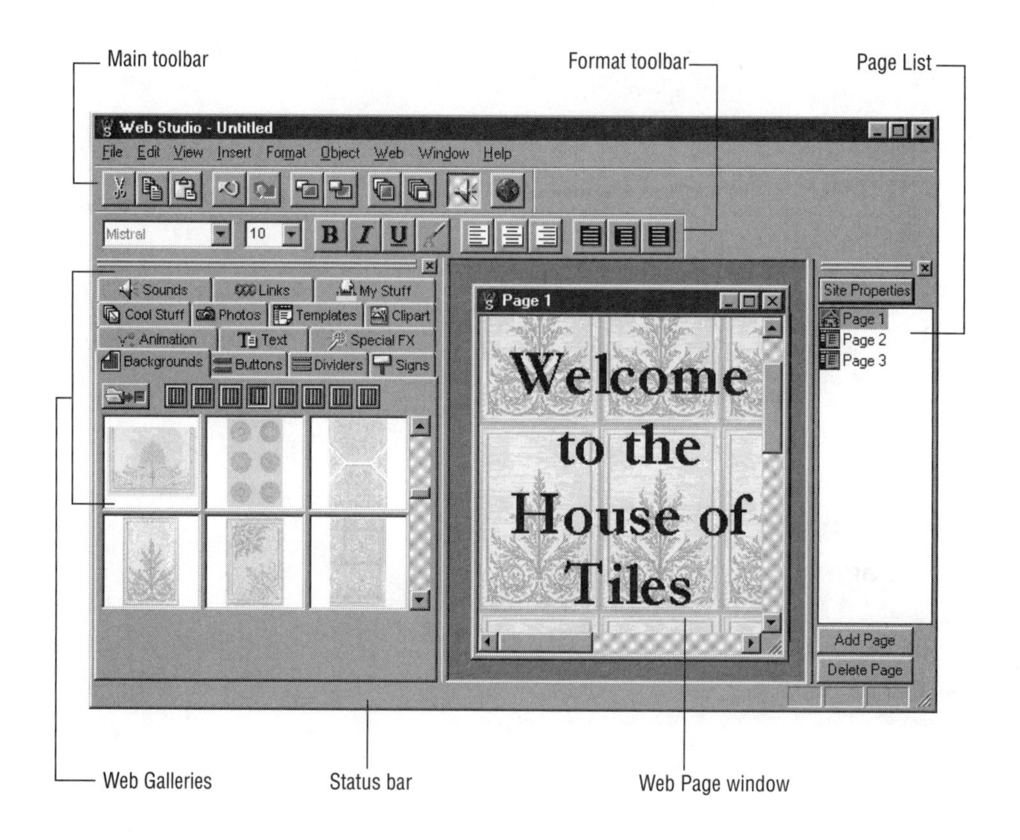

A Look at the Different Parts of the Web Studio Screen

The Web Studio screen offers many tools for constructing Web pages and Web sites. So that you don't get lost in the shuffle, here are the main parts of the Web Studio screen:

Toolbars The Main toolbar offers commands for editing and arranging items on Web pages. The Format toolbar, also called the Text Format toolbar, is for entering, aligning, and indenting text (the buttons on the Format toolbar are grayed out when you aren't working with text).

Web Galleries Click a Web Gallery tab—Backgrounds, Buttons, Dividers, Signs, and so on—to see the decorative items in a Gallery. To make use of a decorative item, click and drag it from a Web Gallery into the Web Page window.

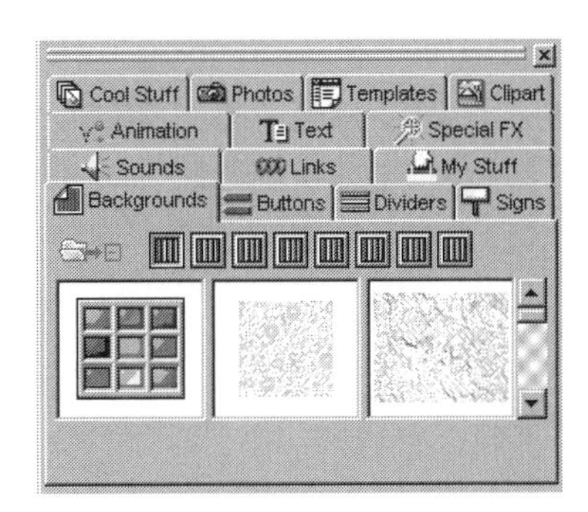

Web Page Window This is where you lay out and create Web pages. The Web Page window shows roughly what Web pages will look like when they are viewed over the Internet.

Page List The Page List displays one icon for each Web page in your Web site. Click an icon to go from page to page.

Status Bar Move the mouse pointer over almost any item in the Web Studio screen and the status bar tells you what you can do with the item or what it is good for. Get used to reading messages on the status bar.

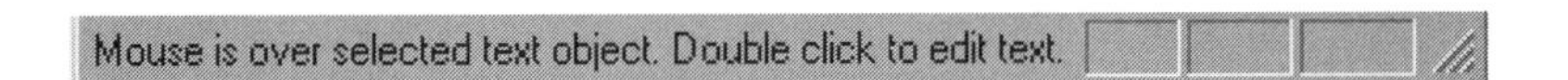

Changing the Web Studio Screen to Your Liking

Most people's first impression of the Web Studio screen is, "My, but it's crowded!" The screen is crowded because the makers of Web Studio have provided many tools for creating exciting Web sites. However, the makers of Web Studio also realize that you need room in which to work, so the program offers many convenient ways to change and rearrange the screen.

Here are techniques for handling different parts of the Web Studio screen:

"Techniques for Handling Page Windows" in Chapter 3 explains how to manage and change the size of the Web Page window.

- Removing and displaying parts of the screen: A check mark appears on the View menu beside the name of each part of the screen that is in view: the Galleries, Page List, Main toolbar, Format toolbar, or status bar. To remove a part of the screen from view, open the View menu and click to uncheck the name of a part of the screen. To place a part back onscreen after you've removed it, open the View menu again and click the screen part's name.

Tip

You can click the Close button (the X) in the upper-right corner of the Web Galleries or Page List to remove them quickly from the screen.

- Moving toolbars out of the way: Besides removing the toolbars, you can drag them to out-of-the-way locations. To do so, carefully click between two toolbar buttons and then drag the toolbar aside. To put a toolbar back where it belongs, double-click its title bar (the blue stripe that states its name).
- Making more (or less) room for the Web Galleries and Page List: To make the Web Galleries or Page List wider or narrower, gently place the pointer over the boundary that separates the Web Galleries or Page List from the middle of the window. When you see the double-headed arrow, click and start dragging.

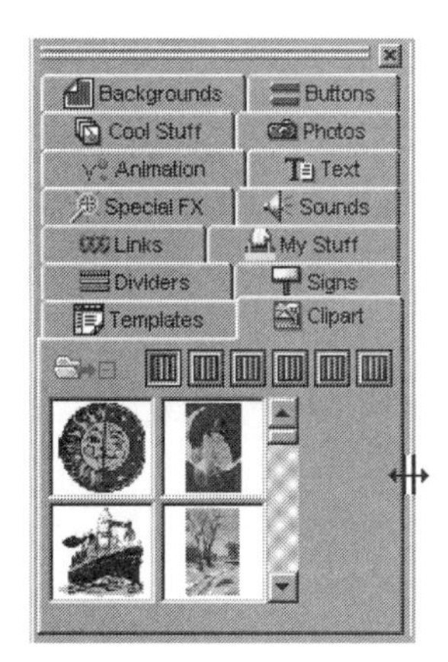

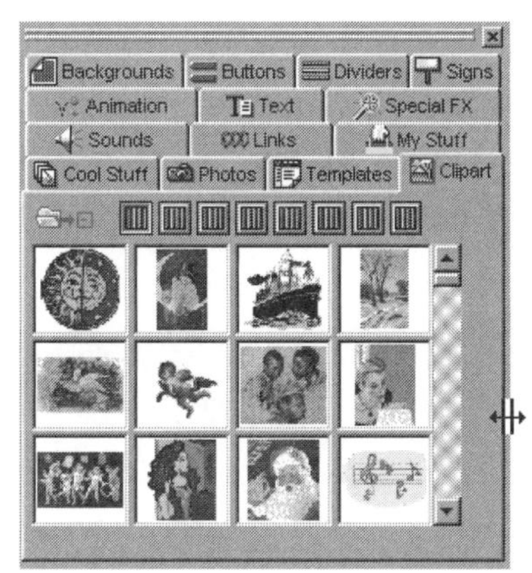

A Quick Look at the Web Galleries

The Web Galleries—and all the clever ways you can use them to decorate Web pages—are explained throughout this book. Here is a quick rundown of the different Web Galleries so you can begin thinking of ways to dress up your Web pages:

Web Gallery	What It Offers
Animation	Images that move onscreen. See Chapter 9.
Backgrounds	Background patterns, designs, and colors for Web pages. See Chapter 6.
Buttons	Buttons that you can use in hyperlinks and lists. See Chapter 8.
Clip art	Clip art images for decorating Web pages. See Chapter 8.
Cool Stuff	A variety of items, including a calendar, clock, and search engine to make your Web site stand out from the crowd. See Chapter 10.
Dividers	Dividers for breaking a Web page into different parts. See Chapter 6.
Links	Links to pages on your Web site and to your favorite Web sites (the sites in your browser's Favorites folder). See Chapter 7.
My Stuff	A place for storing your own clip art images, photos, or graphics so you can find them easily. See Chapter 8.
Photos	Photographs you can place on Web pages. See Chapter 8.
Signs	Special signs that you can use as headings or hyperlinks to other Web sites. See Chapter 6.

Depending on how you installed Web Studio, you may need to put the Web Studio CD in your computer to take full advantage of the Web Galleries. Appendix A explains the installation procedure.

Web Gallery	What It Offers
Sounds	Sound effects and sound bites. See Chapter 9.
Special FX	The means to enhance the graphics on your site—to rotate them, flip them, colorize them, emboss them, and do a number of other things. See Chapter 8.
Templates	Ready-made Web pages that you can adopt for your own. See Chapter 3.
Text	Various fonts for the headings on Web pages. See Chapter 5.

Tip

When you are searching for an item in a Web Gallery, try choosing the View ➢ Small Thumbnails command. You see more items, but sometimes telling what's what is hard because the items are smaller. Choose the command a second time to see items at normal size.

Getting Your Money's Worth from the Web Galleries

Don't forget to drag the scroll bar to investigate all the items that are available in a Web Gallery. While you're at it, try clicking a Hue button or double-clicking a Subfolder button to search farther afield for the item or image that is right for your Web site.

- Changing the hue of items: Click a Hue button to change the tint or shade of items in a gallery.
- Opening a subfolder: Double-click a Subfolder button (a folder icon with a plus sign beside it) to open a subfolder and view items that are similar to the item in question. To return to the Web Gallery, click the open folder icon.

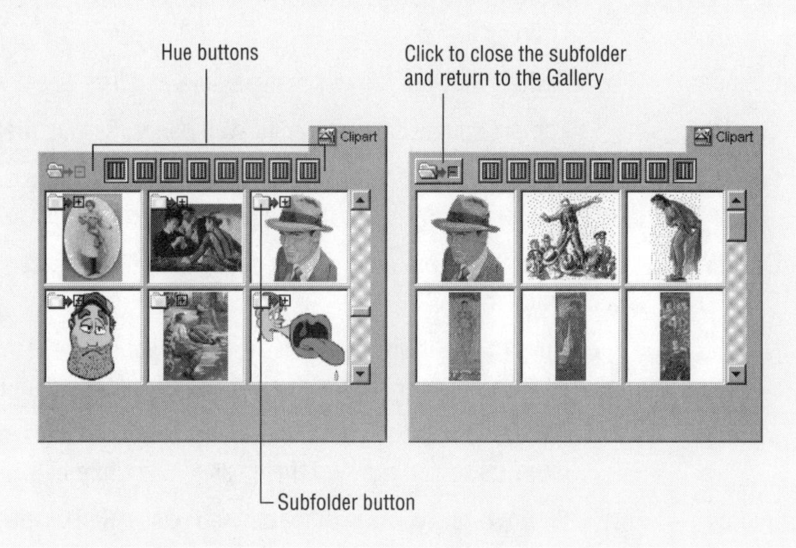

Chapter 2

What You Need to Know before You Begin

This chapter explains the handful of things you need to know before you create a Web page. We'll look at choosing an Internet Service Provider for hosting your Web site, how Web pages are constructed in Web Studio, and what HTML is. You'll learn how to save the work you've done in Web Studio and also how to preview your work in the Preview window. Finally, this chapter offers ten tidbits of advice for designing Web sites.

- Choosing an Internet Service Provider
- Using objects to build Web pages
- Saving your work
- Previewing Web pages in a Web browser
- Tips for designing Web pages

Selecting an Internet Service Provider (ISP) to Host Your Web Site

Internet Service Provider (ISP)
A company that provides customers access to the Internet. Some ISPs also allow customers to post Web pages.

Web Server
The computer at an ISP where Web pages are stored (or hosted). When you visit a Web site on the Internet, you're actually downloading the site from an ISP's Web server.

Very likely, you already subscribe to an **Internet Service Provider (ISP)** so that you can access the Internet and send and receive e-mail. Maybe you've heard of popular ISPs such as AOL, CompuServe, and Earthlink. However, subscribing to an ISP doesn't necessarily mean you can post your Web site on the Internet. To post your Web site, your ISP must offer its subscribers Web-hosting services.

These days, many ISPs *host* Web sites for their members. Most of them do it at no extra charge or for a small monthly fee. Call your ISP and pop the question, "Can I post my Web site on your **Web server**?"

If your ISP doesn't host Web sites for its members, your next task is to find an ISP that offers Web-hosting services. Some outfits offer Web-hosting for free. What's the catch? Usually, you have to carry an advertisement of some kind on your Web site. Sometimes you meet with narrow restrictions as to how large (in megabytes) your Web site can be. What's more, the Web servers at free sites often work slowly, which causes pages to take longer to download.

Tip

Paying the extra money each month to host your Web site with the ISP you now use is the way to go if you can afford it. That way, you spare yourself the hassle of signing up with a new ISP. However, if you've never created a Web site and you want to experiment before you decide whether the Web site thing is for you, sign up with a free service. If you get cold feet, you can abandon your Web site without spending any money.

The first of the following tables describes places you can go on the Internet to find ISPs that offer Web-hosting services. The second of the following tables describes where you can go to investigate ISPs that offer Web-hosting services for *free*. You can find hundreds if not thousands of Web-hosting sites by going to the Web pages listed in both tables.

Web Site	Address
FINDaHOST.com	www.findahost.com
HostFinders.com	www.hostfinders.com
HostIndex.com	www.hostindex.com
The List	http://thelist.internet.com

Upload
To send Web pages across the Internet to an Internet service provider so that the Web pages can be displayed on the Internet.

Web Site	Address
Free Homepage.com	www.freehomepage.com
Free Webpage Provider Review	http://fwpreview.ngworld.net
Free Webspace.net	www.freewebspace.net

Tip

If you decide on a free Web-hosting service, the makers of Web Studio recommend using one of these five: Xoom, Geocities, Fortune City, America Online, or Talk City. Go to this Web page on the Sierra Web site to learn more about these five free Web-hosting options: www.sierra.com/sierrahome/web/titles/webstudio/post.

When you shop for an ISP that offers Web-hosting services, get the answers to the following questions:

- Can I dial in without having to call a long-distance number? When you go on the Internet, the modem in your computer calls the ISP's computers. Make sure that telephone call isn't a long-distance call. If it is, you will be charged long-distance rates each time you **upload** your Web site to the ISP's Web server.
- What is the set-up fee? Most ISPs charge a one-time set-up or enrollment fee. The fees vary from no charge at all to $30.
- What is the monthly service charge? Monthly service charges usually range from $5 to $30.
- How much storage space am I allowed for the Web pages I want to post on the Internet? Most ISPs allow from 1 to 2MB to as much as 50MB of file storage space.

- Does the ISP offer technical assistance? Typically, ISPs that charge a low monthly rate do not offer very much technical assistance to customers, but even if you go with an expensive ISP, find out how long the company takes to reply to e-mail queries for technical assistance. Find out as well if the ISP maintains a telephone line that you can call if you forget your password or can't go online to ask for help

Warning

After you sign on with an ISP that hosts Web sites, the ISP sends you a user name and password. Don't lose them! You will need them to upload your Web site when you have finished creating it.

Constructing Web Pages One Piece, or Object, at a Time

Chapter 4 is devoted to handling objects on Web pages.

Web Studio has removed much of the drudgery from creating Web pages. You don't have to know a line of HTML code. You don't even have to be adept at placing items on Web pages. However, you do have to understand what objects are and how to construct Web pages from objects.

Object

An element of a Web page—a graphic, a box that encloses text, a divider.

All the items in the Web Galleries are **objects**. To construct a Web page, you build it from objects. To be precise, you drag an object from a Web Gallery and place it on a Web page. To arrange graphics, text, and other items on Web pages, you drag them into position.

Visitors to your Web site will never know that it is composed of objects. All they see are text, graphics, and other elements. Visitors don't see the objects because, when you save your Web site, Web Studio converts the objects to HTML code. Web browsers read the code and display your Web pages.

In the following illustration, you can see three objects in the Web Page window: two text boxes and a clip art image. Square selection handles surround the objects. Meanwhile, on the right side of the illustration, the Preview window shows what the Web page will look like in a Web browser. Notice that the objects are nowhere to be seen.

What about that HTML Stuff?

By now you must be wondering, "What about that HTML stuff?" HTML stands for Hypertext Markup Language. Browsers read HTML codes in order to display Web pages on the Internet.

You have probably heard about HTML codes, but, as a user of Web Studio, you don't have to worry about them. The HTML coding is all done in the background. All you have to do is enter the text, graphics, and other items on your Web pages. When you choose Web ➢ Preview Web Site or click the Preview Web Site button (explained shortly), Web Studio codes your file for you.

However, Web Studio *does* permit you to do HTML coding on your own. If you include a banner ad on your site, for example, you *have to* enter HTML codes. The Cool Stuff Web Gallery offers an HTML object that you can drag onto Web pages and fill with HTML codes. Chapter 12 explains one or two nifty tasks—creating a table, for example—that can't be done in Web Studio without resorting to HTML codes.

HTML codes are not for beginning users of Web Studio, but once you become a Web Studio expert, you may want to experiment with HTML coding. To see HTML codes in action, choose View ➢ Source in your browser the next time you visit a Web site. For that matter, try right-clicking a Web page in the Preview window and choosing View Source. The Notepad application opens onscreen and you see the HTML codes with which the Web site was made.

www.sybex[1] - Notepad

File Edit Search Help

```
<HTML>
<HEAD>
        <TITLE>Welcome to Sybex, Inc. - Quality Computer Books</TITLE>
        <META NAME="keywords" CONTENT="Sybex, Sybex Inc., Sybex compute
<META NAME="Description" CONTENT="Sybex Inc. is an independent publishe
<META NAME="copyright" CONTENT="&copy; 1999 Sybex Inc.">
</HEAD>
<BODY BGCOLOR="#FFFFFF" BACKGROUND="/images/bg.gif" TOPMARGIN=8 LEFTMAR
<!--Top Banner-->
<TABLE CELLSPACING=0 CELLPADDING=0 BORDER=0 WIDTH=590>
<TR>
        <TD ALIGN=CENTER VALIGN=TOP WIDTH=85>
        <A NAME="top"><IMG SRC="/images/top_banner/logo.gif" WIDTH=59 H
        </TD>
        <TD ALIGN=LEFT VALIGN=TOP WIDTH=505 COLSPAN=2>
        <IMG SRC="/images/top_banner/header_sybex.gif" WIDTH=457 HEIGHT
" ALIGN=TOP></A><IMG SRC="/images/top_banner/top_home_on.gif" WIDTH=51
```

Saving Your Web Site

The Web pages you create in Web Studio, like all computer files, need to be saved. Not only that, they need to be backed up in case your computer fails. In this section, you'll learn how to save the work you've done in Web Studio, back up your work to a floppy disk or other place where you keep spare copies of computer files, and save a Web site under a new name.

The Different Save Commands

Web Studio offers a bunch of different saving options on the File menu. What are all these commands for? Here is a rundown of the Save commands:

File ➢ Save: Saves the file on your hard disk. Choose this command when you want to save a file for the first time or save the work you recently did to it.

File ➢ Save As: Lets you save the file under a different name, save it to a floppy drive, or save it to another backup device.

File ➢ Save Page As Graphic: Saves the Web page as a bitmap (.bmp) graphic so you can treat it as a graphic. For example, you can paste it into other Web pages. Instead of being a conglomeration of different elements—text boxes, graphics, and so on—your Web page is a single graphic and is therefore easier to manipulate.

File ➢ Save Web Site to Internet: Uploads the Web site to the Internet so that others can view it there. Chapter 14 explains this command.

File ➢ Save Web Site to Hard Drive: Use this command to save your file so that others can view it with their browsers over a network.

Saving the Work You Do in Web Studio

From time to time as you construct your Web pages, be sure to save your work. You can save your work by choosing File ➢ Save (or pressing Ctrl+S). The first time you save your work, Web Studio asks you to name the file and choose the folder in which you want to put it.

Warning

In most computer programs, saving early and often is the best course to follow. But in Web Studio, saving a file has one disadvantage: When you save, you prevent yourself from taking advantage of the Edit ➢ Undo command. Choosing the Edit ➢ Undo command (or pressing Ctrl+Z) reverses your most recent action (especially useful if you've made a mistake). Choose it again, and it reverses the action you did before that. However, after you save a file, Web Studio erases the slate and starts tracking your actions anew, so you can't reverse the actions you did before you saved. The moral: Save often, but only after you have reached a point where you don't have to reverse any errors.

Follow these steps to save a file for the first time.

1. Choose File ➢ Save (or press Ctrl+S). You see the Save As dialog box.

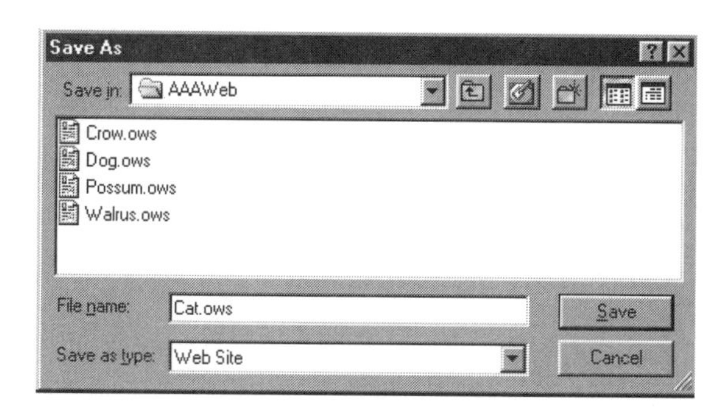

2. Use the standard tools in this dialog box—the Save In drop-down menu, the Up One Level button—to locate the folder where you want to store the file. You can store it in any folder you wish.
3. Click the folder's name. Its name appears in the Save In box.
4. Enter a name for the file in the File Name text box. Be sure to choose a descriptive name that you will remember later. If three-character file extensions appear in the dialog box, make sure the extension *.ows* appears after the file name you enter.
5. Click the Save button.

The File ➢ Save (and File ➢ Save As) command saves a Web Studio version of the file. As yet, Web browsers cannot read the file you saved. However, as you'll learn in "Previewing Your Site" later in this chapter, Web Studio creates a second version of your file when you preview it for the first time. That second version can be read by Web browsers and be seen in the Preview window, where it looks very much if not exactly like a Web site.

Tip

Suppose you want to change the name of a file. To do so, choose File ➢ Save As. The Save As dialog box appears. In the dialog box, enter a new name, and click the Save button.

Saving a Backup Copy of Your Work

Backing up your work is essential. What if something goes wrong with your computer? Unless you backed up your Web Studio files, you might lose the Web site you worked so hard to build.

Follow these steps to back up a Web Studio file to a floppy disk, tape drive, zip disk, or other storage medium:

1. Open the Web Studio file you want to back up.
2. Choose File ➢ Save As. The Save As dialog box appears.
3. Open the Save In drop-down menu and choose where you want to copy the file.

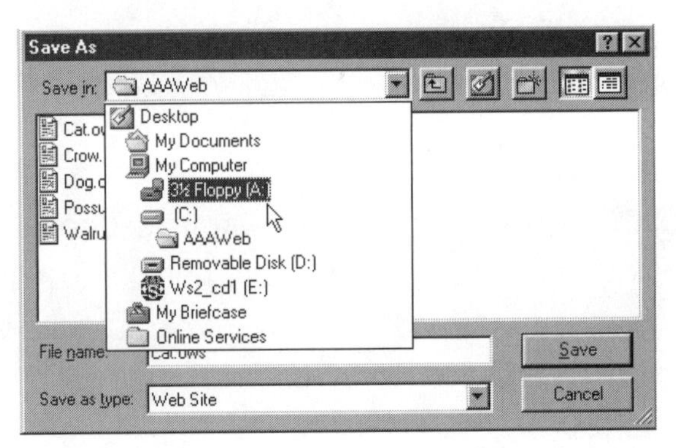

4. Click the Save button.

Tip

You can also use the File ➢ Save As command to save a second copy of a Web site on the hard disk under a different name. Why save a Web site under a new name? Perhaps you want to experiment with a second version of your Web site. To save under a new name, choose File ➢ Save As and enter a new name in the File Name text box.

Seeing What Your Web Page Will Look Like to Web Surfers

The Web Page window in Web Studio is a fine place to lay out your Web pages. Still, to see what visitors to your Web site will see, the Preview window is the best place to go. Read on to learn how to see Web pages in the Preview window, take advantage of the Web toolbar in the Preview window, and switch between the Preview and Web Page windows.

Previewing Your Web Site in the Preview Window

As long as you have saved your Web site file with the File ➢ Save command, you can open it in the Preview window. As the following illustration shows, a Web site looks more like a Web site in the Preview window than it does in the Web Page window. By looking in the Preview window, you can get a very good idea what the visitors who come to your Web site will see. And if something needs changing, you can quickly return to the Web Page window and change it.

Web Studio offers three different ways to open the Preview window and study your Web page there:

- Choose Web ➢ Preview Web Site.
- Press F5.
- Click the Preview Web Site button on the Main toolbar.

As soon as you give the command, you see the Building Site dialog box, and very shortly the Preview window appears.

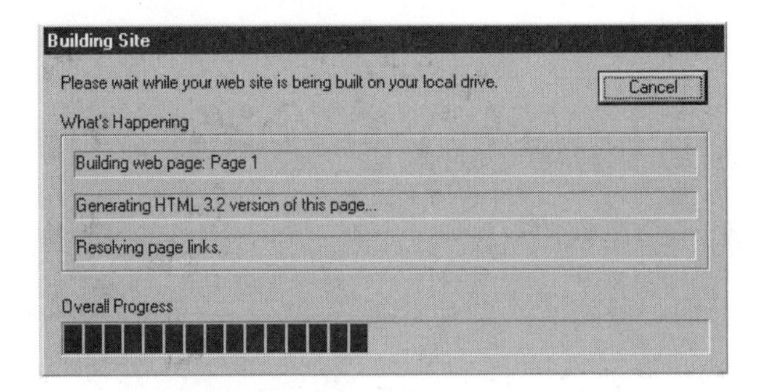

Tip

How can you tell if you're looking in the Web Page window or the Preview window? Glance at the title bar. A Web Page window title bar reads "Page," but a Preview window title bar reads, "Play."

The Preview window is really a stripped down version of Internet Explorer 5. If you were to open your Web site in Internet Explorer, it would look exactly like the Web site you see in the Preview window. For the record, the HTML-encoded files are stored in the `C:\Sierra\Web Studio2\Preview\Filename` folder in case you want to open a file in your browser.

Notice the Web toolbar buttons in the Preview window. These are browser buttons and they work like so:

Back to Preview Takes you to the home page—the first page—in your Web site.

Go To Opens the URL dialog box so you can enter the address of a site and visit it. This button is an aid when creating hyperlinks.

Back Takes you to the Web page you previously viewed.

Forward Takes you to the Web page you just retreated from.

Refresh Reloads the page in the Preview window. Click this button after you make changes and save them in the Web Page window. The changes will not appear in the Preview window until you click the Refresh button.

Stop Keeps a Web page from loading. Click the Stop button if you change your mind about visiting a page.

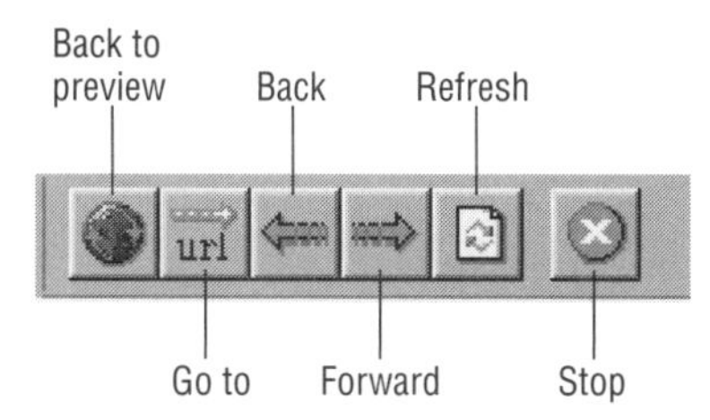

For people who prefer menu commands to toolbar buttons, the Web menu on the menu bar offers the same commands as the Web toolbar.

Switching between the Preview Window and Web Site Window

The Window menu on the menu bar offers commands for switching back and forth between windows. Learn the following commands so you can move quickly from window to window and find out how your Web page is shaping up:

- Window ➢ 1, 2, and so on: Choose the name (or number) of the window you want to go to on the Window menu. The windows are listed at the bottom of the menu.
- Window ➢ Cascade: Arranges the windows in cascade fashion so you can see their title bars. Click the title bar of the window you want to visit.
- Window ➢ Tile: Arranges the windows so that all can be seen, however small they might be. Click the title bar of the window you want to visit and then click its Maximize button. This is the command to choose when you aren't sure which window you want to go to.

To close the Preview or Web Site window, close it as you would any program window—by clicking its Close button (the X in the upper-right corner).

Tip

After you maximize the Preview or Web Site window, how do you minimize it again? Here's how: Look below the Web Studio window buttons in the upper-right corner of the screen for a second set of window buttons. By clicking the Restore button there, you can shrink the Preview or Web Studio window.

Ten Tips for Designing an Attractive Web Site with Web Studio

The last part of this chapter is devoted to what your Web pages will look like. It explains how to make professional-looking Web pages that others will admire. By heeding this advice, you can create Web pages that are useful, pleasant to look at, and easy to read.

1. Ask Yourself, "Who's My Audience?"

The cardinal rule for developing Web sites is to always remember who your audience is. Obviously, a Web site whose purpose is to publicize an amusement park needs to be livelier than a Web site whose purpose is more solemn, say, to post students' final examination scores. Likewise, a Web site that posts pictures of a newborn baby should be brighter and more colorful than one that promotes a small business.

More so than "Who's my audience?" a better question to ask might be, "Why exactly am I developing this Web site?" You are doing the hard work of creating a Web site for a good reason. Ask yourself what that reason is and then you can think of compelling ways to present the topic so that others become as passionate about it as you are.

2. Be Consistent from Page to Page

If you opened a magazine at a newsstand and discovered that the text on each page had a different font, each page was laid out differently, and each page was a different size, you wouldn't buy the magazine. The same goes for Web sites. A Web site that isn't consistent from page to page gives a bad impression. Visitors will conclude that little thought was put into the site and they won't stick around.

Home Page
The first page, or introductory page, of a Web site. Usually the home page offers hyperlinks that you can click to go to other pages on the Web site.

To be consistent, lay out your Web pages in a similar manner. Make sure headings are the same size. Use similar dividers on each page. Pages don't have to have the same background, but backgrounds should be similar. For example, you can use the same pattern but a different hue. Or you can use different shades of the same color.

The point is to give visitors the impression that a lot of thought was put into your Web site and that you care very much about its presentation.

3. Use the Home Page as an Introductory Page to Your Site

Because visitors go to the **home page** first, be sure that the home page makes a fine introduction to your Web site. The home page should include lots of hyperlinks to the other pages on the site. It should be enticing. It should be alluring. It should make people want to stay and explore your Web site in its entirety.

However, to make the home page serve as an introduction, you have to do a little planning. You might sketch a diagram showing how the introductory stuff you will write on the home page will be linked to the other pages on the Web site.

4. Divide Your Web Site into Distinct Topics, One to a Page

An unwritten rule of Web site developers is to never create a Web page that is so long you have to scroll far to reach the bottom. Topics on Web pages should be presented in small, bite-sized chunks. Rather than dwell upon a topic at length, divide the topic across several pages.

What's more, a Web site isn't like a book or article. No one reads Web sites from start to finish. A Web site is like a garden of forking paths in that visitors can click hyperlinks and take different routes through a Web site. (Visitors don't hesitate to try different routes because they know they can always click the Back button to return to where they came from.)

When you build your Web pages, consider using hyperlinks like the ones in the following illustration. These hyperlinks take visitors to other pages in the site, to other places on the same Web page, and to other sites on the Internet. Use hyperlinks to give your visitors the option of going many different places. Instead of presenting long pages that visitors have to scroll to read, let visitors choose what to read next. Hyperlinks are the subject of Chapter 7.

Looking through back issues of the LA TIMES, I came upon many stories that mentioned MAYOR YORTY. I even found a PICTURE of him in his youth. About his run for president in 1968, check out this CARTOON by Paul Conrad whose caption reads: "The sap is running early this year in New Hampshire."

5. Hyperlink Your Site to Other Sites on the Internet

Most Web sites include a page called "My Favorite Links" or "Other Sites of Interest" or "More Sites Worth Visiting." Go to that page, and you find hyperlinks that you can click to go other places on the Internet.

Everybody knows how hard it is to find interesting sites. A "My Favorite Links" page is always appreciated because visitors can be sure that the sites on the page are worth visiting. By including a "My Favorite Links" page, your site could become one of those places that people go to when they want to find a list of interesting sites to visit.

Including hyperlinks on your site gives you another advantage: It helps make your site part of the Internet community. Link your site to someone else's and often the other person reciprocates. Pretty soon your site starts popping up on

"My Favorite Links" lists. The traffic on your site increases. You site becomes a known quantity on the Internet.

Tip

When you link your site to another site on the Internet, send an e-mail message to the other site's **Webmaster**. Tell the Webmaster that your site includes a hyperlink to his or her site. The Webmaster on the other site might reciprocate by adding a hyperlink to your site.

Webmaster
The person responsible for maintaining a Web page. Usually, the Internet address of the Webmaster can be found on the home page of a Web site.

6. Choose Page Backgrounds Carefully

One of the hardest design decisions you have to make concerns page backgrounds. Choose a dark background and visitors to your site have trouble reading the text. A busy background also distracts visitors. You can, of course, opt for white text and a dark background, but too much white text has been known to strain the eyes. What the person who designed the following Web page was thinking when he or she chose this background is hard to say, since you can't read the text. Don't make this mistake yourself.

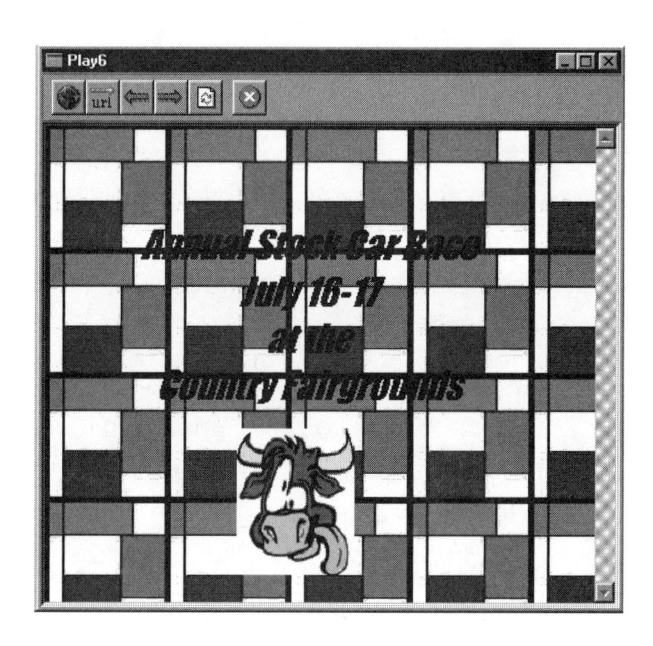

Choose the background before you make any other design decision. That way, as you construct your Web pages, you will be sure to decorate them with items that work well on the background.

7. Write the Text and Assemble the Graphics Beforehand

Download
To transfer a copy of a file or program from a site on the Internet to a personal computer.

Before you start constructing your Web site, write the text. As you will discover in Chapter 5, rewriting and editing text after it has been placed on a Web page isn't easy. Open your word processor, start typing, say exactly what you want to say on your Web pages, correct all misspellings and grammatical errors, and save the file. Later, you can import the text from the word-processed file to the Web page (Chapter 5 explains how).

Web Studio comes with a great many graphics, animations, and other doodads that are easy to put on your Web page. However, if you intend to use graphics, pictures, or sound files apart from the ones that Web Studio offers, set them aside in a folder where you can find them easily. While you're at it, take a good look at them. Which graphics you use will influence the design decisions you make as you construct your Web page. Make sure you know the graphics and sound files you intend to use intimately so that you can use them wisely and well.

8. Don't Overload Your Pages with Too Many Gizmos

More than a few Web site developers have ruined their efforts by loading their sites with too many exotic gizmos. Yes, those toys are fun to play with, and yes, they make for a nice Web site. Problem is, visitors to a site have to wait for all those gizmos to **download** before they can appreciate them. Not only that, all those gizmos can be very distracting.

No doubt you have waited impatiently for a Web site to appear in your browser screen and have given up. Next time you are tempted to load down your Web pages with sounds, video, animations, and other fancy stuff, consider the poor person who has to wait for them to appear onscreen. Fancy gizmos on a Web page are like pieces of rich, gooey chocolate. Eat one and you can really appreciate it. Eat three or four and you get a stomachache.

9. Learn the Many Ways to Align Objects

A Web page in which the graphics and text are aligned horizontally and vertically is a thing of beauty. Fortunately for you, Web Studio offers many tools for aligning objects on the page. You can align them with one another horizontally or vertically. And you can do it without any trouble at all.

Chapter 4 describes the various ways to align items on a Web page. After you have learned how to put items on a page, make sure you learn how to align them.

10. Use Web Studio's Special FX Tools to Tweak Images

The graphic images and other items in the Web Gallery are mighty nice, and you can make them even nicer by tweaking them with the Special FX tools in the Special FX Web Gallery. What's more, by tweaking them, you make these images and items your own. You make them unique. Nobody tweaks a Web Gallery item in quite the same way.

Chapter 8 explains the Special FX tools.

Part 2

The Basics: Creating Web Pages

In Part 2, you really get going in Web Studio. Part 2 shows you how to create and manage the Web pages in a site, build it piece by piece with objects, and lay out objects on Web pages. You learn how to enter the text, decorate Web pages in different ways, and place hyperlinks on your Web pages.

The Basics: Creating Web Pages

Chapter 3 • Constructing Your Web Pages 31
Chapter 4 • Laying Out a Web Page 43
Chapter 5 • Entering the Text for Your Web Page 59
Chapter 6 • Decorating Your Web Pages 75
Chapter 7 • Putting Hyperlinks on Your Web Pages 95

Chapter 3

Constructing Your Web Pages

This chapter explains how to set up the framework of a Web site—it tells how to create Web pages, delete pages, and name them. You'll also learn how to make one page the home page and why choosing a home page carefully is so important. This chapter also describes another important task: how to establish the size of Web pages and the size of the margins.

But, first things first. The start of this chapter explains how to create a new Web site and how to resume working on a Web site you've been building.

- Creating and opening Web sites
- Adding and deleting Web pages
- Changing the names of pages and choosing the home page
- Choosing the size of Web pages
- Managing the Page windows

Creating a Web Site

Template
A special kind of file that is used as the starting point for creating other files. When you create a Web site with a template, the Web page you get is already created and laid out for you—you just need to customize it to make it your own.

Before you can create Web pages, you have to start a new Web site file to put the pages in. Web Studio makes doing that easy. When you open Web Studio, you see the Welcome to Web Studio 2.0 screen. From there, you can create a Web site from the ground up or rely on a **template** to create the first page in your new Web site.

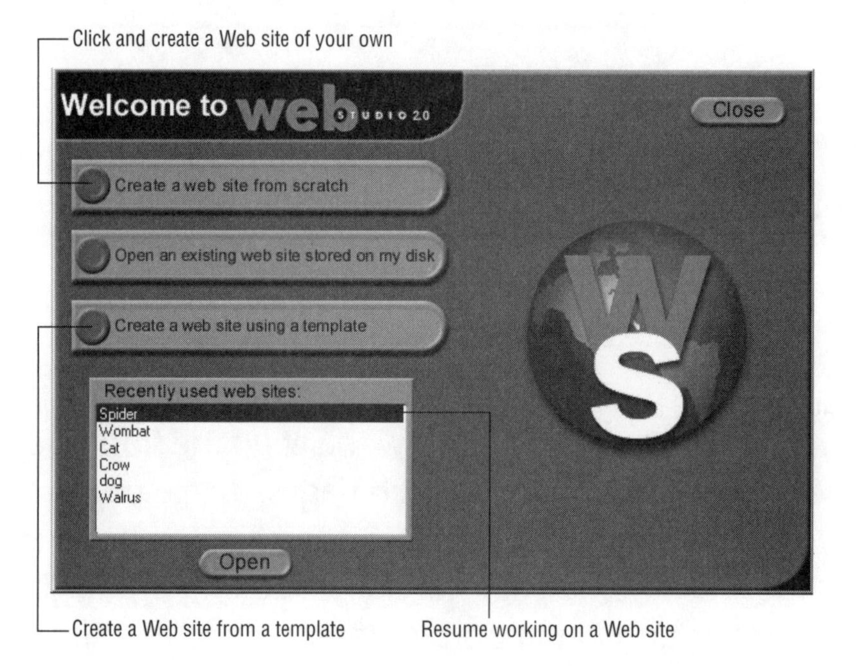

To create a Web site from the ground up, click the Create a Web Site from Scratch button. The Web Studio window opens to a new Web site. The Web site has but one page–a blank one that you can see in the Page View window.

To create a Web site from a template, follow these steps:

1. Click the Create a Web Site Using a Template button in the Welcome window. The Open Page Template dialog box appears.

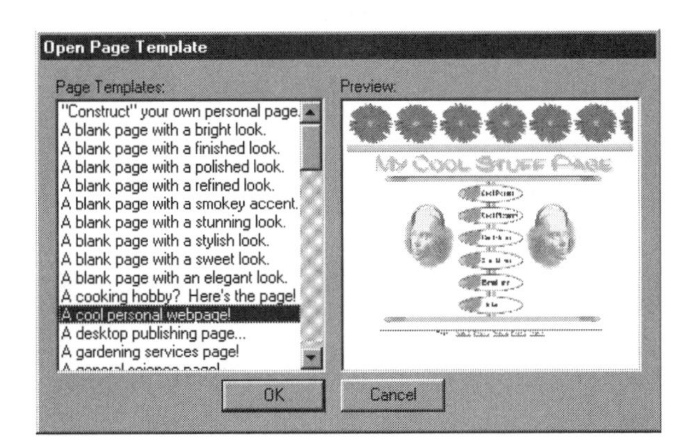

2. Scroll through the list of templates and click the one that interests you. When you click a page on the list, the Preview window shows what the Web page you chose looks like.

3. Click OK when you have found and selected the page that is right for you. The Web Studio window opens, and, in the Page View window, you see a Web page designed after the template you chose.

You can create a new Web site file after Web Studio is up and running. To do so, save the file you are working on and choose File ➢ Close. The Welcome to Web Studio 2.0 dialog box appears so you can start anew.

Later in this chapter, "Adding a New Page to a Web Site" explains how you can make use of the templates when you add a new page to a Web site.

Chapter 2 explains how to save and name a new Web site file.

The Pros and Cons of Templates

Templates are a mixed blessing. Creating a Web page from a template spares you the trouble of doing most of the layout work. Professional artists designed the templates, so you can be sure that a Web page made from a template looks good. The artwork and headings are also already in place. To complete the page, all you have to do is enter your own words and graphics where the placeholder text and graphics are.

That's the good news. The bad news is that sometimes templates are more trouble than they're worth. You have to know Web Studio well to turn a Web page made from a template into a Web page that is genuinely your own. You have to know how to move objects around, handle objects that overlap, and, most importantly, remove the things you don't want without upsetting the page design. Sometimes, modifying a page you made from a template is more trouble than building a Web page from scratch.

Web Studio offers a second, more useful way to create a Web page from a template—by opening the Templates Web Gallery and dragging a template onto the page (see "Adding a New Page to a Web Site" later in this chapter). When you create a Web page this way, Web Studio provides dialog boxes that you can fill out to write your own headings, provide your own graphics, and make the new Web page your own.

Opening a Web Site You Have Been Working On

The Welcome to Web Studio 2.0 dialog box lists the Web sites you created with Web Studio. To resume work on a Web site, click its name in the Recently Used Web Sites box and then click the Open button. Or, if you're in a hurry, double-click a name in the Recently Used Web Sites box to open a Web site.

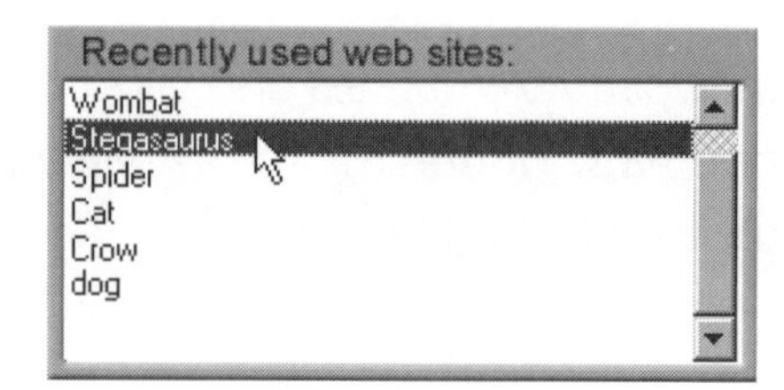

Adding and Removing Web Pages

Most Web sites comprise more than one Web page. The home page, which is the first page visitors go to and serves as an introduction to the Web site, typically includes hyperlinks to the other pages. Your first task as a Web site developer is to decide which pages you will need and create them. This section explains how to create and remove pages from a Web site.

See "Changing the Name of a Web Page" later in this chapter to learn how to give meaningful names to Web pages in place of the numbers that Web Studio gives them.

Adding a New Page to a Web Site

Web Studio offers two ways to create a new Web page:

Creating a Blank Page Click the Add Page button or choose File ➢ New Page to create a blank page. You will find this button at the bottom of the Page List. A new Web Page window opens after you

create the page. Meanwhile, another page icon appears in the Page List window.

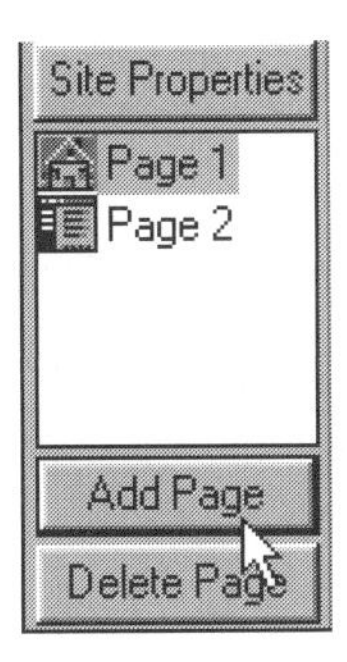

Creating a Page from a Template Click the Templates tab in the Web Gallery to see the templates. After you've found the page design template you want, drag it into the Page View window.

Because creating a Web page from a template can be kind of tricky, here are step-by-step instructions for doing it:

1. Click the Templates tab in the Web Gallery to display the page templates. If necessary, choose View ➢ Galleries to see the Web Gallery.
2. Scroll to find the template you want to add. When you move the pointer over a page, a description of the page appears on the status bar (choose View ➢ Status Bar if the status bar isn't showing).

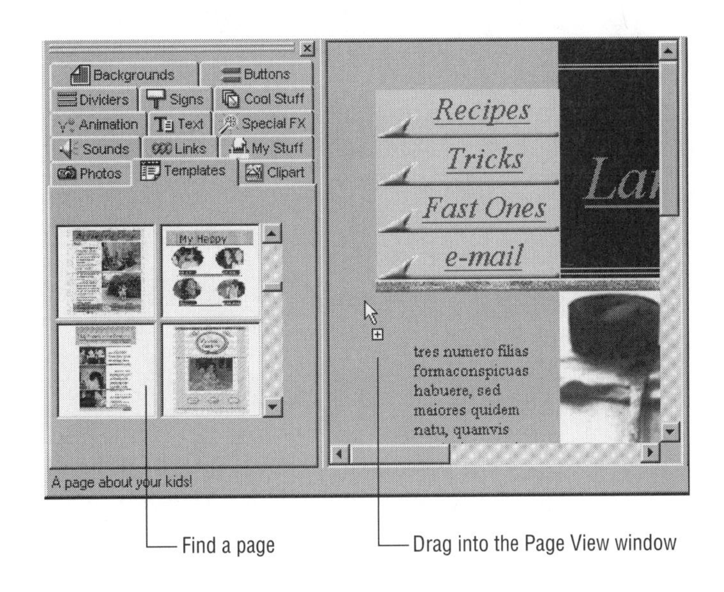

3. Click the template you want and then drag the pointer over the Page View window—it doesn't matter where.
4. When you see a plus sign (+) below the pointer, release the mouse button. The first Page Wizard dialog box appears.

   The plus sign (+) appears below the pointer only if the pointer isn't over an object. If the pointer is over a text box, graphic, button, or other object, the plus sign doesn't appear and you can't create a new Web page from a template.

Tip

If you prefer *not* to negotiate the Page Wizard dialog boxes, press the Ctrl key as you drag the pointer into the Page View window. Your new Web page is created instantly.

5. Click the Next button and follow the instructions in the Page Wizard dialog boxes. Depending on which template you chose, you get the opportunity to choose a page background, write headings of your own to take the place of the generic headings on the template page, choose buttons, import your own photos and graphics, and do any number of things.

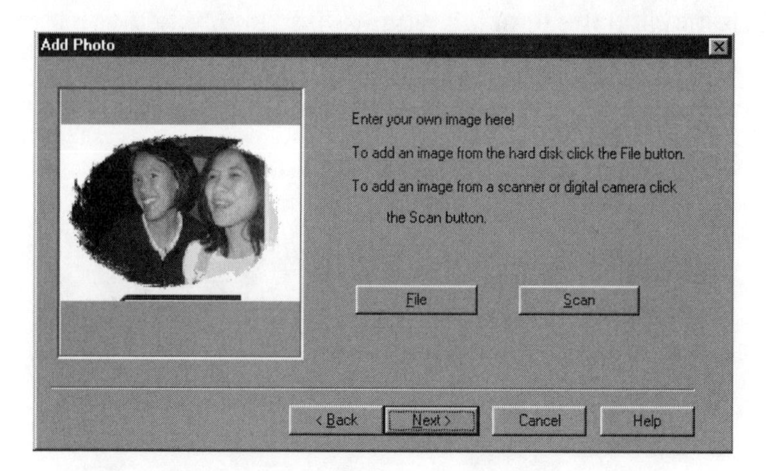

6. Click the Finish button when you are done.

Your new page appears in the Web Page window. Meanwhile, a new icon shows up in the Page List. Notice that, for the time being, your new page is named after the template you chose.

Deleting a Web Page from a Web Site

It so happens now and then that you have to delete a Web page from a Web site. Perhaps the information on the page is outdated. Or maybe you made a mistake and you need to correct it. Deleting a Web page is simple:

1. Click the name of the page in the Page List.

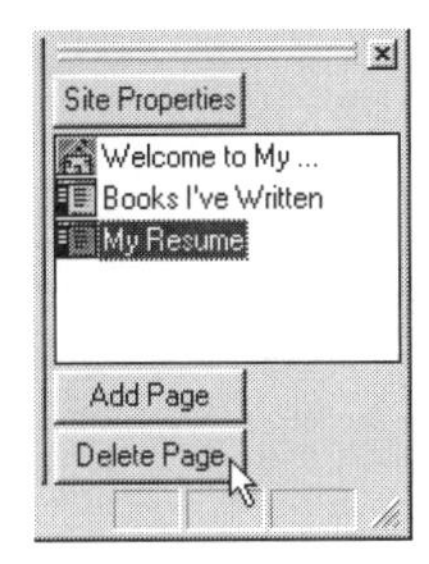

2. Click the Delete Page button. A dialog box asks if you really want to delete the page.
3. Click OK.

Warning

Before you delete a Web page, ask yourself whether hyperlinks on your Web site go to the page you want to remove. If hyperlinks on your Web site target a page that you've removed, those hyperlinks are rendered invalid. Before you delete a page, choose View ➢ Highlight Objects ➢ With Links. Red boxes appear around the hyperlinks on the page you are viewing. Right-click a link and choose Link Info to find out where it goes.

Changing the Name of a Web Page

Web page names serve an important purpose apart from helping you identify Web pages in the Page List. When a Web surfer opens one of your Web pages in his or her browser, the name you gave the page appears in the browser's title bar. If someone bookmarks your Web site, the name you gave appears in the

Favorites list. Be sure to choose descriptive names so that visitors to your Web pages can glance at the title bar and know what your Web pages are all about.

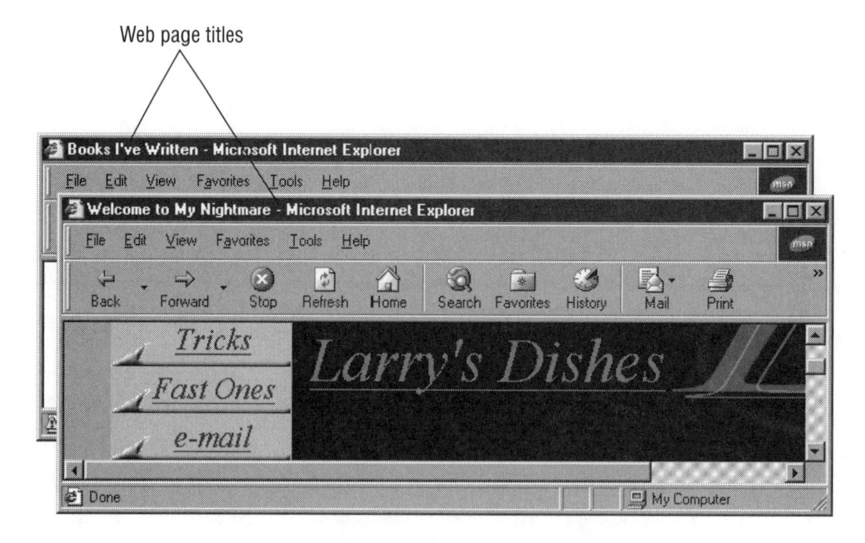

Follow these steps to change the name of a Web page:

1. In the Page List, click the name of the Web page that needs a new name.

2. Slowly, delicately, without double-clicking, click the Web page name again. A box appears around the highlighted page name.

3. Type a new name for the page.

4. Press the Enter key.

Choosing Which Page Is the Home Page

Perhaps you've noticed the small house icon next to one of the page names in the Page List. The house icon marks the home page in the Web site.

The home page gets special treatment. When visitors come to a Web site, their browsers open the home page first—no ifs, ands, or buts. Make sure that the home page on your Web site—the page you want visitors to see first—is marked with the house icon.

To mark a Web page with the house icon and make it the home page, right-click the icon beside the page's name.

Pixels
The thousands upon thousands of dots from which images on a monitor screen are constructed. The term stands for "picture element."

Establishing the Page Size and Page Margins

The size and height of a Web page is measured in **pixels**, as is the size of page margins. Read on to find out how to change the size of Web pages and the size of page margins. More importantly, read on to learn why tampering with page sizes is a risky endeavor.

Changing the Size of Web Pages

Unless you tamper with the default settings, Web pages are 576 pixels wide and 720 pixels high. The settings were chosen to accommodate people whose monitors are set to the smallest possible screen area, 640 by 480 pixels.

Tip

Want to know what screen area your monitor is set to? Right-click the Windows desktop and choose Properties on the shortcut menu. In the Properties dialog box, click the Settings tab and look under Screen Area. Windows users can change the screen area on their monitors in the Properties dialog box.

Changing the width and height settings of Web Studio Web pages is not recommended. Here's why:

Maximum Page Size Width On a page that is wider than 640 pixels, people whose monitors are set to 640 by 480 pixels have to scroll from side to side onscreen to see a complete Web page. And having to scroll from side to side to see what's on a page is mighty inconvenient.

Maximum Page Size Height On a page that is higher than 720 pixels, a lot of blank space can appear at the bottom of the page. To a person whose screen area is 480 pixels high, 720 pixels makes up about a screen and a half. The person has to scroll 1.5 screens to reach the bottom of the page. At more than 720 pixels high, the person has to scroll far beyond 1.5 screens.

Still, if you want to defy the experts and change the width and height of the Web pages in your Web site, follow these steps:

1. Choose File ➢ Web Site Properties or click the Site Properties button. You will find this button above the Page List. The Web Site Properties dialog box appears.

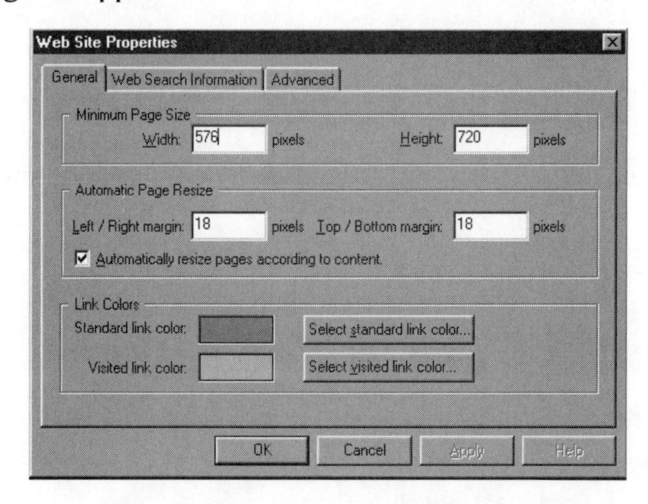

2. On the General tab, enter new settings in the Width and Height boxes.
3. Make sure the Automatically Resize Pages According to Content box is checked. As long as it is checked, Web pages are enlarged automatically when you drop an item in the margin and force the Web page to be wider or higher.
4. Click OK.

Changing the Size of Page Margins

Web Studio puts 18 pixels of empty space in each **margin**. Margins put a little breathing room between the side of the browser window and the **content** on the page—the text, graphics, and so on. Without margins, a Web page can look cluttered.

Follow these steps to enlarge or reduce an 18-pixel margin setting or allow items to appear in the margin:

1. Click the Site Properties button, which you will find above the Page List. You see the Web Site Properties dialog box.
2. On the General tab, enter new margin settings in the Left/Right Margin and Top/Bottom Margin boxes.

Margin
The empty space along the left side, right side, top, and bottom of a Web page.

Content
The droll term that Web site developers use to describe what is presented on a Web site. The person responsible for writing the text on a site is sometimes called the "content provider."

Tip

Uncheck the Automatically Resize Pages According to Content check box if you want to place items in the margin. When the box is checked and you put an item in the margin, Web Studio maintains the margin and enlarges the page to accommodate the item. But if you uncheck the box, items can appear in the margin without the page being resized.

3. Click OK

Techniques for Handling Page Windows

Suppose you are working on a complex Web site. Many Page Preview windows are open. How do you quickly get to the window you want to work in or see? For that matter, how do you enlarge or shrink windows so you can work in them or set them aside?

Here are techniques for handling windows:

- Opening a Web Page window: Either click the window's name in the Page List or choose its name on the Window menu.

- Opening a Page Preview window: Choose the window's name on the Window menu.

Tip

In the case of Page Preview windows, take advantage of the hyperlinks in your site to go from window to window. Make like a visitor to your Web site, click hyperlinks, and click the Back or Forward button on the Web toolbar to travel to different windows.

- Enlarging a window: Click the window's Maximize button. The window fills as much of the screen as it can, allowing for the Web Galleries, Page List, and toolbars.
- Shrinking a window after it has been enlarged: Click the Restore button in the upper-right corner of the screen. Be careful which Restore button you choose. As the following illustration shows, you should choose the Restore button in the second set of buttons.

Chapter 4

Laying Out a Web Page

Welcome to what may be the most important chapter of this book. This chapter explains objects, the elements with which Web pages are constructed. Here, you learn how to place objects on a Web page, change their size, position them, select them, exhibit them, and copy them. The advanced layout techniques in this chapter will help you achieve a professional look for your Web site.

- Dragging objects onto a Web page
- Selecting, positioning, and changing the size and shape of objects
- Merging objects so they are easier to handle
- Aligning objects and spreading them evenly and carefully over a Web page
- Managing objects that overlap

Placing Objects on a Web Page

Objects are explained in Chapter 2.

In Chapter 1,"A Quick Look at the Web Galleries" describes the different galleries and how to view them.

In Chapter 8,"Bringing in a Photo or Graphic of Your Own" explains how to land your original artwork on a Web page.

What is an object? All the items in the Web Galleries are objects. To construct a Web page, you drag objects from the Web Galleries onto Web pages. To place an object on a Web page, start by putting the Web Studio CD in your computer's CD-ROM drive. Depending on how you installed Web Studio, most or all of the objects in the Web Galleries are not loaded on your computer (Appendix A explains installing Web Studio). To make use of objects, Web Studio has to grab them from the CD.

With the CD ready to go, find the object you need in a Web Gallery, click it, hold down the mouse button, drag the pointer over the Web Page window, and release the mouse button. Placing objects on a Web page is as simple as that. After the object is in place, you can think about positioning it, a topic I explain later in this chapter.

Follow these steps to place an object from a Web Gallery on a Web page:

1. If necessary, open the Web page that is to receive the object in the Web Page window.
2. Locate the object you want in a Web Gallery.
3. Click the object, hold down the mouse button, and drag the pointer over the Web Page window. As long as the pointer is not over an object that has already been placed on the Web page, you see the outline of a box and a plus sign (+) appears below the pointer.
4. Release the mouse button when the box is roughly where you want the object to be.

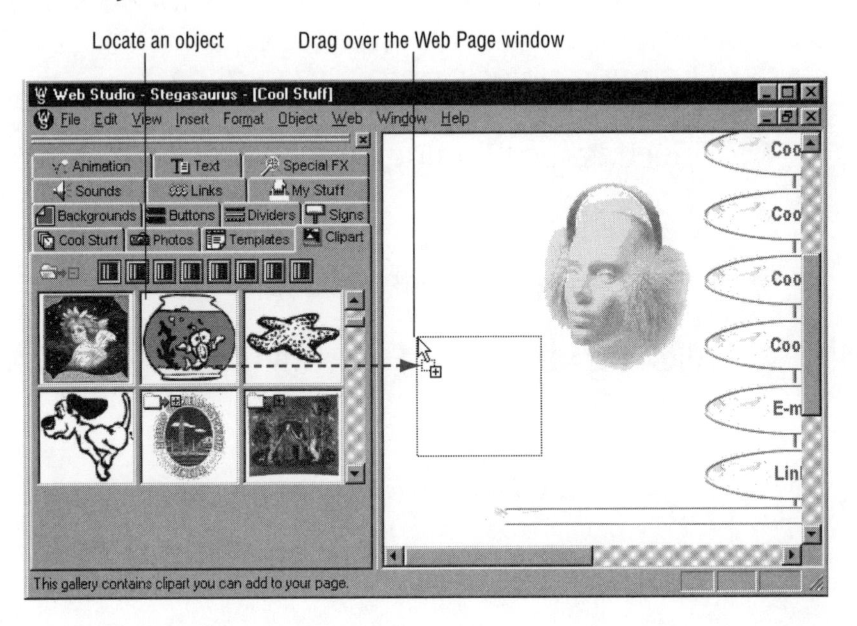

To remove an object, click to select it, and then press the Delete key or choose Edit ➢ Clear. You can also choose Edit ➢ Undo Add From Gallery (or press Ctrl+Z) to remove an object, but to do so, you must have just finished placing the object.

Tip

Remember: You can click the Close button (the ×) to remove the Web Galleries and get more room to work onscreen.

Searching the Web Galleries for the Right Object

If you aren't careful, a search of the Web Galleries for the right object can turn into an expedition. Here are a few tips for finding an object suitable for your Web page:

Opening Subfolders to Find More Objects Most Web Galleries offer many more objects than can be seen by scrolling. Double-click a Subfolder button (a folder icon with a plus sign beside it) to open a subfolder and look at the items there. Click the open folder icon (you will find it in the upper-left corner of the Gallery tab) to return to the Web Gallery.

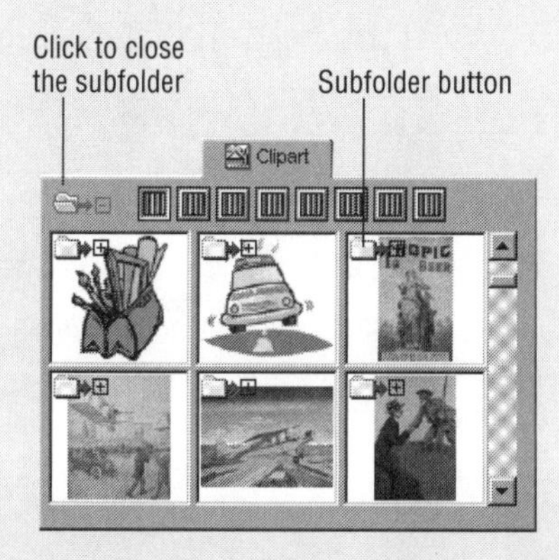

Changing the Hue of Objects Click a Hue button to experiment with the shading and tint of objects. Each time you click, the objects take on a different tone.

Seeing More Objects at Once Choose View ➢ Small Thumbnails to see more objects at once in a Web Gallery.

Making Use of the My Stuff Gallery As Chapter 8 explains, you can store replicas of your own graphics on the My Stuff Gallery and thereby make use of them quickly.

Selecting an Object or Objects

Selection Handles

The squares that appear on the perimeter of an object when it is selected. By dragging a selection handle, you can change an object's size or shape.

Before you can copy, move, alter the position of, or change the size of an object, you have to select it. Knowing how to select an object is an essential skill. And knowing how to select more than one object at the same time is important as well. By selecting more than one object, you can copy, move, reposition, realign, or resize several objects at once.

Here are instructions for selecting objects:

Selecting an Object Click the object.

Selecting More Than One Object Hold down the Shift key as you click the objects.

Selecting Objects That Are Nearby One Another Web Studio lets you draw a box around the objects you want to select. Click one corner of the box, hold down the mouse button, and drag to the opposite corner. Web Studio draws the box onscreen. When you release the mouse button, all the objects in the box are selected.

Selecting All the Objects on a Web Page Choose Edit ➢ Select All.

Tip

Selecting several objects at a time is especially helpful when you need to move objects on a Web page. Instead of moving them one at a time, you can move them all at once.

You can tell when an object has been selected because black **selection handles** appear on its perimeter. Use the handles to change the size of objects.

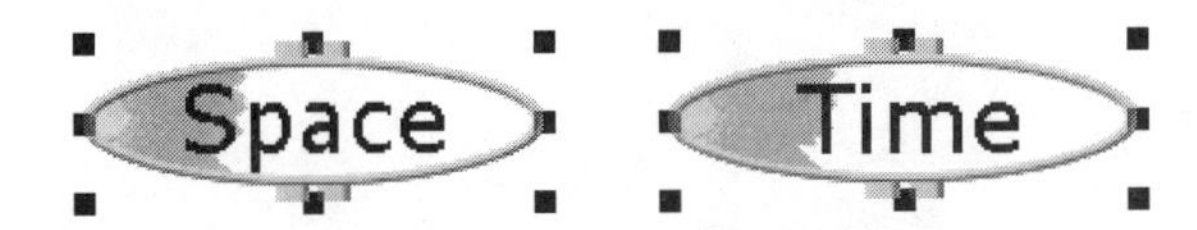

Warning

Be sure to hold down the Shift key, not the Ctrl key, to select more than one object. Holding down the Ctrl key *copies* the object. Not only that, but the copy is placed behind the original, so you might not know it's there.

Positioning an Object on a Web Page

The simplest way to position an object on a Web page is to drag it to a new location. To do so, click the object to select it. Then, holding down the mouse button, drag the object where you want it to go. Finally, release the mouse button in the new location.

Shift+click
To hold down the Shift key as you click to select items. In this way, you can select several items at once.

Tip

You can move several objects at once by Shift+clicking to select them before you start dragging. To **Shift+click**, hold down the Shift key as you click, and select, the objects.

Web Studio offers a second way to position objects on a Web page—by entering Vertical and Horizontal coordinates in the Object Properties dialog box. At first glance, positioning objects this way seems like a good opportunity for aligning objects. After all, you could give several objects the same Vertical coordinate and in so doing be sure that all the objects line up the same distance from the top of the Web page. However, Web Studio offers easier ways to align objects than the Object Properties dialog box (see "Aligning Objects on the Page" later in this chapter).

Still, the Object Properties dialog box can be a useful means of securing objects in a corner of a Web page. And you can also go to the Object Properties dialog box to lock an object and thereby keep it from being moved. Follow these steps to position an object by way of the Object Properties dialog box:

1. Click the object whose position you want to change.
2. Either choose Object ➢ Object Properties or right-click and choose Properties. You see the General tab of the Object Properties dialog box.

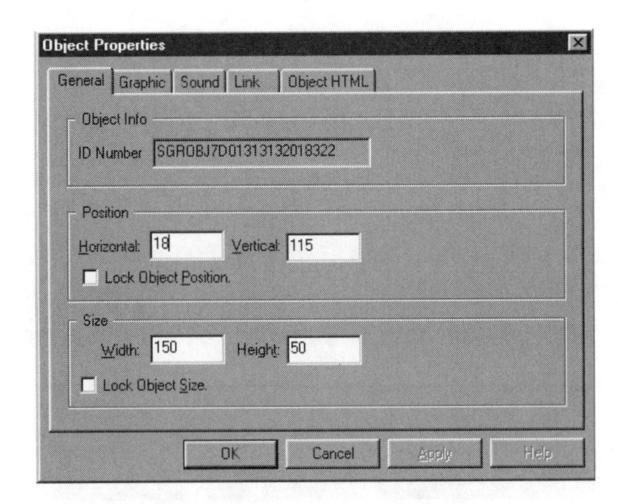

3. Enter coordinates in the Horizontal and Vertical text boxes. The numbers you enter represent pixels.

   By default, a Web page is 576 pixels wide by 720 pixels high. When positioning objects in the Object Properties dialog box, it helps to think in terms of fourths. A Horizontal entry of 144 places the object a fourth of the way into the page from the left margin; an entry of 299 puts it halfway across the page. A Vertical entry of 180 places the object a fourth of the way down the page; an entry of 360 puts it halfway down the page.

4. Check the Lock Object Position check box if you want to prevent the object from being accidentally moved.

5. Click OK.

Changing the Size and Shape of Objects

Web Studio offers a bunch of different commands for changing the size of an object. Read on to learn how to enlarge an object, shrink it, stretch it, or squeeze it. You also find out how to lock objects so their sizes won't change.

Changing an Object's Size or Shape

Select an object and you see its selection handles, the eight black squares that appear on its sides and corners. Selection handles are for changing an object's size and shape. By dragging selection handles, you can enlarge, stretch, shrink, or squeeze objects. Notice how the pointer turns into a double-arrow when you move it over a selection handle. To change an object's size or shape, click and start dragging when you see the double-arrow.

Dither
A graphic-editing technique whereby different colors in a graphic are merged into a single color when the graphic is shrunk or enlarged.

Follow these instructions to change an object's size or shape:

Changing the Size but Keeping an Object's Proportions Drag a corner selection handle to change the size of an object but retain its proportions.

Changing the Size and Proportions of an Object Drag a selection handle on the side of an object to change its shape.

Tip

A graphic can start to look grainy when you enlarge it. To prevent that, try holding down the Ctrl button as you enlarge it. Web Studio **dithers** objects when you hold down the Ctrl key. Dithering softens the edges so they don't look as coarse.

In the following illustration, the object on the left is the original object. For the middle object, I dragged a corner selection handle, so the object kept its proportions when it was enlarged. I dragged a side handle and stretched the object on the right.

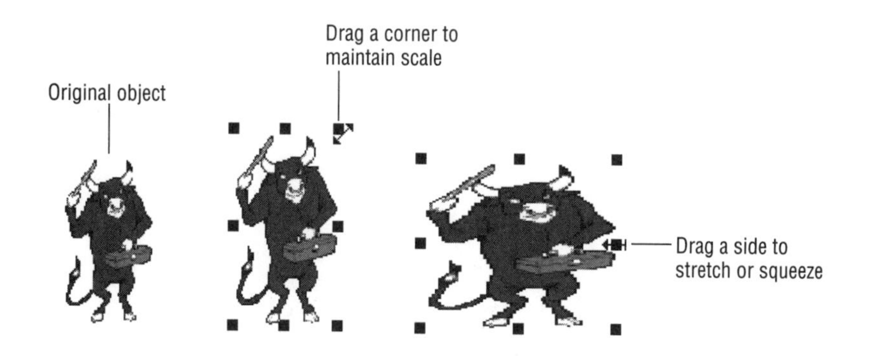

Preventing an Object from Changing Size

Another way to change an object's size or shape is to visit the Object Properties dialog box and enter Width and Height settings in the text boxes. Changing an object's size in the Object Properties dialog box is far more trouble than dragging its selection handles. The chief reason for going to the Object Properties dialog box is to prevent anyone else from changing the size of an object.

Follow these steps to keep an object from changing size:

1. Click the object that is to stay the same size.
2. Either right-click and choose Properties or choose Object ➢ Object Properties. The General tab of the Object Properties dialog box appears.
3. Check the Lock Object Size check box.

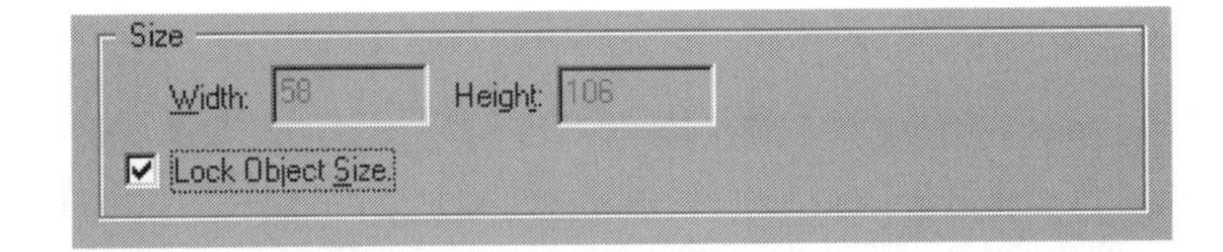

4. Click OK.

Making Objects the Same Size

Web Studio offers a special command for making objects the same size—the Make Equal Size command. Follow these steps to make several different objects the same size:

1. Choose one object in the group and make it the size you want all the other objects to be.
2. Select the object whose size you just changed, if the object isn't already selected.
3. Hold down the Shift key and click the other objects in the group to select them.

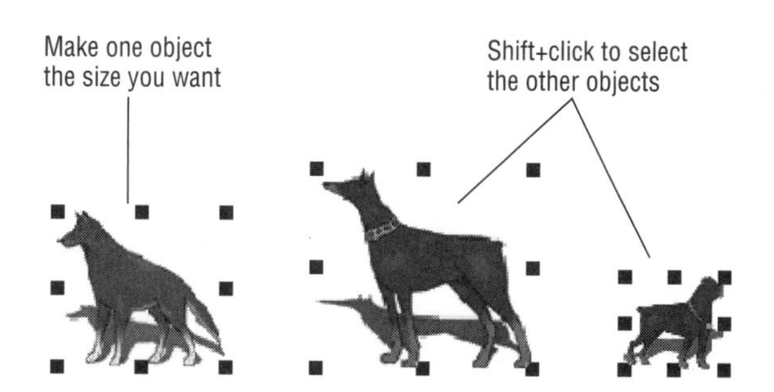

4. Choose Object ➢ Make Equal Size or right-click one of the objects you selected and choose Make Equal Size on the shortcut menu.

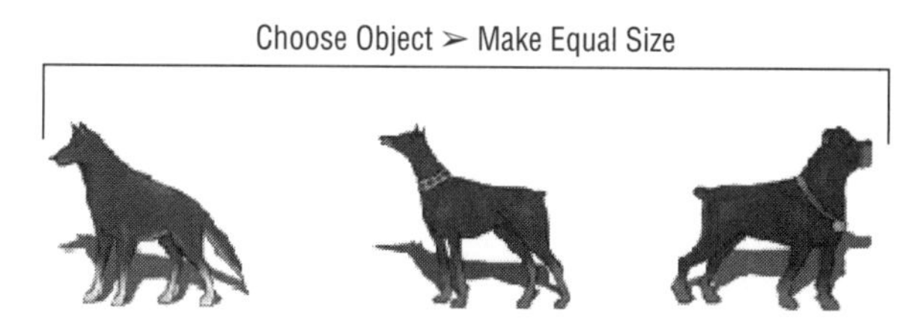

Warning

On the surface, the Make Equal Size command seems like a good way to impose the same dimensions on a row or column of objects. However, when objects change size they sometimes lose clarity. Carefully examine objects after you make them the same size. If they look fuzzy, choose Edit ➢ Undo Resize Objects.

Merging Objects So They Are Easier to Work With

Here's a trick for making objects much, much easier to work with: Merge them. After objects are merged, you can treat them as a single object. Instead of having to move several objects, you only have to move one. Instead of enlarging several objects, you only have to enlarge one.

Warning

Short of choosing the Edit ➢ Undo Object Merge command, objects that you have joined together cannot be cast asunder. In other words, you cannot "unmerge" objects.

To see the value of merging, consider the objects in the following illustration. Three objects were needed to create the cartoon on the left: a clip art image, a bubble caption, and a text box. To move the cartoon, I have to move three objects, unless I merge the objects first. After the objects are merged, as they are on the right side of the illustration, I can move them all at once.

Chapter 8 explains how to place your own images and images you copied from the Internet on Web pages.

Follow these steps to merge objects:

1. Shift+click to select the objects you want to merge.
2. Choose Object ➢ Merge Selected Objects or right-click an object you selected and choose Merge Selected Objects.

Quickly Copying an Object

Knowing how to copy an object is an essential skill because certain kinds of objects—especially buttons, dividers, and signs—usually appear in sets. Instead of placing the objects one at a time on a Web page, you can place one object and then copy it. By copying it, you can rest assured that all the buttons, dividers, and signs are identical.

Copying is very simple: Click the object to select it, hold down the Ctrl key, and drag the object aside. Instead of the object moving when you drag, a copy of the object appears.

So much for copying an object you want to use a second time on a Web page. Suppose you want to borrow an image from one Web page and use it in another. Follow these steps to copy objects from Web page to Web page:

1. Click the object you want to copy.

2. Choose Edit ➢ Copy, press Ctrl+C, or right-click and choose Copy. The object is copied to the Windows Clipboard.
3. Open the Web page where you want the copy to go.
4. Choose Edit ➢ Paste, press Ctrl+V, or right-click and choose Paste. A copy of the object lands on the Web page.
5. Drag the object where you want it to be.

Aligning and Spacing Objects on the Page

The aligning and spacing commands are designed to keep Web pages from looking sloppy. Instead of objects lying hither and yon on the Web page, the objects line up. Or, in the case of the spacing commands, objects are equidistant, not cluttered together.

Read on to learn how to make objects line up with one another and how to space objects evenly across or up and down the page.

Aligning Objects with Respect to One Another

Do not try to align objects by carefully dragging them here or there. Why do that when you can take advantage of an Align command? These commands line up objects on their left sides, right sides, top, or bottom. And the Align commands do their work quickly. The Align commands are essential for lining up buttons and other objects that appear in sets.

Next time you notice objects scattered about a Web page, follow these instructions to make them snap to attention and stand in line:

1. Click the object that you want the others to line up with.
2. Shift+click to select the other objects you want to line up.

3. With all the objects selected, either open the Object menu and choose an Align command, or right-click and choose an Align command:
   - Align Left Sides: Lines up objects along their left sides.
   - Align Right Sides: Lines up objects along their right sides.
   - Align Tops: Lines up objects along the top.
   - Align Bottoms: Lines up objects along the bottom.

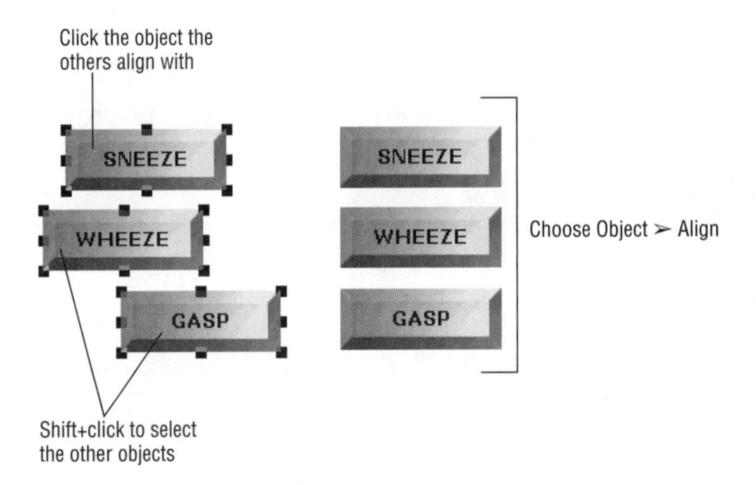

Spacing Objects Evenly on the Page

Like the Align commands, the Spacing commands are essential for handling objects such as buttons that appear in sets. Unless the same amount of distance appears between buttons, a Web page looks sloppy indeed.

Follow these steps to put an equal amount of horizontal or vertical space between objects on a Web page:

1. Move the outermost objects—the first and last object in the set—where you want them to be. Web Studio will distribute the objects equally between the two outermost objects.
2. Shift+click to select all the objects.
3. Either open the Object menu and choose a Space Evenly command or right-click and choose a Space Evenly command:
   - Space Evenly Across: Distributes objects evenly across the page between the leftmost and rightmost objects.

- Space Evenly Down: Distributes objects evenly up and down the page between the uppermost and bottommost object.

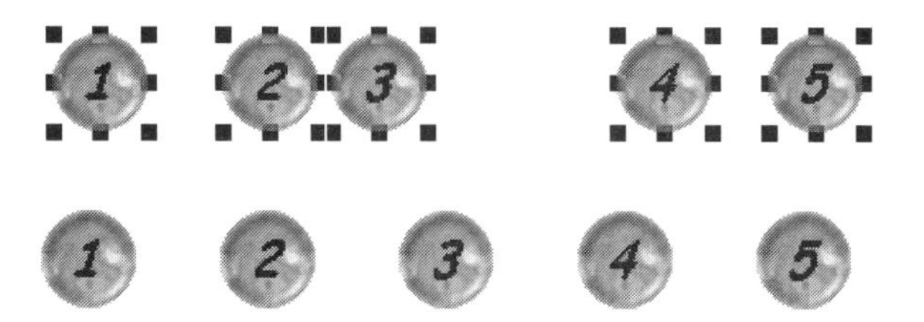

When Objects Overlap: Deciding Which Goes Where

Objects have a tendency to overlap on Web pages. And when objects overlap, you have to decide which should appear in the foreground and which in the background. To complicate matters further, when three or more objects overlap, you have to tell Web Studio where each object stands on the totem pole: on top, on bottom, or in the middle.

The commands for handling objects that overlap can be found on the Main toolbar, the Object menu, and the shortcut menu you get when you right-click an object that you selected. The commands are as follows:

- Send to Back: Moves the object you selected to the bottom of the stack. Except where other objects are not overlapping it, you can't see the object. In the following illustration, the bottle of champagne has been sent back and is now behind the sign.

- Bring to Front: Moves the object you selected to the top of the stack, where it obscures the objects it overlaps. Here, so you can read it, a text object with the word "Hootenanny" has been brought to the front of the clipart image.

- Move Backward: Moves the object lower in the stack. If it was the top-most object in a stack of three, it moves to the middle position. If it was in the middle position, it moves to the bottom. Here, the red button over the mannequin's mouth has been moved backward in the stack. It still overlaps the mannequin, but not the text object.

- Move Forward: Moves the object higher in the stack. If it was on the bottom of a stack of three, it moves to the middle position. If it was in the middle position, it moves to the top. Here, the grass was at the bottom of the stack, but it has been moved forward. Now it obscures the elephant's feet, but the text object with the words "Elephant Land" overlaps it.

To determine how an object overlaps or is overlapped by other objects, follow these steps:

1. Click the object to select it.
2. Choose one of the following overlap commands:
   - Click a button that pertains to overlapping on the Main toolbar.
   - Choose the command from the Object menu.
   - Right-click the object and choose the command.

Being Alerted When Objects Overlap

On a crowded Web page with many objects, sometimes it is hard to tell where objects overlap. Sometimes, in fact, objects get hidden underneath other objects and you can't even tell that they are there.

To help you manage objects that overlap, Web Studio offers the View ➢ Highlighted Objects ➢ That Overlap command. Choose it, and red boxes appear around all objects that overlap or are overlapped by other objects. The red boxes show precisely where overlapping objects are so you can get at them or manipulate them more easily.

Chapter 5

Entering the Text for Your Web Site

A picture is not worth a thousand words—not anymore. These days, anybody can drop a picture in a Web site. All you have to do is drag the mouse. What really matters is the text. Does it communicate a message? Is it laid out well and easy to read? You could argue that the old formula has been reversed: Now a word is worth a thousand pictures.

This chapter offers techniques for laying out the text so it is just right. You discover shortcuts for getting text on the page and find out how to change the font and font size of text. This chapter also explains how to format text in different ways, and, finally, how to drop one of those scrolling text doodads in a Web page.

- Entering and editing text on Web pages
- Changing the font, font style, font size, and color of text
- Choosing a background color for text
- Aligning and indenting text
- Making text scroll on a Web page

Putting Text on a Web Page

Web Studio offers no less than three ways to put text on a Web page. The standard technique is to drag a text object from the Text Gallery to the Web Page window and start typing. Another technique is to paste the text from the Clipboard with the Edit ➢ Paste command. And you can choose Insert ➢ Text from File to appropriate an entire file for the Web page you are working on.

A *font* is a typeface design. Later in this chapter, "Making Sure Visitors See the Fonts You Want Them to See" explains how to make sure that people who visit your Web pages see the fonts you chose.

Which technique is best? For headings, which are only a few words long, dragging an object from the Text Gallery is the way to go. But if you want to present several paragraphs, start by writing them in a word processor. When you are done, use the Edit ➢ Paste or Insert ➢ Text from File command to bring the text into Web Studio. Writing and editing a page or more in Web Studio is nothing but trouble.

Read on to learn the different ways to put text on a Web page.

Dragging a Text Object onto the Page

Follow these steps to place text on a Web page by dragging it from the Text Gallery:

1. Click the Text Gallery tab in the Web Gallery. If need be, choose View ➢ Galleries to see the Web Galleries.
2. Click the font you want for the text, and, still holding down the mouse button, drag the mouse into the Web Page window. A plus sign (+) appears below the pointer and a box shows where the text object will land when you release the mouse button.

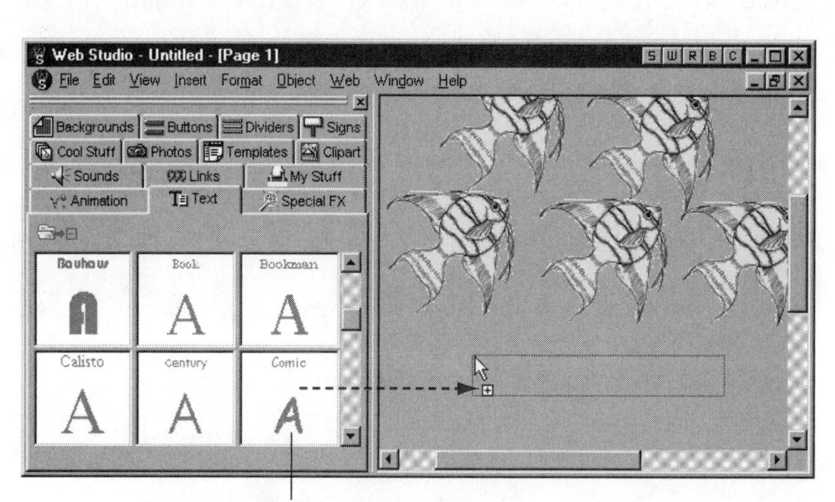

Choose a font and drag into the Web Page window

3. Release the mouse button. Black lines appear on the corners and sides of the text box.

4. Start typing. The text object increases in size if you write more than a few words.

Fish Tales

5. Click outside the text object when you are finished typing.

"Placing Objects on a Web Page" in Chapter 4 explains the details of handling objects from the Web Galleries.

Tip

Here's a shortcut for creating a text object: Hold down the Alt key, click anywhere in the Web Page window, and start typing.

Getting Text from a File You've Already Written

As I mentioned earlier, getting text you've already written is the way to go when you want to place more than a few paragraphs on a Web page. Writing the text in a word processor such as WordPerfect or Word is easier than wrestling with a text object in Web Studio. Follow these instructions to import an entire file into the Web Page window:

1. Open the file you want to import. Choose File ➢ Save As, open the Save As Type drop-down list, choose Rich Text Format (RTF) or Text Only (TXT), and click the Save button. Only files in these formats are acceptable. Of the two, choose rich text format if you can. Under this format, boldface and italics, text alignments, and a few other formats from the original file are retained. Saving a file under a different format creates a second copy of the file—the original copy isn't disturbed.

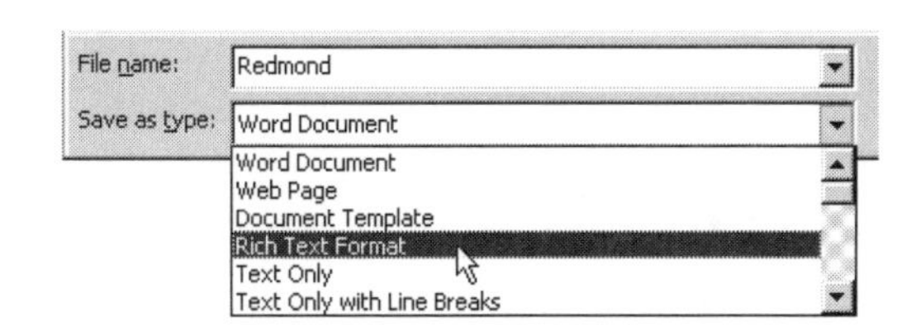

2. In Web Studio, choose Insert ➢ Text from File. You see the Open dialog box.
3. Locate and select the file you want to import. You might have to choose Text, Rich Text, or All Files in the Files of Type drop-down list to find the file you want.

Clipboard
A holding tank to which you can copy or move text and graphics. Text and graphics can be pasted from the Clipboard onto a Web page.

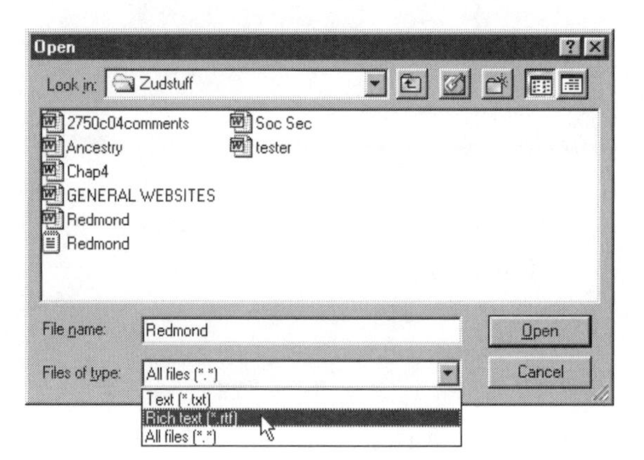

4. Click the Open button. The text lands in the upper-left corner of the Web Page window.
5. Drag the text where you want it to be.

Importing a Paragraph or Two with the Paste Command

Maybe you only need a paragraph or two from a file you've already written. In that case, make use of the Windows **Clipboard**:

1. Select the text in the word-processed file and choose Edit ➢ Copy (or press Ctrl+C).
2. Click in the Web Page window and choose Edit ➢ Paste (or click the Paste button on the Main toolbar). The text lands in the upper-left corner of the Web Page window.
3. Drag the text to a new location.

Editing the Text

You have a sentence that needs rewriting? You found a misspelled word? To edit text, double-click it. Black lines appear around the text object. The black lines (they are not the same as selection handles) are your signal to go into the text, enter or erase characters, and fix the error. Press the Delete or Backspace key to erase characters. To erase several words or sentences, drag across them before pressing Delete or Backspace.

Selection handles are the squares that appear on the perimeter of an object when you select it. See "Selecting an Object or Objects" in Chapter 4.

Neither a burrower nor a lender be.

You can't edit text if you click instead of double-clicking the text object. Click a text object to display its selection handles and move it. Compare the following illustration to the previous one. In this illustration, I clicked the text object instead of double-clicking it, and, instead of black lines, selection handles appear.

Neither a borrower nor a lender be.

Spell-Checking a Web Page

Spelling errors in a printed document are one thing, but spelling errors on a Web page that all the world sees on the Internet are another! You owe it to yourself to check Web pages for spelling errors before you put them on the Internet.

To check for spelling errors, start by clicking a text object to select it. The Check Spelling command can only examine one text object at a time. With a text object selected, choose Edit ➢ Check Spelling and click the Start button in the

Check Spelling dialog box. The spell-checker stops on the first misspelling it finds and lists it in the Word Not Found in Dictionary box.

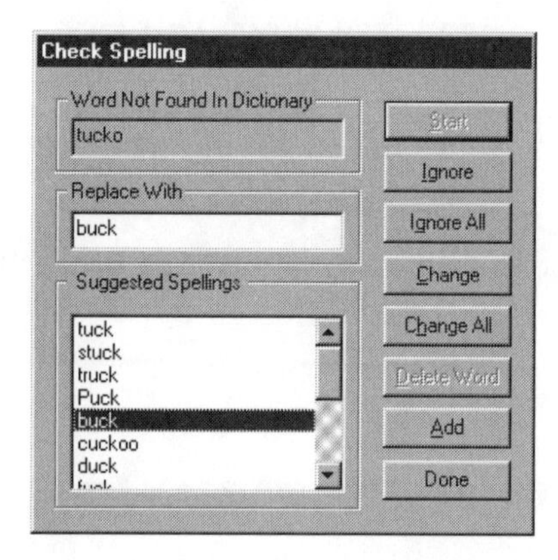

Correct the misspelling by clicking one of the buttons, choosing correctly spelled words, or entering a word in the Replace With box. Your options are as follows:

- Replace With: Lists the word that will replace the misspelling if you click the Change or Change All button. You can type a word in this box.
- Suggested Spellings: Provides a list of words to use in place of the misspelling. Click the word that you want to replace the misspelled one.
- Ignore: Ignores the misspelling, but stops on it again if it appears later in the text object.
- Ignore All: Ignores the misspelling wherever it appears.
- Change: Exchanges the misspelled word for the word in the Replace With box.
- Change All: Changes not only this misspelling of the word in the Replace With box, but all identical misspellings.
- Delete Word: Erases the second of two words that appear in a row ("the the," for example).
- Add: Adds the word in the Replace With box to the words in the dictionary so the word is no longer considered a misspelling. Click this button the first time that the spell-checker stops on your last name to add your last name to the spelling dictionary.
- Done: Click this button to quit using the spell-checker.

Warning

The smell-checker can't catch all spelling errors. If you type *sweat* but mean to type *sweet,* the spell-checker won't catch the error because *sweat* is a legitimate word. The moral: Proofread Web pages carefully. Don't rely on the spell-checker to catch all your smelling errors.

Formatting Headings and Other Text

This part of the chapter looks into how to decorate the text. A Web page doesn't have to look dull and dreary. Here, you learn how to italicize, boldface, and underline text. These pages explain fonts and font sizes, too. Not all fonts can be displayed on browser screens, and this section looks into how to get around that thorny problem. Finally, you discover how to change the color of text and choose a background color for text.

Boldfacing, Italicizing, and Underlining Text

The simplest way to make a heading stand out is to **boldface**, *italicize*, or underline it. The Format toolbar offers buttons for doing just that. Follow these steps:

1. Select the text you want to boldface, italicize, or underline:
   - Some of the text: Double-click the text object and drag the pointer across the letters or words you want to format. To select an entire word, double-click it.
   - All of the text: Click the text object. The black selection handles appear. Formatting commands you give will apply to all the text.
2. Click the Bold, Italic, or Underline button on the Format toolbar. In the following illustration, the text has been boldfaced and italicized. Notice how the Bold and Italic button are pressed down on the toolbar.

Warning

Most Web surfers who see underlined text on a Web page think they are seeing a hyperlink. Don't underline text unless you have a good reason to do so. A viewer of your Web page who clicks underlined text but doesn't go to a new Web page will be sorely disappointed.

Font
The catch-all name for a type style and type size.

Choosing a Font and Font Size for Text

When you change **fonts**, you choose another style of type or change the size of the letters. By custom, headings and text are displayed in different fonts. A Web page with well-chosen fonts gives a good impression, so choose fonts carefully. And don't go overboard with fonts. Too many fonts on a page can make your head start to spin.

Tip

Unless you want a whimsical Web page, be consistent in your choice of fonts. Headings should be the same font. Choose the same font for the text in paragraphs as well. Visitors get a bad impression when they come to a page on which many different fonts are used. The page looks sloppy, as if the designer didn't put much thought into it.

Follow these steps to choose a font and font size for text:

1. Select the text that needs a new font:
    - All of the text: Click the text object. The Font commands you give will apply to all the text.
    - Some of the text: Double-click the text object and drag the pointer across the letters or words that require a new font. You can double-click a word to select it.
2. Open the Font drop-down menu and choose a font.
3. Open the Font Size drop-down menu and choose a font size. If the measurements on the drop-down menu aren't suitable, type your own measurement in the box and press the Enter key.

Type is measured in **points**. For reading, most Web page designers prefer 10- or 12-point type. For headings, choose a larger point size.

Point
A unit for measuring the height of type. One point equals 1/72 of an inch.

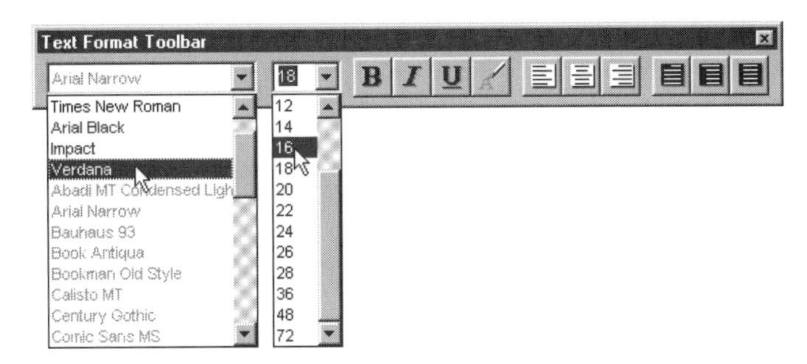

The other way to change fonts and font sizes is to start from the Font dialog box. After you have selected the text, choose Format ➢ Font. The advantage of going this route is that you can change a font style—Italic, Bold, or Bold Italic—as well as change fonts and font sizes. And the Sample box shows precisely what the text will look like after you format it.

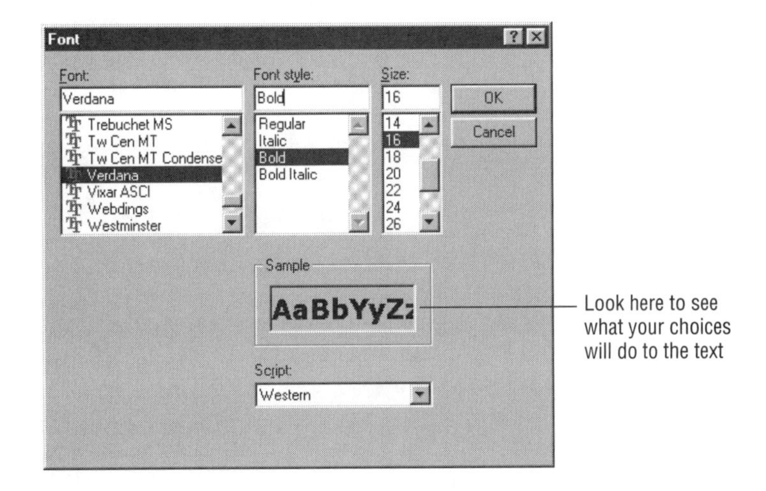

Tip

A quick way to change fonts is to find the font you need in the Text Gallery and simply drag it over a text object you already created.

Making Sure Visitors See the Fonts You Want Them to See

Take a look at the Text Gallery or the Font drop-down menu and you will notice that some font names are black, some are blue, some are orange, and some are red. Web Studio has color-coded these fonts for a very important reason: The colors tell you whether all visitors to your Web sites will see the fonts.

- Fonts whose names are black or blue are found on everyone's computer. These are standard Windows fonts. When you assign a black or blue font to text, you can be sure that visitors to your Web page will see exactly what you see on your computer screen.
- Fonts whose names are orange or red are *not* found on everyone's computer. A visitor to your Web page, depending on which fonts are loaded on his or her computer, may not see the font you chose. When a computer can't display a font, it uses the next best font. Choose a font whose name is red or orange and you take a gamble as to whether visitors to the Web page will see the letters the same way you see them.

Only six fonts on the Font menu—Arial, Courier, Times, Arial Black, Impact, and Verdana—are standard Windows fonts. To be sure that others see your Web pages the same way that you see them, you can stay with the six fonts, or you can use other fonts as well but convert the text objects in which they appear to graphics.

Follow these steps to convert a text object to a graphic:

1. Click to select the text object in which a non-standard Windows font appears.
2. Right-click the text object and choose Properties or choose Object ➢ Object Properties. You see the Object Properties dialog box.
3. Click the Text tab.
4. Under Fonts, click the Always Convert Object to Web Page Graphic check box.

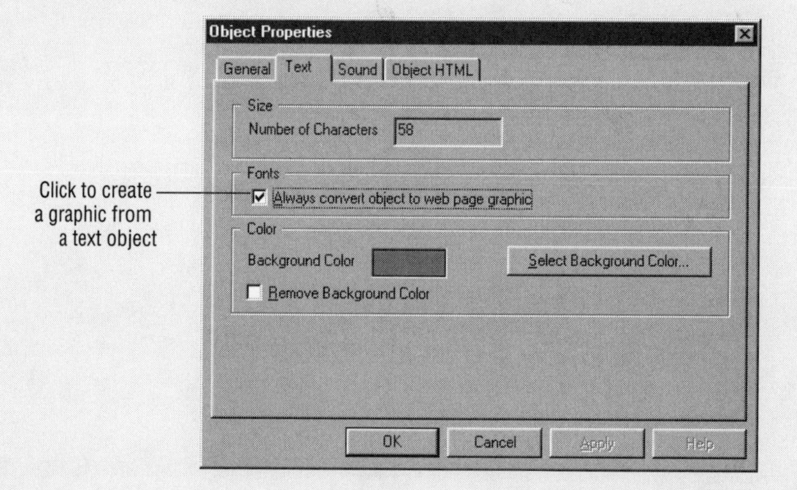

5. Click OK.

Web Studio creates a Graphic Interchange Format (GIF) image from the text box and displays it instead of the text. However, visitors to your Web site can't tell the difference. All they see is the text, in the font you chose, exactly as you want them to see it.

Those are the advantages of converting a text object to a graphic. The disadvantages are that the Web page takes longer to download because it includes an extra graphic, and the text isn't text anymore, so a search engine can't recognize or index it.

By the way, you can tell which text objects on a Web page have been turned into graphics: Choose View ➢ Highlight Objects ➢ Text Objects Converted to Graphics on Your Web Page. On the page, red boxes appear around text objects that have undergone a conversion. The red boxes also appear around text objects that overlap.

Changing the Color of Text

All text needn't be black. You are hereby invited to choose another color for text, although page backgrounds have to be considered when you make your choice. To be read comfortably, the text must be a different color from the page background. And be careful about using too many colors in headings and other text. Too many colors can be a distraction.

Follow these steps to change the color of text:

1. Select the text that needs a new color:
   - All of the text: Click the text object. As long as the black selection handles are showing, the formatting commands you give will apply to all the text.
   - Some of the text: Double-click the text object and either drag the pointer across the letters or words that need a new color, or double-click a word to select it.
2. Either click the Text Color button on the Format toolbar or choose Format ➢ Text Color. You see the Color dialog box.

3. Click a color to select it.
4. Click OK.

Tip

The Color dialog box offers a Define Custom Colors button that you can click to select from more colors than the 42 in the dialog box. But if you choose a color apart from the 42, you run the risk of choosing a color that can't be displayed in everyone's browser. The 42 colors in the dialog box are safe colors. Every browser can display them.

Choosing a Background Color for Text

To start with, a text object is transparent: The background color or pattern on the Web page shows through. But you can change that. You can fill a text object with its own color to make it stand out on the page. In the following illustration, the text objects on the left are transparent; the ones on the right have been assigned a text background color.

Chapter 6 explains how to choose a background color or pattern for a Web page.

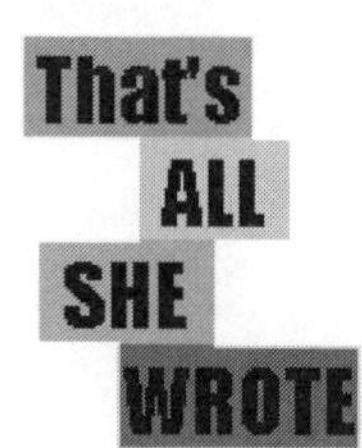

Follow these steps to assign a background color to text:

1. Click to select the text object.
2. Either right-click and choose Text Background Color ➢ Text Background Color or choose Format ➢ Text Background Color ➢ Text Background Color. You see the Color dialog box.
3. Click a color to select it.
4. Click OK.

To make a text object transparent, click to select it and either right-click and choose Text Background Color ➢ Transparent Text Background or choose Format ➢ Text Background Color ➢ Transparent Text Background.

Making Text Appear in Front of a Graphic

Making text appear in front of a graphic is an elegant trick. And it's easy to do as well. Start by placing a graphic and text object on the page. Then click the text object and drag it over the graphic. If you can't get the text to go over the graphic, select the graphic and click the Bring to Front button on the Main toolbar.

Laying Out Text on a Web Page

Besides dragging text objects here and there, you can lay out the text inside a text object in appealing ways. Text can be centered across a text object or aligned with its left side. And you can indent text in several different ways. The following pages are devoted to the premise that Web pages look more interesting when the text gets to dance on the page instead of sit there.

Justify
To align text on its left side or right side.

Left-Justifying, Centering, and Right-Justifying Text

Justifying refers to how lines of text fit in a text object—flush left, flush right, or across the center. By playing with the Justify commands, you can achieve elegant layouts like the ones in the following illustration. Here, the text on the left is left-justified; the text in the middle is center-justified; and the text on the right is right-justified.

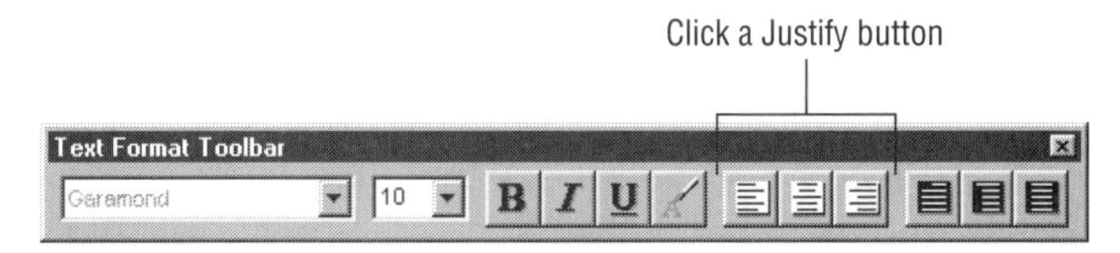

Hours	**Hours**	**Hours**
The fair starts at 11:00 and closes at 10:00. We hope to see you there.	The fair starts at 11:00 and closes at 10:00. We hope to see you there.	The fair starts at 11:00 and closes at 10:00. We hope to see you there.

Tip

Unfortunately all the text in a text object must be justified the same way. Centering a word or two above a column of left-justified text, for example, is impossible to do with the Justify commands. To do it, justify the two text boxes in different ways and then merge them. See "Merging Objects So They are Easier to Work With" in Chapter 4.

Follow these steps to left-justify, center, or right-justify the text in a text object:

1. Click to select the text object.
2. Either click a Justify button on the Format toolbar or choose Format ➢ Left Justify, Format ➢ Center Justify, or Format ➢ Right Justify.

Indenting Text

Indenting text moves text away from the left side and toward the center of a text object. Web Studio offers three ways to indent text: by indenting the first line of paragraphs, by indenting all but the first line of paragraphs, and by indenting all the lines.

First-line indents help mark the beginning of paragraphs. The reader knows precisely where one paragraph ends and the next begins.

> I begin to sing about Pallas Athena, renowned goddess, with bright eyes, quick mind, and inflexible heart, chaste and mighty virgin, protectress of the city, Tritogeneia.
>
> Wise Zeus himself gave birth to her from his holy head and she was arrayed in her armor of war, all gleaming in gold.

In a *hanging indent*, all but the first line is indented away from the left side of the text object. Typically, hanging indents are used in numbered and bulleted lists to make the numbers or bullets stand out.

> 1. I begin to sing about Pallas Athena, renowned goddess, with bright eyes, quick mind, and inflexible heart, chaste and mighty virgin, protectress of the city, Tritogeneia.
> 2. Wise Zeus himself gave birth to her from his holy head and she was arrayed in her armor of war, all gleaming in gold.

In a *paragraph indent*, all the text is moved away from the left side of the text object. Indent text this way when your text object has a color background and you want to put some space between the text and the left side of the text object. In the following illustration, a combination of indents was used. The first lines of paragraphs and the paragraphs themselves are indented.

> I begin to sing about Pallas Athena, renowned goddess, with bright eyes, quick mind, and inflexible heart, chaste and mighty virgin, protectress of the city, Tritogeneia.
>
> Wise Zeus himself gave birth to her from his holy head and she was arrayed in her armor of war, all gleaming in gold.

Follow these steps to indent text:

1. Click the text object whose words and letters need indenting.
2. Either click an Indent button on the Format toolbar or choose Format ➢ First Line Indent, Format ➢ Hanging Indent, or Format ➢ Paragraph Indent.

Tip

If you indent text too far, keep clicking an Indent button. Eventually, the text will bounce back to where it was before you started indenting it.

Making Text Scroll on the Page

Before you learn anything about *scrolling text*, you should know that some people find it annoying. Scrolling text refers to a message that leaps, loops, glides or slides onscreen. It keeps doing that. It continues to get viewers' attention whether viewers like it or not. Web Studio offers no less than eleven different ways to scroll text on a Web page.

Follow these steps to place a scrolling, marquee-style message on your Web site:

1. Open the Cool Stuff Gallery.
2. Find the Text F/X box and double-click its subfolder button. A selection of scrolling text effects appears in the gallery.

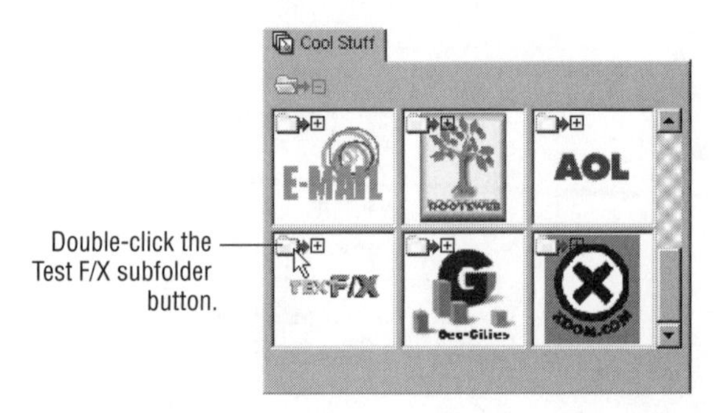

3. Click the one you want and drag into the Web Page window. Very likely, you will have to experiment with different effects until you find one that suits you. The Cool Text Effects dialog box appears.

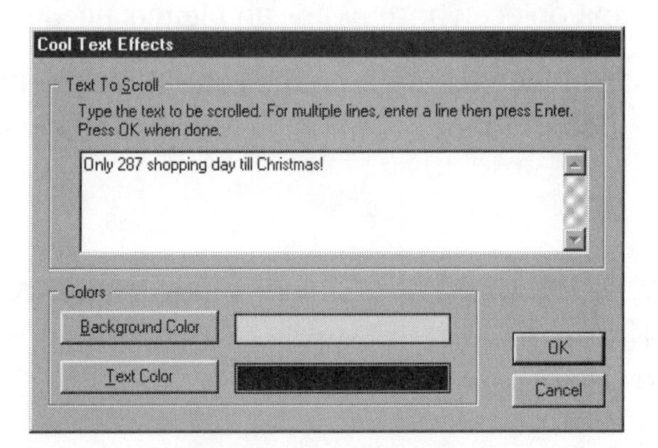

4. Enter a message in the Text to Scroll box.
5. If you want a background color different from the one on the Web page, click the Background Color button and choose a color in the Color dialog box.
6. If you want the scrolling text to be a certain color, click the Text Color button and choose a color.
7. Click OK.
8. Click the Preview Web Site button or press F5 to open the Page Preview window and watch the text scroll.

Chapter 6

Decorating Your Web Pages

This chapter is dedicated to the proposition that Web pages should be pleasing to the eye and easy to read. Here, you learn about page backgrounds and the many ways to create them—with colors, patterns, text, and graphics. You find out how to make the background show through an object, how to stretch a divider across a Web page, and how to use signs to make a livelier Web page.

- Using a solid color or pattern as a Web page background
- Tweaking backgrounds with the Special FX tools
- Using text or a graphic as the background
- Making the background scroll on the page
- Sprucing up a page with dividers and signs

Choosing a Background Color, Pattern, or Picture

Go to the Backgrounds Gallery to put a background on a Web page. How many backgrounds are there? About a million. Between the colors, the various patterns, the different hues you can give each pattern, and the special effects you can apply to patterns, the choice of backgrounds is enormous.

Read on to learn about backgrounds and how to choose them, change them, tweak them, and remove them. You also find out how to use a graphic of your own as the background, use text as a background, and make the background scroll.

Tips for Choosing Page Backgrounds

Choosing the right background for a Web page is like choosing the right clothes for a job interview. The background sets the tone. Viewers see the background first. It tells them what kind of Web page they are viewing—a sober Web page with a white background, for example, or a playful Web page with a colorful pattern.

Changing the page background is easy, so it's not as if you can't change backgrounds when a page is nearly complete. Still, the objects you choose for a page have to harmonize with the background. Green text, for example, doesn't work on a green background because no one can read it. Graphics are hard to see on a busy background. By choosing a background early, you can examine each object as you put it on the page to make sure it harmonizes with the background. By contrast, if you choose a background or change backgrounds late in the game, you run the risk of choosing a background that clashes with the objects that are already there.

One more thing: Backgrounds in a Web site should be consistent from page to page. This does not mean that backgrounds have to be the same. Different backgrounds set the pages apart and make it plain to visitors when they have come to a new Web page. However, if you go with different backgrounds, try to be consistent. Choose the same pattern with different hues. Or choose different shades of the same color. Visitors get a mighty jolt when they click a hyperlink, go to a new page, and discover a page that is radically different from the page they came from.

Using a Solid Color as the Background

Maybe the most elegant background is a solid color. A pale blue or green is easy on the eyes and doesn't obscure the text. And Web Studio offers numerous shades of each color. You can choose different shades of the same color for different Web pages.

Follow these steps to use a solid color as the background of a Web page:

1. Open the Backgrounds Gallery. To do so, choose View ➢ Galleries, if necessary, and then click the Backgrounds tab.
2. Click the color thumbnail, the first item in the Backgrounds Gallery, and drag it into the Web Page window. The Color dialog box appears.

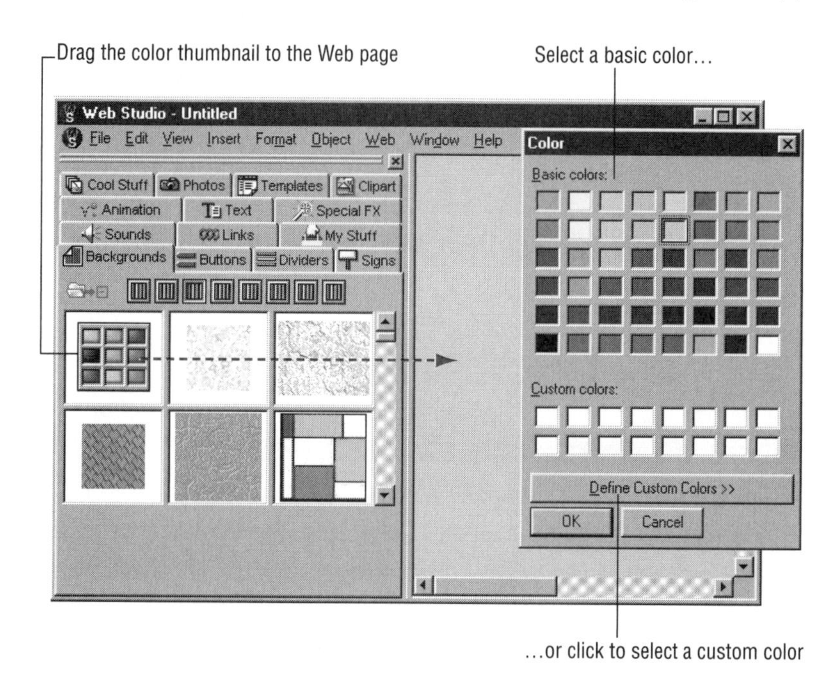

3. In the Color dialog box, select a basic color, or, if the basic colors aren't suitable, choose a color shade. You can choose one of the following from the Color dialog box:
   - Basic color: Click a color under "Basic Colors" at the top of the dialog box, and then click OK.
   - Color shade: Click the Define Custom Colors button. A color spectrum appears. Click different places across the color spectrum until you find the color you want, and then click in the box on the right to choose a color shade. The Color|Solid box shows the color and shade you have chosen. Click OK.

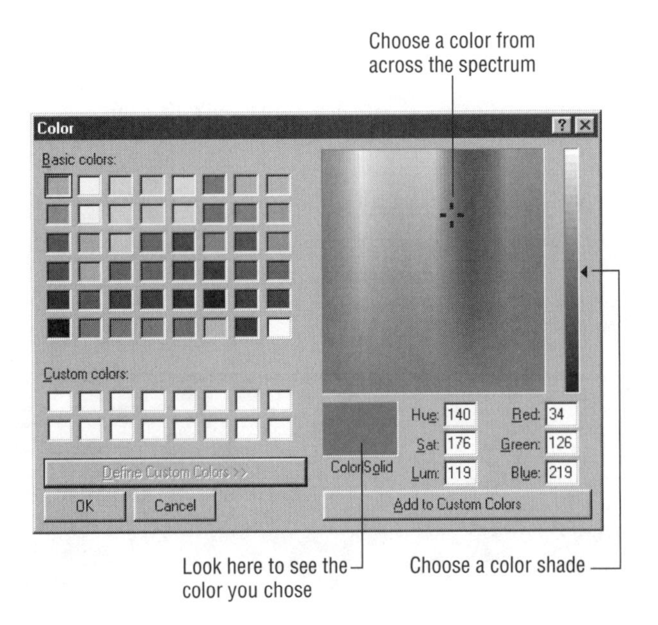

Warning

Be careful about choosing red and green backgrounds, because text hyperlinks on the page are red and text hyperlinks that have been clicked are green. If you are fond of red and green backgrounds, you can still use them without obscuring hyperlinks. To do so, choose new colors for hyperlinks. See "Changing the Color of Text Links" in Chapter 7.

When you're in a hurry, you can choose a solid color as the background of a Web page without visiting the Backgrounds Gallery. To do so, either right-click the page and choose Page Properties or choose Object ➢ Page Properties. In the Object Properties dialog box, click the Select Background Color button to view the Color dialog box and take it from there.

Later in this chapter, "Tweaking a Background in the Special FX Gallery" describes more ways to alter a pattern to your liking.

Decorating Pages with a Pattern

Given the number of patterns you can choose from, the different hues that can be applied to each pattern, and the numerous ways to tweak a pattern in the Special FX Gallery, you can spend a lot of time choosing a pattern background for a Web page. More than likely, finding the right pattern will take more than

one try. Keep experimenting, however, and soon you will find a background that suits the Web page you want to build.

Follow these steps to use a pattern as the background of a Web page:

1. Go to the Backgrounds Gallery by choosing View ➢ Galleries, if necessary, and clicking the Backgrounds tab.
2. Find a suitable pattern for your Web page:
   - Open folders to view different patterns
   - Click Hue buttons to change the shade or tint of a pattern you've chosen.
3. Drag the pattern into the Web Page window.

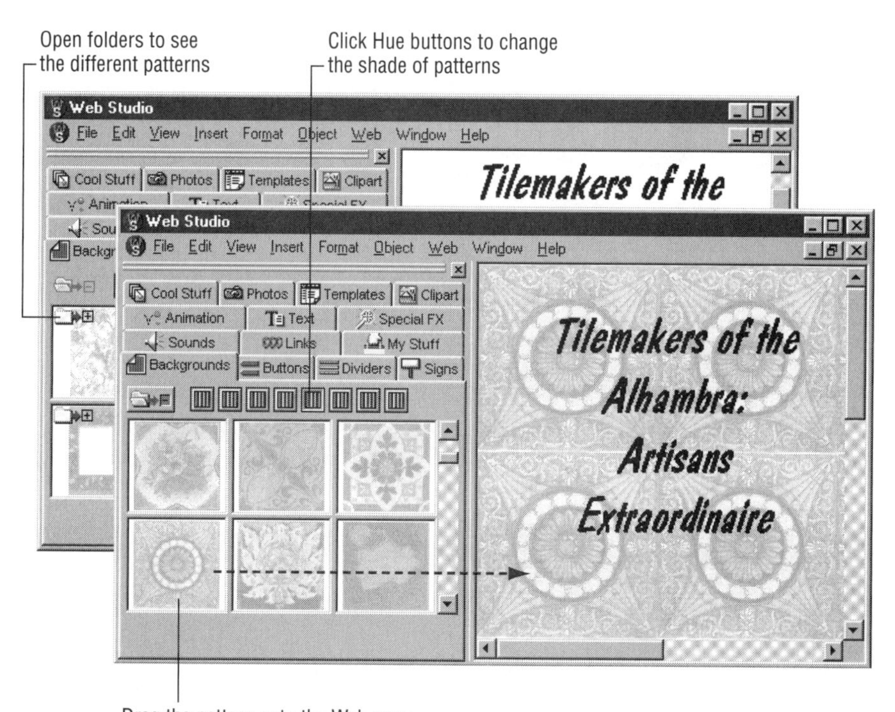

Tip

The Hue buttons in the Backgrounds Gallery are especially useful for choosing a background. Before you select a pattern, experiment by clicking different Hue buttons to find the right shade or tint.

Look closely and you will see that background patterns are formed from tiles that are laid side by side on the page. Sometimes you can see the tiles and sometimes you can't–it depends on the pattern.

Choosing a "Web Style" Background Pattern

Personally, I like the "Web Style" backgrounds that you can get by opening the Web Styles folder in the Backgrounds Gallery. "Web Style" backgrounds lend a touch of color to Web pages, but leave enough white space for text and graphics. The color appears along the left side of the Web page. You can devote the rest of the page to whatever you please.

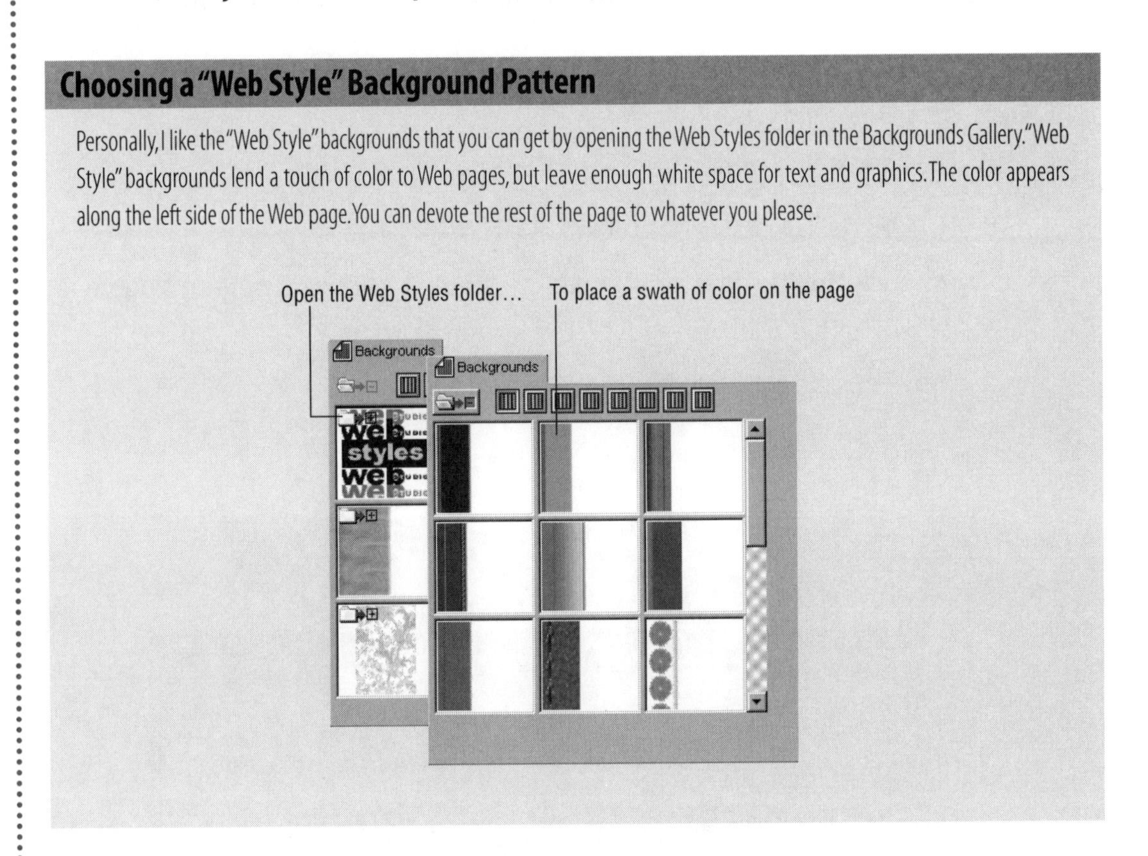

Tweaking a Background in the Special FX Gallery

As if the number of patterns in the Backgrounds Gallery isn't enough, you can tweak a pattern you've chosen to make it more original. To tweak a background pattern, go to the Special FX Gallery, drag a special effect into the Web Page window, and see what happens.

The Special FX Gallery offers 36 ways to tweak a background. What's more, you can tweak the same background one, two, three, or several different ways. As you experiment with special effects, keep the pointer on the Undo button

(or be prepared to choose Edit ➢ Undo Special Effect). Choosing special effects for a page background is decidedly a trial-and-error undertaking.

Not all the special effects are applicable to backgrounds, but following are descriptions of the ones that are.

The first special effect, Shadow, makes the design elements of the background cast a shadow.

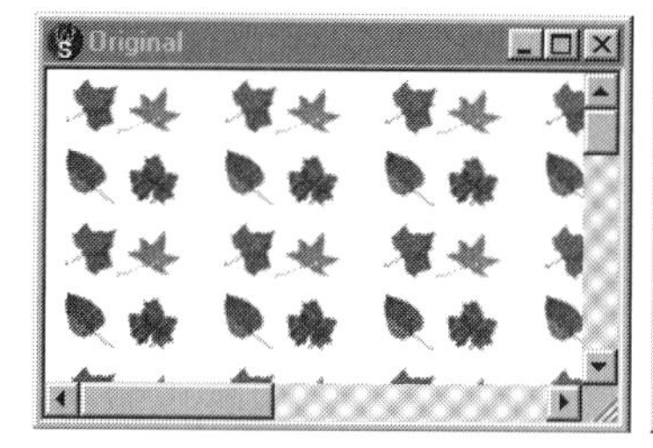

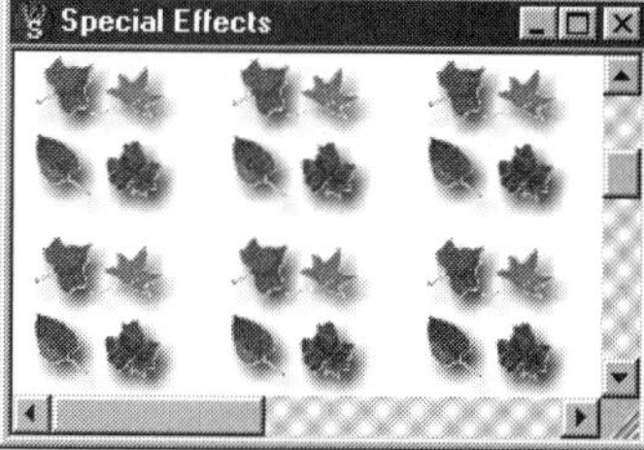

The next two special effects, Oilpaint and Paint by Numbers, give the impression that the background was hand-painted.

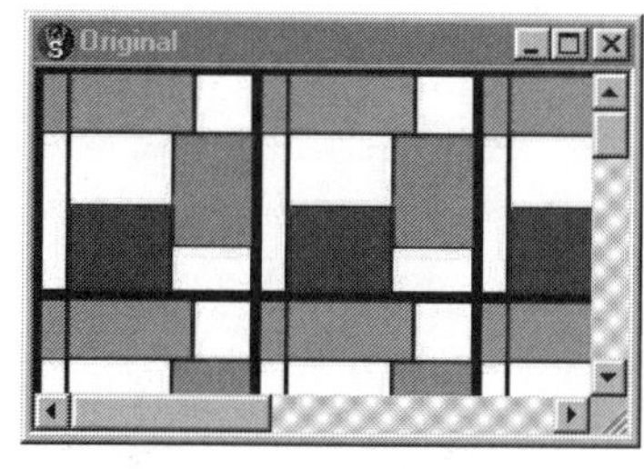

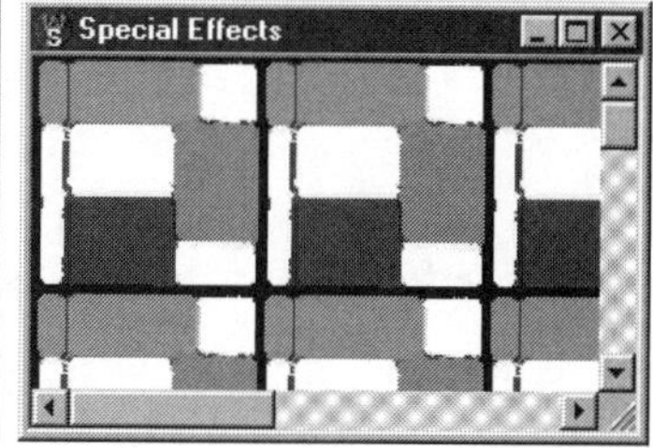

The Hue special effect merely does what clicking Hue buttons in the Web Gallery does—it changes the background's tint or shade. Keep applying the Hue special effect until you discover the shade you want. You can choose from eight hues.

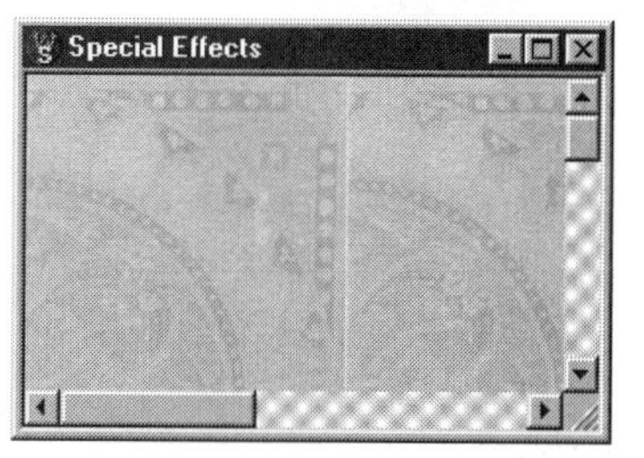

A Pattern special effect imposes a pattern—bricks, canvas, tiles (shown here), diamonds, barrels, vertical bars, or horizontal bars—over the pattern that is already on the background.

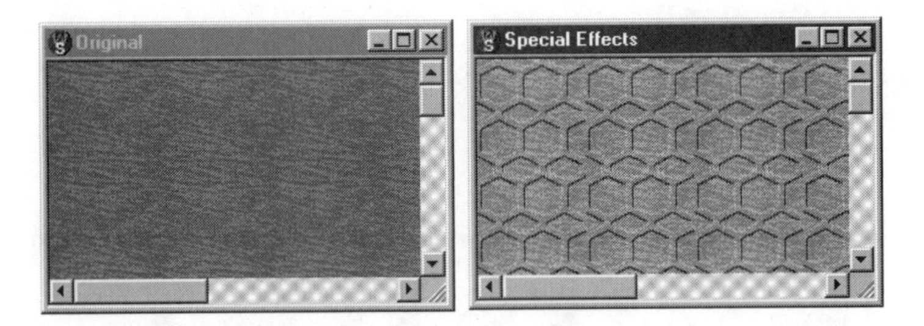

An Edges special effect makes the tiles that form the background pattern stand out. The edges around each tile are plain to see.

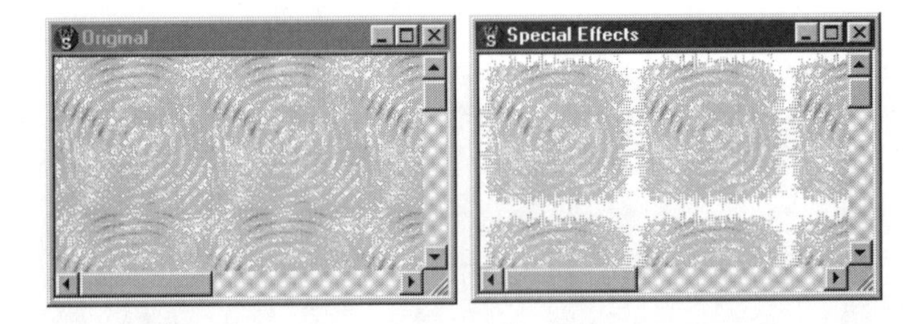

The Lighten and Darken special effects make backgrounds lighter or darker. In combination with the Hue special effect, Add Contrast, and Contrast special effects, these two are very useful for getting the background you want.

The Add Contrast special effect increases the contrast between dark and light colors on the background to make the background shinier. The Contrast special effect mutes the colors to make the background duller.

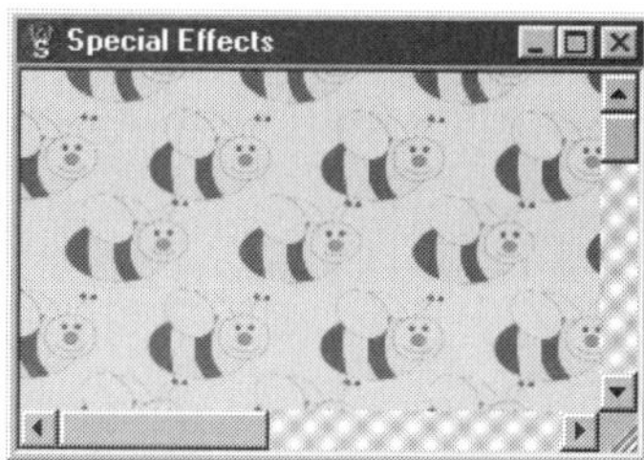

The Rotate, Reverse, and Flip special effects change the direction of the tiles on the background. Rotate turns the tiles 90 degrees. Reverse presents the mirror image of tiles. Flip turns tiles upside-down.

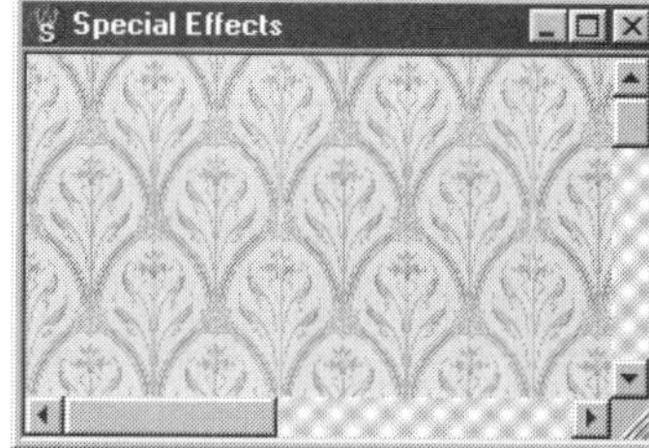

The Colorize special effect changes the color pattern of the background. When you drag the Colorize special effect into the Web page window, you see the Color dialog box. Choose a new color for the background pattern and click OK.

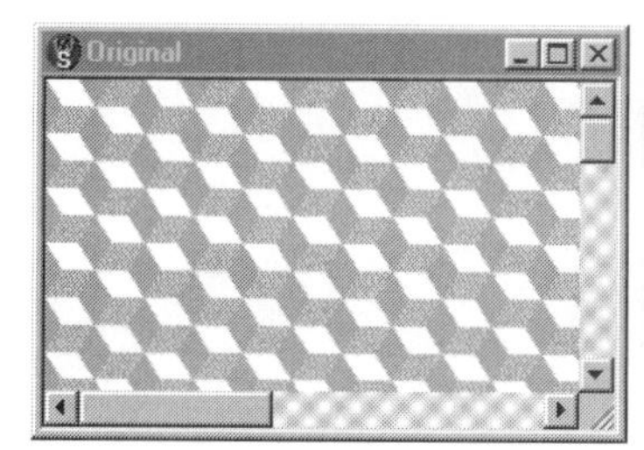

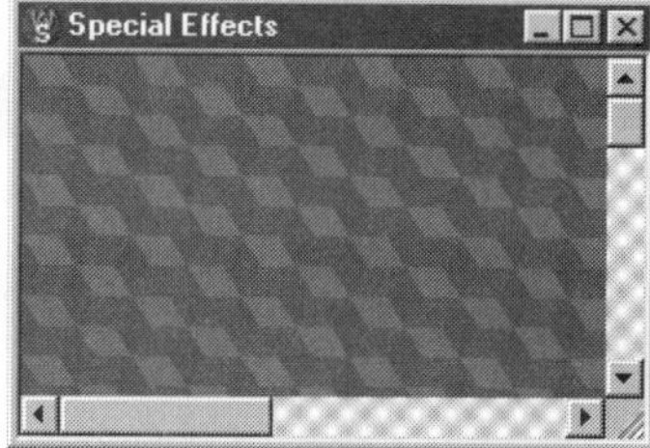

The Emboss special effect gives the impression that the background is embossed—that the lines are raised from the surface of the Web page.

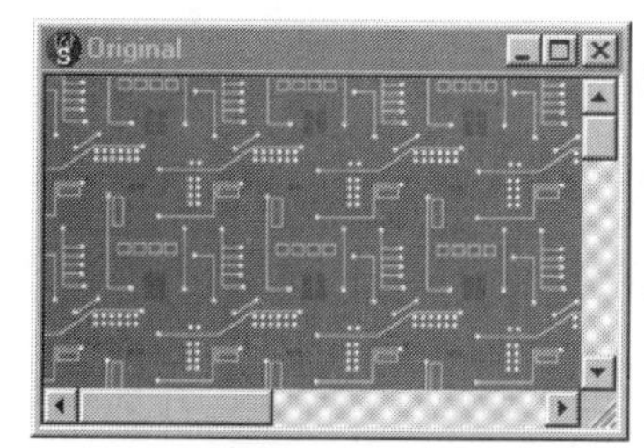

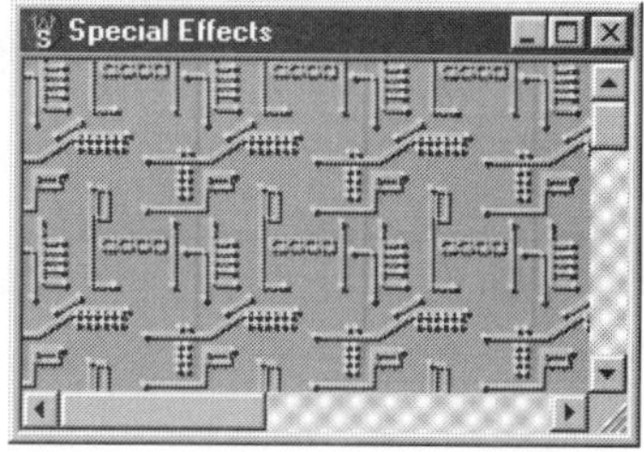

The Solarize and the Invert Colors special effects present the negative image of the background. Use them with caution. They turn the background into its opposite.

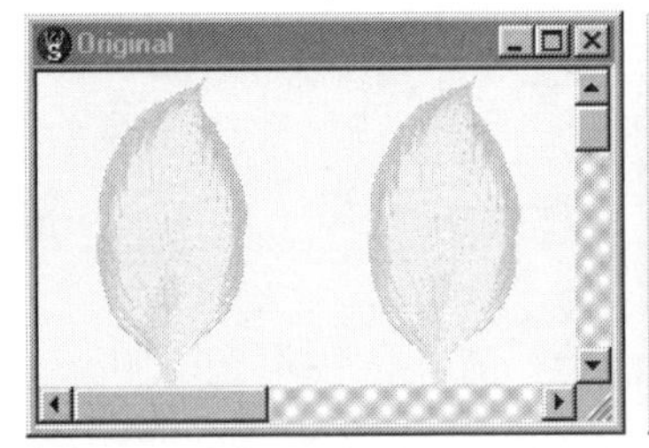

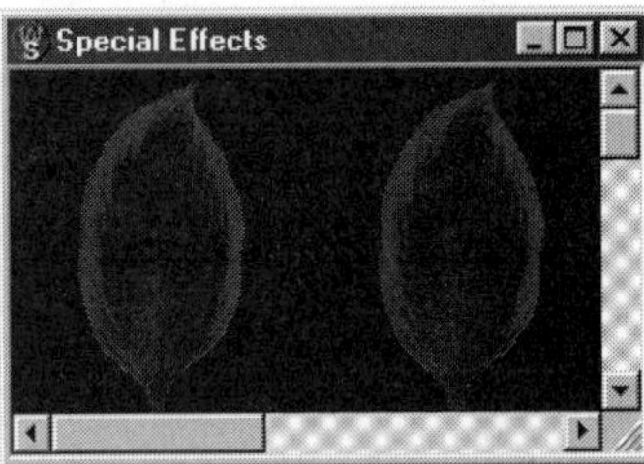

The Posterize special effects idealize the contrast between the different colors of the background to make the background look like a poster.

The Sharpen special effect and Blur special effects (found closer to the bottom of the Special FX Gallery) make backgrounds sharper or blurrier.

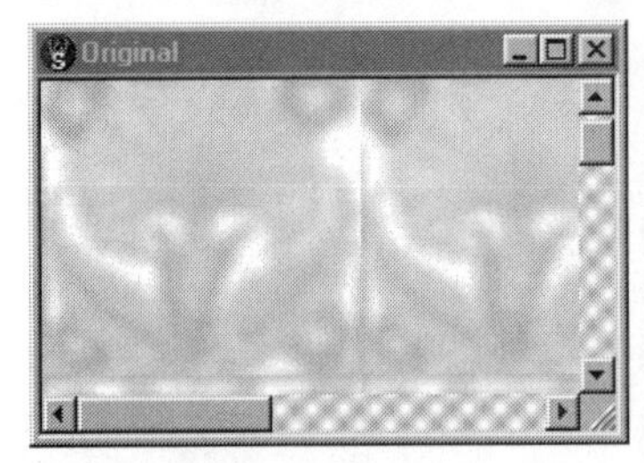

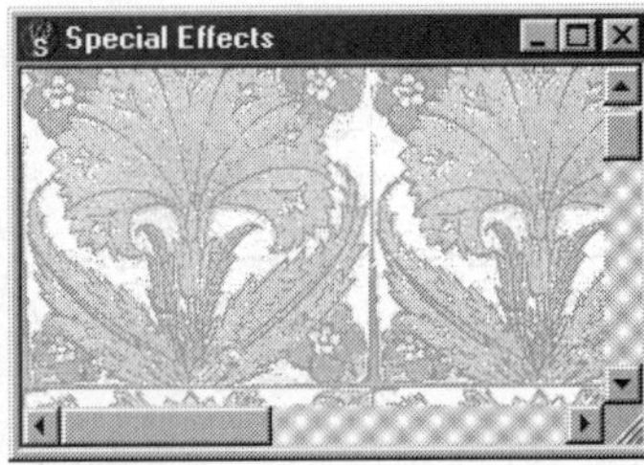

The Gray special effect renders a *film noir* version of the background. Instead of color, the background appears in shades of gray.

The Color Noise and Noise special effects make the colors of the background look coarser and grainier.

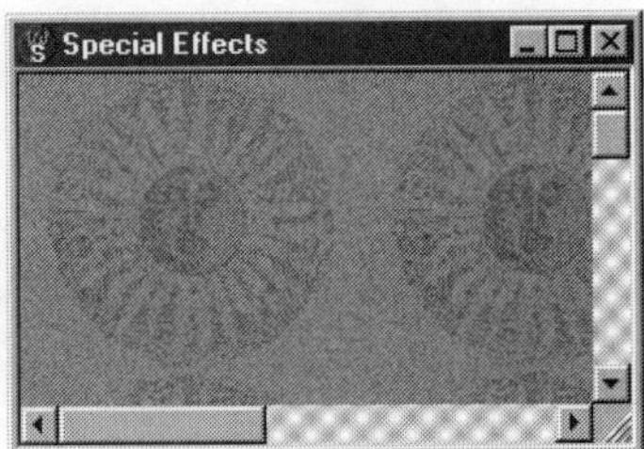

The Small, Medium, and Large Mosaic special effects give the impression that the background was constructed from small, medium, or large mosaic tiles.

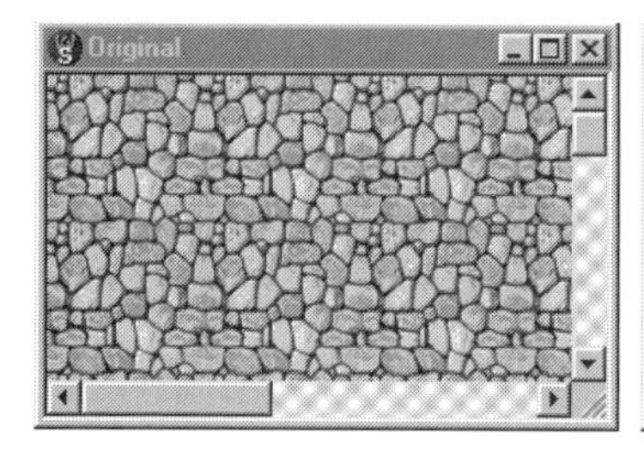

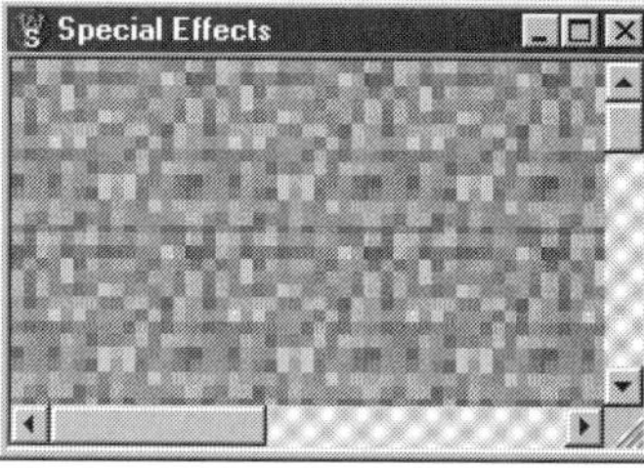

The Halftone and Halftone 2 special effects turn a color background into grainy shades of black and white.

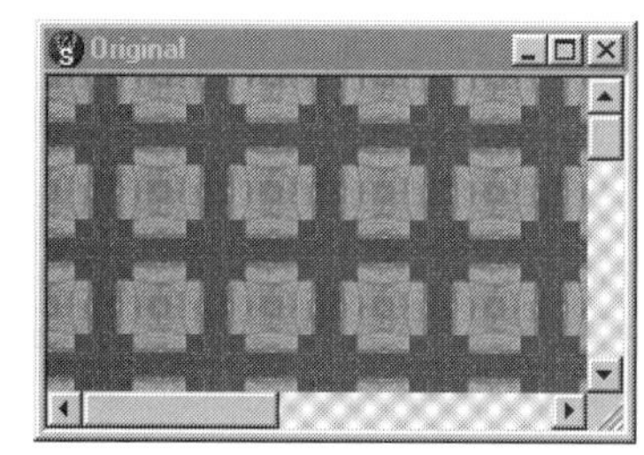

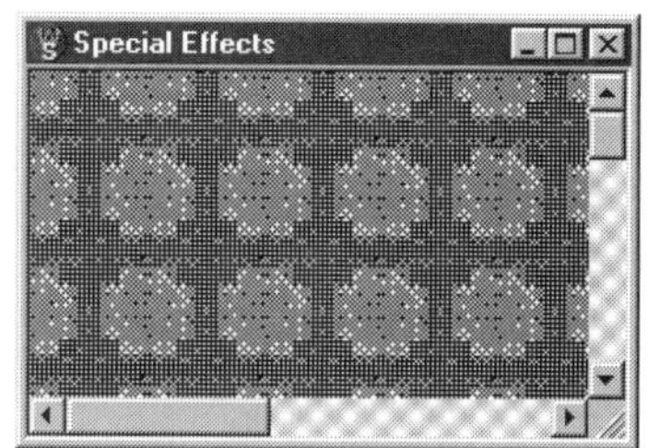

Importing a Graphic for Use as the Background

If the backgrounds in the Backgrounds Gallery don't do the trick, try using a graphic of your own for the background. Remember, however, that a graphic is tiled when it is used in the background. It appears repeatedly. Most graphics weren't designed to appear as tiles, and they don't interlock very well when they are placed side by side.

Warning

Stick with GIF and JPEG images when you choose a graphic for the background. GIF and JEPG files are not large, and therefore don't take long to download from the Internet. A visitor to your Web page doesn't have to wait long for the background to appear if you use a GIF or JPEG image.

Borrowing the Background from a Page on the Internet

Suppose that you are traveling the Internet, you come to a Web page whose background looks enticing, and you say to yourself, "I'd like to borrow that background for one of my Web pages."

You can do it. Follow these steps to borrow a background from a Web page:

1. Right-click the Web page and choose Copy Background on the shortcut menu.
2. Open Web Studio and display the Web page that will receive the background you are about to borrow.
3. Either choose Edit ➢ Paste As Background, or right-click in the Web Page window and choose Paste As Background.

Better yet, you can save backgrounds as you find them on the Internet, store them in a folder, and call on them when you need them. Follow these steps to save a page background so you can make use of it later:

1. Right-click the Web page whose background you want for your collection and choose Save Background As. You see the Save Picture dialog box.
2. Save the file where you can find it later on. You might give it a descriptive name if it doesn't already have one.

Earlier in this chapter, "Importing a Graphic for Use as the Background" explains how to make use of a background you saved with the Save Background As command.

Follow these steps to commandeer a graphic for use as the background of a Web page:

1. Choose Insert ➢ Background from File. The Open dialog box appears.
2. Locate the folder where the graphic you want is stored.
3. Click the Details button. You will find it in the upper-right corner of the dialog box. The size of files and the file type are shown after you click the button. Now you can find JPEG and GIF files more easily.

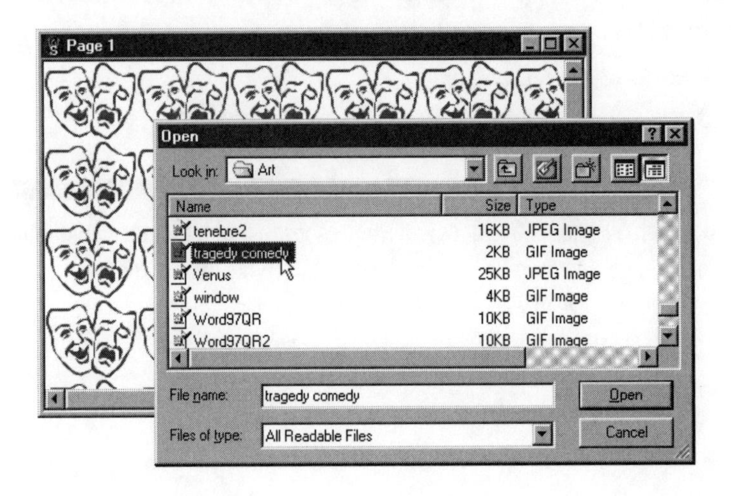

4. Select the file you want.
5. Click the Open button.

All of the special effects in the Special FX Gallery can be applied to a graphic you imported on your own. The previous section in this chapter explains the Special FX gallery.

Using Text as the Background

Using text as the background of a Web page is simply a matter of creating a text object, converting it to a graphic, and pasting it into the Web Page window. Follow these steps if you believe that words, not pictures, make the best backgrounds:

1. Create the text object.

Tip

Used in the background, a text object appears in tiled form. For that reason, make it very large, center the text, and use a fat font such as Arial or Impact so that people can read the text. What's more, change the text color to gray or another light color that won't obscure the text and graphics on the page.

2. Click the text object and choose Edit ➢ Cut (or press Ctrl+X).
3. Choose Edit ➢ Paste As Background

These Special FX commands are especially useful with text backgrounds:

- Shadow: Gives the text a three-dimensional quality.
- Hue: Lets you change color shades without starting all over.
- Lighten: Permits you to make the text lighter if it obscures other items on the Web page.
- Rotate: Lets you turn the text on its ear.
- Sharpen: Makes the letters crisper.

See "Tweaking a Background in the Special FX Gallery" earlier in this chapter to learn about the Special FX commands.

- Gray: Turns the letters a shade of gray.

Making the Background Scroll

The Cool Stuff Gallery offers a command for making the background scroll ever so slowly toward the top of the page. Depending on your point of view, I should say, either the background scrolls upward or the text and graphics on the page scroll downward. Be careful with this command—a scrolling background can be annoying.

Follow these steps to see if a scrolling background is right for you:

1. Open the Cool Stuff Gallery. To do so, choose View ➢ Galleries, if necessary, and click the Cool Stuff tab.
2. Look for the red arrow and the letters BG (for Background), and click them.
3. Drag the letters BG into the Web Page window. Don't worry about the letters getting in the way of text or graphics. The BG is there only to let you know that the background of this Web page is supposed to scroll. The letters don't actually appear on the Web page, as the next step demonstrates.

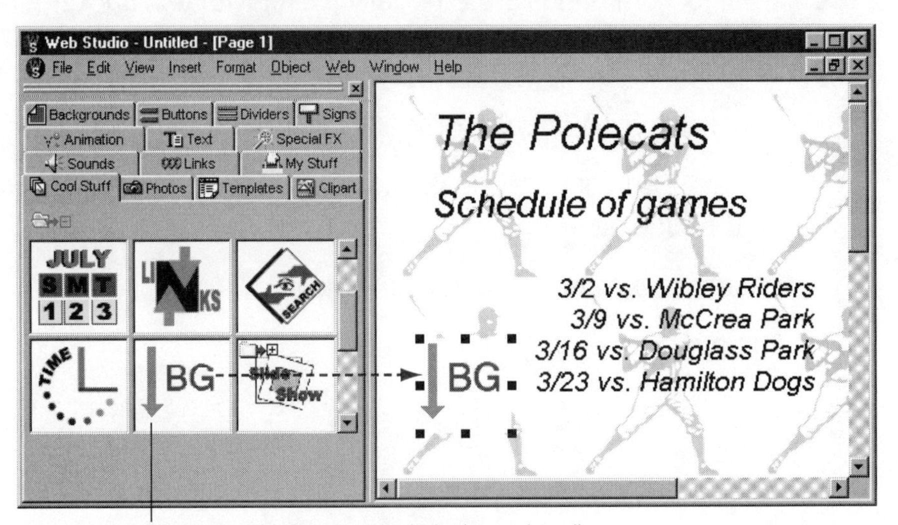

Drag the letters BG onto the Web Page to make the background scroll

4. Click the Preview Web Site button or press F5.

See the background scroll in the Page Preview window? What do you think? If you decide against a scrolling background, return to the Web Page window, click the letters BG, and press the Delete key.

"Choosing a Background Color for Text" in Chapter 5 explains how to change the color of a text object or make it transparent.

Removing the Background

You will be glad to know that removing a background is far easier than creating one. Follow these steps to remove the background from a Web page:

1. Click the page whose background needs removing. Be sure not to click an object of any kind.
2. Either choose Object ➢ Remove Background, or right-click and choose Remove Background.

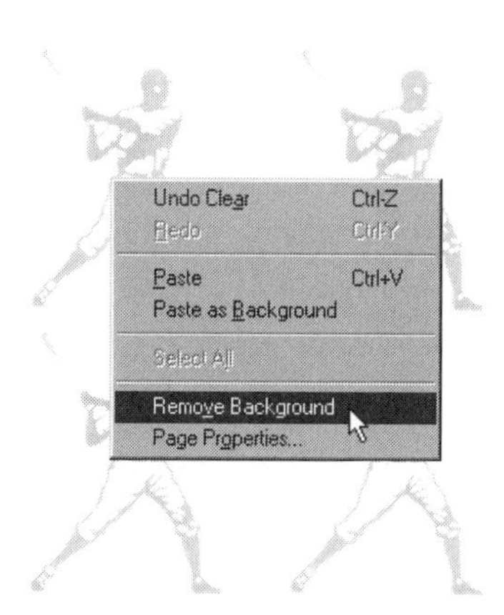

Making the Background Show through an Object

The Transparent commands on the Object menu determine how an object and the background of a Web page cooperate. The commands take some getting used to because they do different things, depending on whether the object is transparent or not.

A transparent object is one through which you can see the background. In this illustration, the angel on the left is transparent. You can see the background of the page through the angel. The angel on the right is not transparent. It appears in a white box.

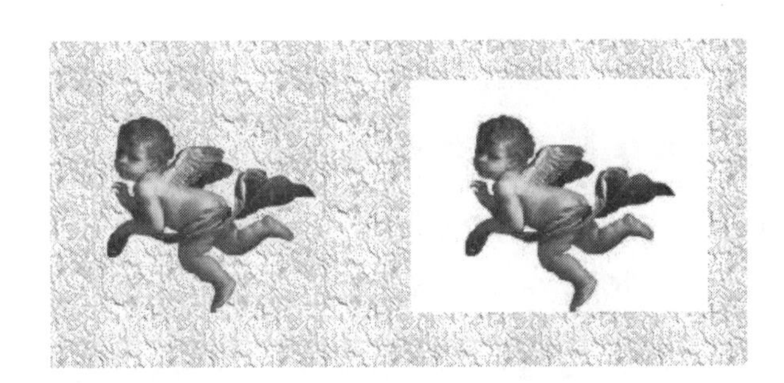

The trick to understanding the Transparent commands is to understand that only one color in each object can be the transparent color—the one that is replaced by the background, whatever it happens to be. In most cases, objects arrive onscreen in a white box, so in most cases, white should be made the transparent color if you want the background to show through. Web Studio offers a special command for turning white into the transparent color: Object ➢ Transparent Color ➢ Transparent White.

However, by choosing Object ➢ Transparent Color ➢ Choose Color, you can select a color besides white as the transparent color. In this illustration, different colors in the same clip art image were chosen as the transparent color. As you can see, the background shows through in different places to make for interesting effects:

Here is the lowdown on handling objects and the background:

Replacing the White Box with the Background Choose Object ➢ Transparent Color ➢ Transparent White to make the background show through. You can also right-click and choose Transparent Color ➢ Transparent White.

Making the Object Appear in a White Box Choose Object ➢ Transparent to remove the checkmark beside the Transparent command.

The white box appears, and the object isn't transparent anymore. You can also right-click the object and choose Transparent.

Choosing a Part of the Object to Be Transparent As I explained, you can choose one color to be transparent and be replaced by the background. To try for an unusual effect and make a color besides white transparent, choose Object ➢ Transparent Color ➢ Choose Color. Then, in the Select Transparency Color dialog box, click the part of the object you want to be transparent. Gray appears in place of the color you chose to show where the background will show through. Click OK.

Divider
A thick line, or bar, on a Web page that divides one part of the page from another.

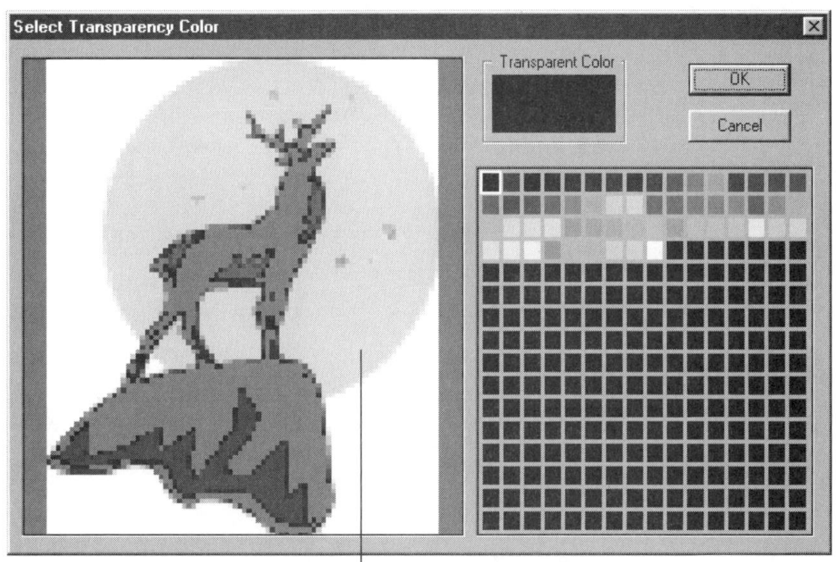

Click the part of the object you want to be transparent

Dividers for Breaking a Page into Different Parts

Dividers separate one part of a Web page from another. They sort of steer the eye from place to place and let visitors know when the Web page presents a new topic. Read on to learn how to place a divider on the page, change the size of a divider, and place a vertical divider on a Web page.

Placing a Divider across a Web Page

Follow these steps to place a divider across a Web page:

1. Go to the Dividers Gallery. To do so, choose View ➢ Galleries, if necessary, and click the Dividers tab.
2. Click Hue buttons to find the dividers that are the right shade.
3. Drag the divider into the Web Page window.

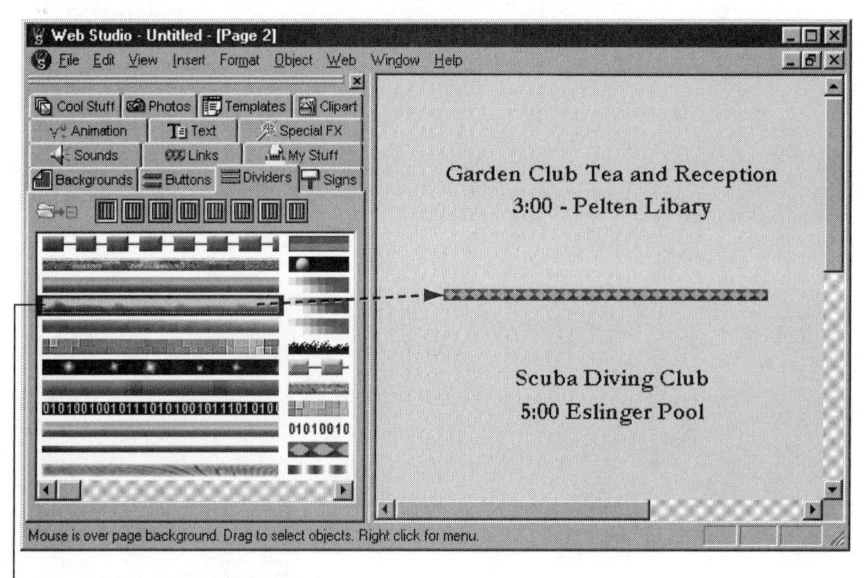

Drag a divider onto the Web page

Although a divider is long and slender, it is still an object. To move it, click and start dragging. The standard techniques for wrestling with objects also apply to dividers:

- Shorter or longer: To make a divider longer or shorter, move the pointer to one end. When you see the double-headed arrow, click and start dragging.
- Wider or narrower: To make the divider wider or narrower, move the pointer over a selection handle in the middle. When you see the double-headed arrow, click and start dragging.

Dividing the Sides of a Page

As well as separating one part of a page from another, you can separate the sides of pages with dividers. For that matter, you can simply use dividers as decorative objects, as they are used in the following illustration.

Follow these steps to create a vertical divider:

1. Place a divider across the Web page.
2. Go to the Special FX Gallery.
3. Find the Rotate object in the gallery and drag it atop the divider to rotate the divider by 90 degrees.

Signs for Sprucing Up Web Pages

Pound for pound, the easiest way to spruce up a Web page is to put a sign on it. Web Studio offers numerous signs in the Signs Gallery, and chances are you can find one that fits nicely on your Web page. Use signs to draw attention to part of a Web page or simply for decorative purposes.

Follow these steps to drop a sign on a Web page:

1. Open the Signs Gallery by choosing View ➢ Galleries, if necessary, and clicking the Signs Stuff tab.
2. Locate the sign you want by searching in folders.
3. Drag the sign into the Web Page window.

Chapter 7

Putting Hyperlinks on Your Web Pages

A hyperlink is a secret passage from one place on the Internet to another. Click a hyperlink and something new appears onscreen—a different Web page, a different Web site, or a new location on the same page. Hyperlinks give Web site visitors the opportunity to choose what they read or view next. Hyperlinks make a Web site livelier and more inviting.

This chapter explains everything you need to know to about hyperlinks, from creating them to changing their color. You'll learn how to manage hyperlinks, create links to different places, and stock the Links Gallery with useful hyperlinks.

- Putting your own links in the Links Gallery
- Turning an object or text into a hyperlink
- Linking a Web page to another site, another page, or another location on the same page
- Removing and editing hyperlinks
- Changing the color of text links

All about Hyperlinks

Uniform Resource Locator (URL)
An address on the Internet. Every Web page has its own URL.

You can tell when you have encountered a hyperlink because when you move the pointer over a hyperlink it changes into a gloved hand. The gloved hand is your signal to click and go elsewhere on the Internet. Anything on a Web page—a graphic, text, a button—can be made into a hyperlink. By convention, a text hyperlink is blue and is underlined.

Next time you are surfing the Internet, glance at the status bar in your browser when you move the pointer over a hyperlink. The status bar lists the **uniform resource locator (URL)**, or address, of the page on the Internet where you will go if you click the hyperlink.

Managing the Links Gallery

As far as hyperlinks are concerned, the Links Gallery is Grand Central Station. You know the routine: To create a hyperlink, drag a hyperlink name from the Links Gallery over an object in the Web Page window. Read on to learn how to

put your own hyperlinks in the Links Gallery so that, later on, you can drag them onto Web pages. Putting together a well-stocked Links Gallery with the hyperlinks you need is the first step in placing hyperlinks in a Web site.

This section explains how the Links Gallery works, how to place your own hyperlinks in the Links Gallery, and how to handle links in the gallery.

A Quick Tour of the Links Gallery

The three boxes in the Links Gallery hold hyperlinks to other pages in the Web site or to other places on the Internet. The three boxes in the Links Gallery are:

- Site Links: Lists other pages in your Web site so you can hyperlink one page to another. *Add Anchor to Object* is for creating a hyperlink to a new location on the same Web page.
- My Links: Lists hyperlinks that you have placed in the box. Place the names of Web sites here to make hyperlinking easier.
- Links: Lists the Web sites you designated as "favorites" in Internet Explorer. Choose Favorites ➢ Links in Internet Explorer to see the same list of Web sites. Web Studio presumes you want to share your favorite Web sites with others, so it puts their names in the Links box to make linking to your favorite Web sites easier.

Appendix C explains how to organize bookmarks by creating subfolders in the Links folder.

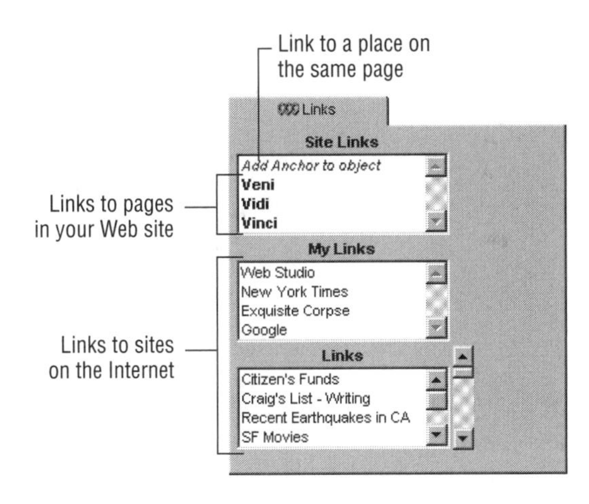

More boxes than these three may be available in the Links Gallery if you organized your favorite Web sites into subfolders in Internet Explorer. Inside the Links folder, I created subfolders called Newspapers, Search Engines, Research, E-Zines, and Addie for holding my favorite Web sites. By enlarging the Links Gallery, I can see all my subfolders.

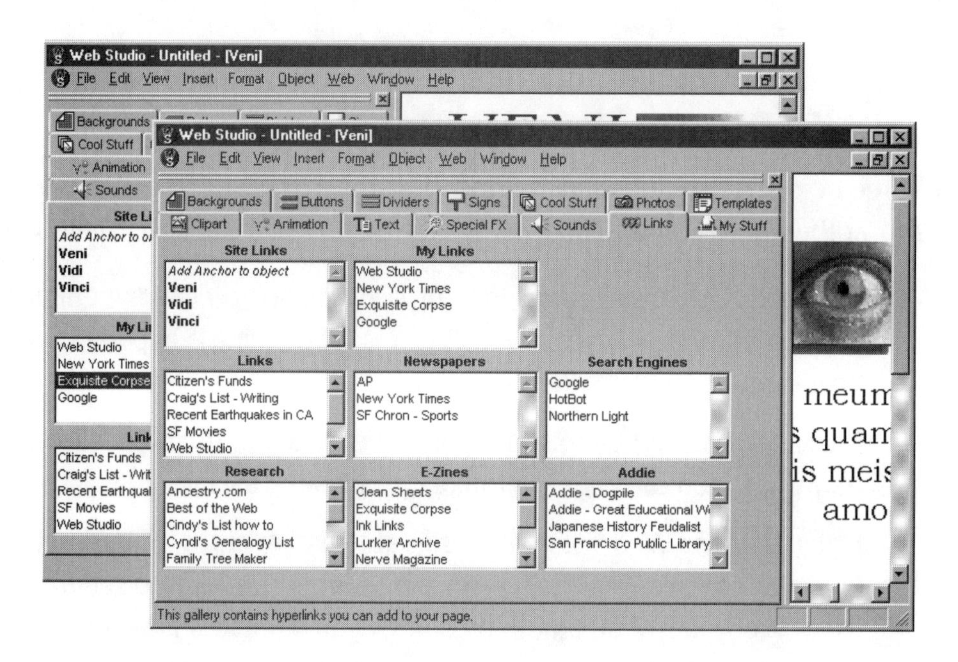

Later in this chapter, "The QuickWay to Turn a Graphic, Button, or Sign into a Hyperlink" explains how to create a hyperlink without visiting the Links Gallery.

Adding Your Own Hyperlinks to the Links Gallery

You may as well store the hyperlinks you need in the Links Gallery. That way, you can find and make use of them easily.

Follow these steps to create and keep a hyperlink in the Links Gallery so you can use it time and time again:

1. In Internet Explorer, open the Web page you want to make the target of a hyperlink.
2. In Web Studio, open the Links Gallery.
3. Either right-click the My Links box and choose Add Link or choose Insert ➢ My Links Gallery Link. You see the Add Link dialog box.

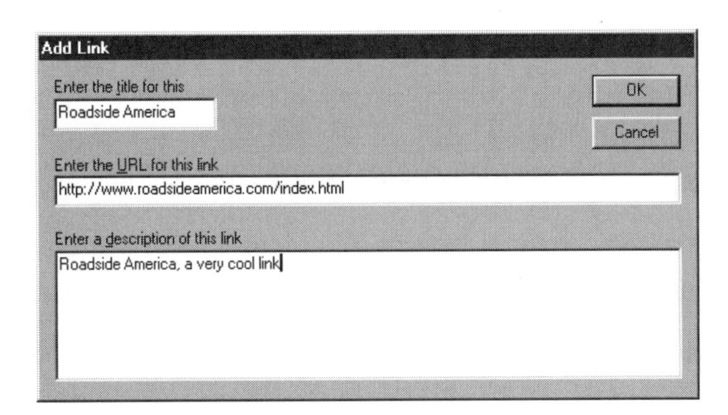

4. Enter a title for the hyperlink in the first text box. The title you enter will appear in the My Links box in the Links Gallery.
5. Enter the URL for the hyperlink in the Enter the URL for This Link box.

Tip

URLs are hard to type. Here's the easy way to enter a URL: Go back to your browser, click in the Address bar to highlight the URL address (choose View ➢ Toolbars ➢ Address Bar if you don't see the Address bar), right-click the address, and choose Copy on the shortcut menu. Then go back to Web Studio, erase the `http://` in the Enter the URL for This Link box, right-click, and choose Paste. The URL address appears in the Add Link dialog box.

6. Describe the hyperlink in the Enter a Description of This Link box. The description is for identification purposes only, in case you forget where the link goes.
7. Click OK.

Now the hyperlink is ready to go. All you have to do is drag it over an object in the Web Page window to turn part of a Web page into a hyperlink. To test your new hyperlink and make sure it goes to the right place, hold down the Ctrl key and double-click its name. If all is well, the Web site to which the link goes opens in your browser.

Tip

Suppose you want to put a hyperlink from the Links box in the My Links box where finding it is easier. To do so, drag it there. Dragging a hyperlink from the Links to the My Links box copies the hyperlink. The original copy remains in the Links box.

Handling Hyperlinks in the Links Gallery

The Links Gallery is a repository of hyperlinks that you can put in your Web pages. Here are instructions for keeping a tidy Links Gallery:

Copying a Hyperlink in the Links Box to the My Links Box Drag the link from the Links box into the My Links box.

Removing a Hyperlink Right-click a link in the My Links box and choose Delete.

Rearranging Hyperlinks Right-click a link and choose Move Up or Move Down to change its position in the list.

Changing the Name or URL of a Hyperlink Right-click a link and choose Edit. You see the Edit Link dialog box. Fill it in the same way you fill in the Add Link dialog box.

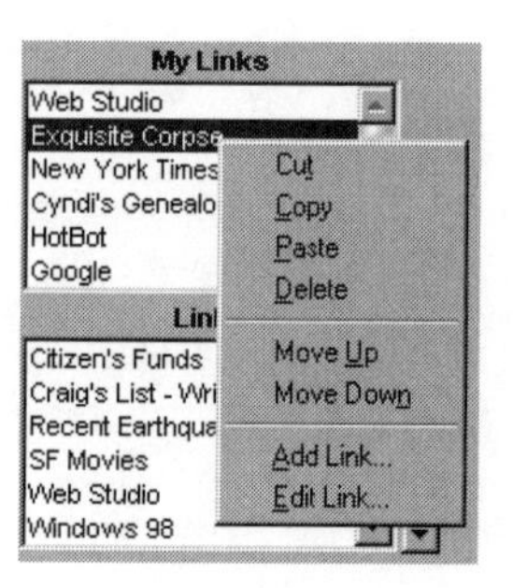

Tip

Here's a fast way to delete several hyperlinks at once in the Links box: Open Windows Explorer and go to the `C:\Sierra\Web Studio 2\linkfldr` folder. In the folder, double-click the My Links document to open it. You see a list of hyperlinks and their URLs. Delete the ones you don't want and choose File ➢ Save. Next time you open Web Studio, the hyperlinks you deleted will be gone.

Hyperlinks for Making Your Web Page Jump

Now that you know how to manage hyperlinks in the Links Gallery, you can get down to business. These pages explain how to turn an object into a hyperlink,

turn text into a hyperlink, and quickly fashion a hyperlink without getting it from the Links Gallery. You also learn how to link one Web page to another and how to create a hyperlink that joins two different places on the same page. Oh, one more thing: You find out how to remove a hyperlink.

Turning an Object into a Hyperlink

A text box, clip art image, photograph, sign, or button can double as a hyperlink. To make an object into a hyperlink, follow these steps:

Earlier in this chapter, "Adding Your Own Hyperlinks to the Links Gallery" explains how to place your own hyperlinks in the My Links box.

1. Open the Links Gallery.
2. In the My Links or Links box, find the hyperlink that you want for the object and click it.
3. Drag the hyperlink you chose over the object. A plus sign (+) appears below the pointer when the pointer is correctly over the object.
4. Release the mouse button.

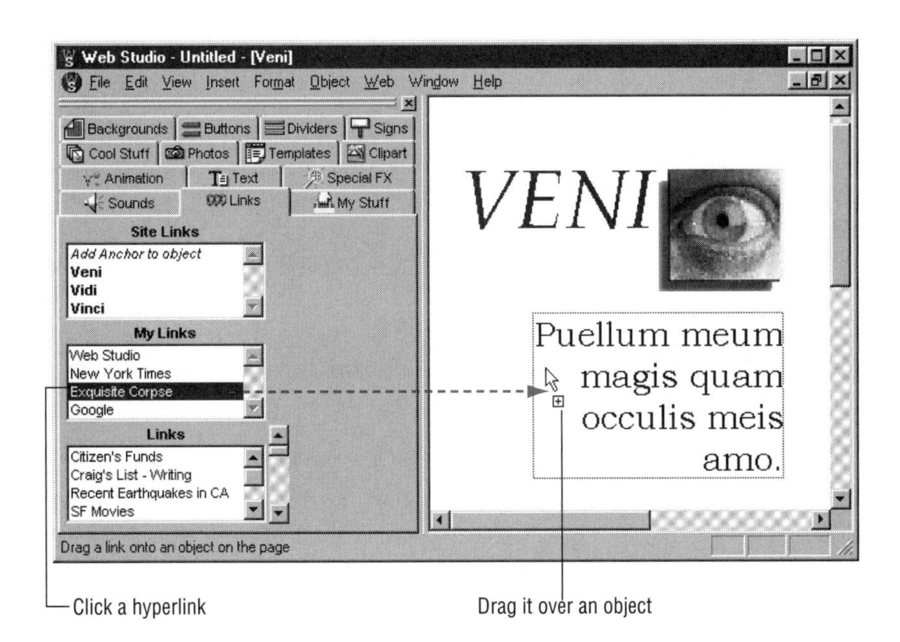

Be sure to test your hyperlink after you create it. To do so, click the Preview Web Site button (or press F5). Then, in the Page Preview window, double-click the hyperlink. Does the Web page to which the hyperlink refers appear?

Visiting a Hyperlink before You Put It on a Web Page

Especially if a lot of links are in the Links Gallery, telling them apart can be difficult. One link is named Peter, for example, and another is named Paul. How can you be sure when you create a hyperlink that you are sending visitors to the right place?

Follow these steps to test-drive a hyperlink in the Links Gallery before you deposit it on a Web page:

1. Hold down the Ctrl key.
2. Double-click the hyperlink in the My Links or Links box.

Internet Explorer opens, and you see the Web site to which the hyperlink refers. Is it the right Web site? If so, you can confidently drag the hyperlink you double-clicked into the Web Page window to create a hyperlink.

The Quick Way to Turn a Graphic, Button, or Sign into a Hyperlink

A graphic, button, sign, or animation for that matter can be turned into an Internet hyperlink without visiting the Links Gallery. Follow these steps to link a graphic, button, sign, or animation to a site on the Internet:

1. In Internet Explorer, open to the Web page where the hyperlink will go.
2. In Web Studio, click the sign, button, graphic, or animation that will form the hyperlink.
3. Either choose Object ➢ Object Properties or right-click and choose Properties. You see the Object Properties dialog box.
4. Click the Link tab.

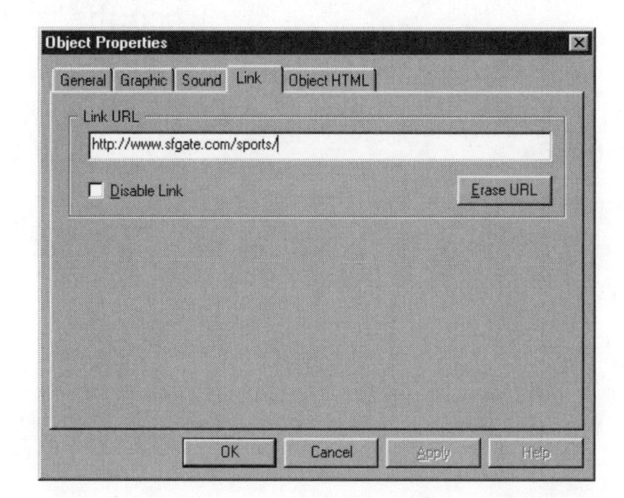

5. Enter the URL for the hyperlink in the Link URL box.

Tip

The fast way to enter a URL in the Object Properties dialog box is to go to your browser, click in the Address bar to highlight the URL (choose View ➢ Toolbars ➢ Address Bar if you don't see the Address bar), right-click the address, and choose Copy. In Web Studio, right-click in the Link URL box and choose Paste. The URL appears in the Object Properties dialog box.

6. Click OK.

To test the hyperlink, click the Preview Web Site button (or press F5). Then, in the Web Preview window, click the link you created and see what happens.

Turning a Word or Phrase into a Hyperlink

Turning all the text in a text object into a hyperlink is easy—just drag the hyperlink from the Links Gallery to the text object. But suppose you want to fashion a hyperlink out of a word or phrase. In this illustration, for example, the name of a newspaper, *The Town Crier,* is a hyperlink. Viewers can click the link to go to the newspaper's home page on the Internet.

Later in this chapter, "Changing the Color of Text Links" explains how to steer away from the standard red color for hyperlinks and the standard green color for links that have been visited.

my hometown, whose newspaper is still
thriving. In fact, The Town Crier is
available on the Internet, and sometimes I

Turning a word or phrase into a hyperlink involves selecting the word or phrase and then following the standard procedure for creating a hyperlink. Follow these steps:

1. Double-click the text object as though you were going to edit the text.
2. Drag the pointer over the word or phrase that will form the hyperlink. The word or phrase is highlighted.

my hometown, whose newspaper is still
thriving. In fact, The Town Crier is
available on the Internet, and sometimes I

3. Open the Links Gallery.
4. Find the hyperlink that you want in the My Links or Links box and click it.
5. Drag the hyperlink over the highlighted word or phrase and release the mouse button.

Two Tricks for Handling Hyperlinks

Here are a couple of tricks for handling hyperlinks:

Finding Out Where Hyperlinks Go Either click a link and choose Object ➢ Link Info or right-click and choose Link Info. The Link Description dialog box appears so you can read the hyperlink's URL. If a description was entered for the link, you can read it there, too.

Finding the Hyperlinks On a Web page with many objects, it is sometimes difficult to tell which are hyperlinks. Of course, you could click each object in the Page Preview window to find out where the hyperlinks are, but there is a faster way to find the links: Choose Views ➢ Highlight Objects ➢ With Links. Red boxes appear around all objects to which a hyperlink has been attached.

Linking One Page on a Site to Another Page

Linking one page to another page on the same site is pretty darn simple. The Site Links box in the Links Gallery lists each Web page on the site. To create the link, click the name of the page you want to link to in the Site Links box. Then drag the page onto an object. Visitors who click the link you created will go to the top of the Web page.

By convention, links to the other Web pages in a Web site sometimes appear at the bottom of each page. The Link Wizard in the Cool Stuff Gallery lets you

enter links to each page in a Web site. The links appear automatically at the bottom of the Web page in which you place them. Here, links to Web pages named Veni, Vidi, and Vinci have been placed at the bottom of a Web page with the Link Wizard. To create the links, open the Cool Stuff Gallery, click the Link Wizard, and drag it onto a Web page.

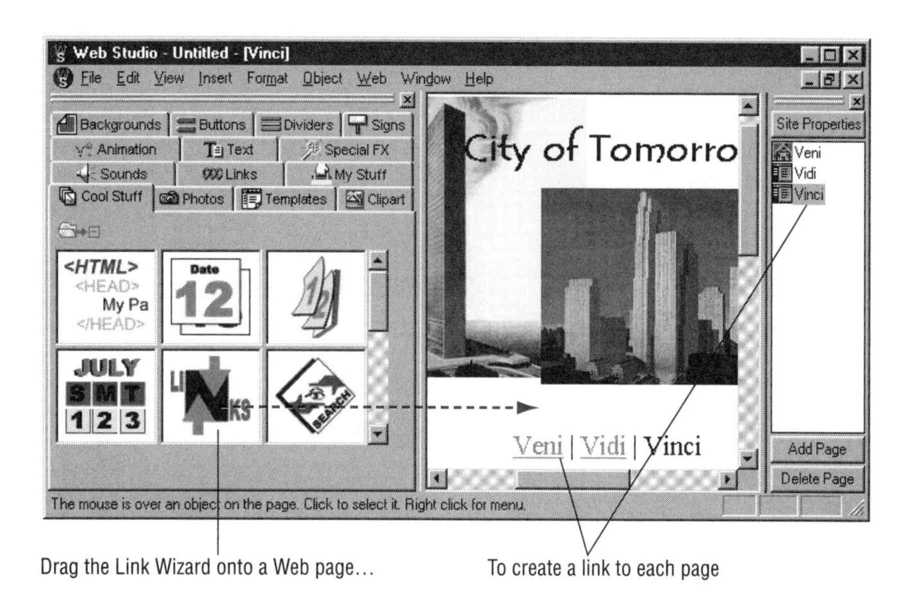

Drag the Link Wizard onto a Web page... To create a link to each page

Linking Two Different Places on the Same Web Page

To keep visitors from having to scroll in a long Web page, sometimes different places on the same page are linked. That way, instead of scrolling, the visitor can click a hyperlink to get from one place on the Web page to another. Here are two situations in which links to different places on the same Web page are used:

- A hyperlink called Return to Top appears at the bottom of the page. Visitors can click it to scroll instantly to the top.
- A series of questions appears at the top of a page. A visitor who wants the answer to a question can click the question and scroll instantly to the answer, which is found further down the page.

Anchor
For the purpose of hyperlinking two places on the same Web page in Web Studio, the target of the hyperlink.

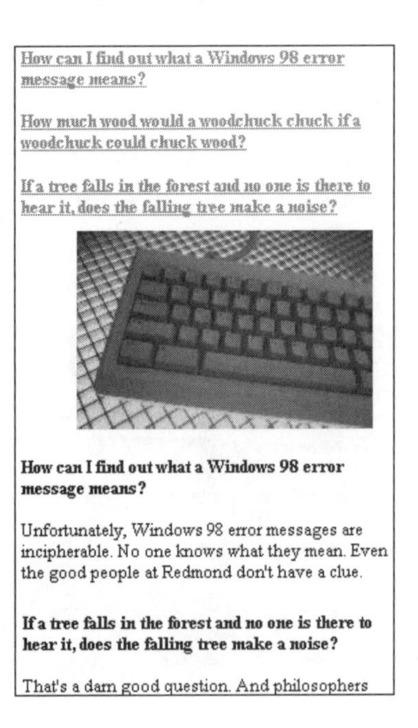

Work from the Site Links box in the Links Gallery to create a hyperlink between objects on the same page. Creating a the hyperlink is a two-step business:

1. Creating the anchor: Create an **anchor**, or target, for the hyperlink. The anchor is the hyperlink's destination. To designate an object as the anchor for a hyperlink, click Add Anchor to Object in the Site Links box and drag it over the object where you want visitors to go when they click the hyperlink. A dialog box asks you to name the anchor. The name you enter appears in the Site Links box. In the following illustration, the Site Links box holds two anchors, each an answer to a question. When visitors click the question, they will go to its answer—an anchor whose name appears in the Site Links box.

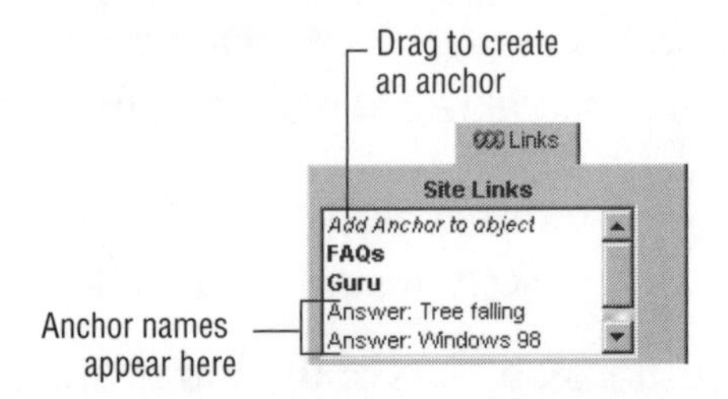

2. Creating the hyperlink: Make the connection between the anchor you created and the object that will form the hyperlink. To do so, drag an anchor in the Site Links box over the hyperlink object. In this illustration, the Answer: Windows 98 anchor is being dragged over the question

"How can I find out what a Windows 98 error message means?" to form a hyperlink. A visitor who clicks the question will go immediately to its answer, a text object further down the screen.

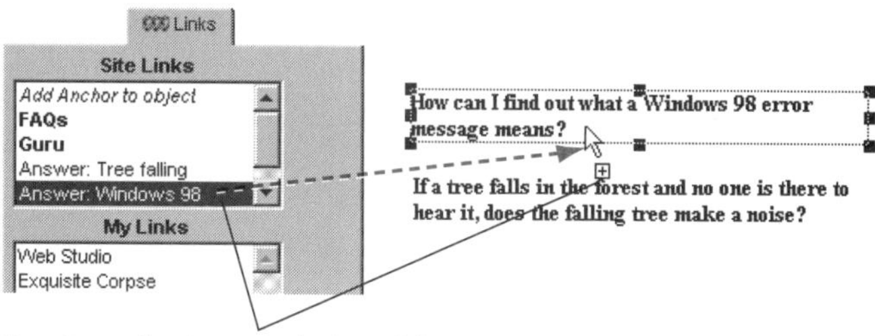

Drag the anchor to create the hyperlink

Follow these steps to create an anchor, a destination where you want visitors to go when they click a hyperlink:

1. Open the Links Gallery.
2. In the Site Links box, click Add Anchor to Object, and drag it over the object where you want visitors to go when they click the hyperlink. You see the Add Anchor dialog box.

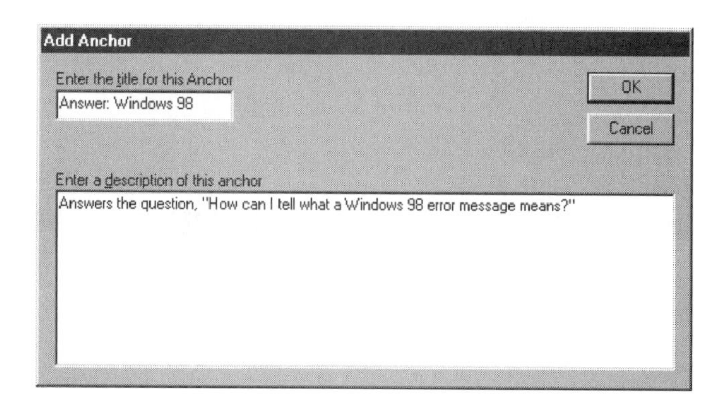

3. Enter a title for the anchor. The name you enter will appear in the Site Links box.
4. Enter a description. Descriptions can be helpful in determining where hyperlinks go. If you right-click a hyperlink and choose Link Info, the description you enter will appear in a dialog box.
5. Click OK.

The name of the anchor you created appears in the Site Links box. Now, to form a hyperlink, all you have to is drag the anchor over an object.

Warning

Sorry. You can't delete, rename, or edit anchors in the Site Links box. The only real chance you get to change an anchor is to start all over after you create it. To start all over, choose Edit ➢ Undo Set Link and try again.

Follow these steps to form a hyperlink between two places on the same Web page after you have created the anchor:

1. In the Site Links box, click the anchor.
2. Drag the anchor over the object that will form the hyperlink.

Click the Preview Web Site button (or press F5) right away to go to the Page Preview window and test the hyperlink. If the hyperlink doesn't go to the right object, return to the Web Page window, choose Edit ➢ Undo Set Link, and start all over.

Removing a Hyperlink

Thankfully, Web Studio has made removing hyperlinks very simple. To remove a link, click it and either choose Object ➢ Remove Link or right-click and choose Remove Link.

Tip

Having trouble telling where hyperlinks are? Choose View ➢ Highlight Objects ➢ With Links. Red boxes appear around hyperlinks so you know where they are.

Changing the Color of Text Links

Unless you change the settings, text hyperlinks are red to begin with. After a visitor clicks a text hyperlink on your Web site, it turns green to show that it has been clicked. Red and green text hyperlinks are fine and dandy as long as the background of your Web pages is not red or green. A green or red background makes text hyperlinks difficult to see.

Follow these steps to change the color of text links to make them easier to see or simply to make them look snazzier:

1. Choose File ➢ Web Site Properties or click the Site Properties button above the Page List. The Web Site Properties dialog box appears.
2. Click the Select Standard Link Color button and choose a new color for text hyperlinks.
3. Click the Select Visited Link Color button and choose a new color for text hyperlinks that have been clicked.
4. Click OK to close the dialog box.

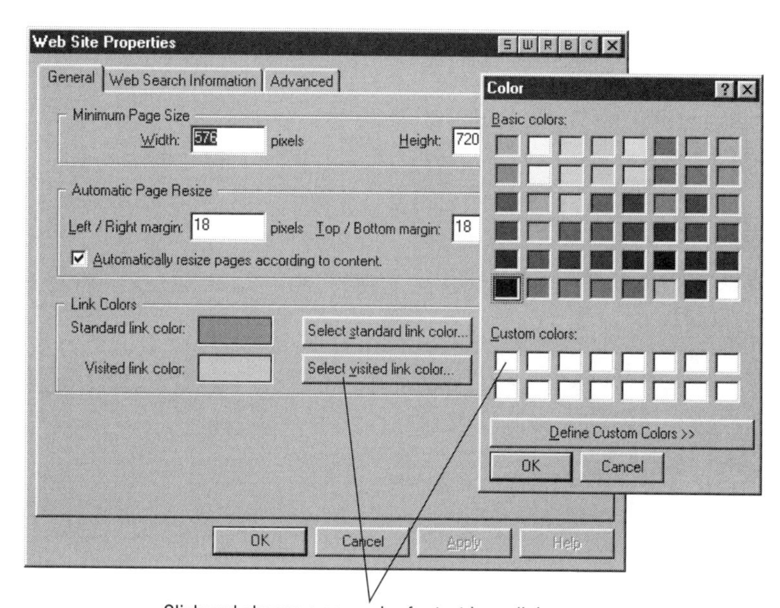

Click and choose a new color for text hyperlinks

Part 3

Advanced Techniques for Advanced Web Pages

In Part 3, you go beyond the basics and learn how to do the fancy stuff. This part explains how to put graphics, photos, animations, sounds, slide shows, and even sophisticated things like search engines on a Web site. You also discover how to print Web pages and try out complex formats that require HTML tags.

Advanced Techniques for Advanced Web Pages

Chapter 8 • Handling Graphics, Photos, and Clip Art Images. 113

Chapter 9 • Doing the Fancy Stuff—Animations, Sounds, and Slides . . . 131

Chapter 10 • Putting "Cool Stuff" on Your Web Pages. 147

Chapter 11 • Printing Your Web Pages 155

Chapter 12 • Entering Your Own HTML in Web Studio 161

Chapter 8

Handling Graphics, Photos, and Clip Art Images

Oscar Wilde said, "Appearances are everything." In this chapter, you learn how to tend to appearances. This chapter explains how to put graphics, photos, and clip art images on a Web page. More importantly, it shows how to alter appearances with the tools in the Special FX Gallery. You learn how to write an alternate text message—a message that appears when visitors to your Web site move their pointers over an image. You also learn how to put buttons on a Web page and use the My Stuff Gallery to store the images you use time and time again.

- Placing photos, clip art, and scanned images on a Web page
- Copying pictures from the Internet
- Writing an "alternate text message" that describes an image
- Altering images by way of the Special FX Gallery
- Placing buttons on a Web page
- Storing your favorite images in the My Stuff Gallery

Putting an Image on a Web Page

Clip art images and photographs are welcome additions to any Web site because they make it livelier. You know the old saying: "All text and no graphics makes Johnny a dull boy."

Read on to learn the whys and wherefores of putting images on a Web page. You will find out how to import an image from the Clipart or Photos Gallery, import an image of your own, get a scanned image, and copy pictures from the Internet. Along the way, I'll show you how to adjust the brightness and sharpness of photographs, which kinds of graphics to use on Web pages, and why to think twice before copying images from the Internet.

Getting an Image from the Photos or Clipart Gallery

Depending on how you installed Web Studio, you might need to put the Web Studio CD in your CD-ROM drive to access clip art images and photos. See Appendix A.

Probably the easiest way to adorn a Web page with an image is to get it from the Photos or Clipart Gallery. The Galleries offer numerous images, so chances are you can find one that does the job. What's more, the images were designed for Web pages. They look good on monitor screens and do not require a long time to download.

Follow these steps to put a photo or clip art image from Web Studio on a Web page:

Chapter 4 explains how to change the size and position of photos, clip art images, and other objects.

1. Go to the Photos or Clipart Gallery. To do so, choose View ➢ Galleries, if necessary, and click the Photos or Clipart tab.
2. Find the photo or clip art image you want. Don't forget to look in the subfolders. There are many images to choose from.

Tip

Try clicking the Hue buttons. Clicking Hue buttons changes the tint of the photos or clip art images.

3. Click the image you want and drag it into the Web Page window.

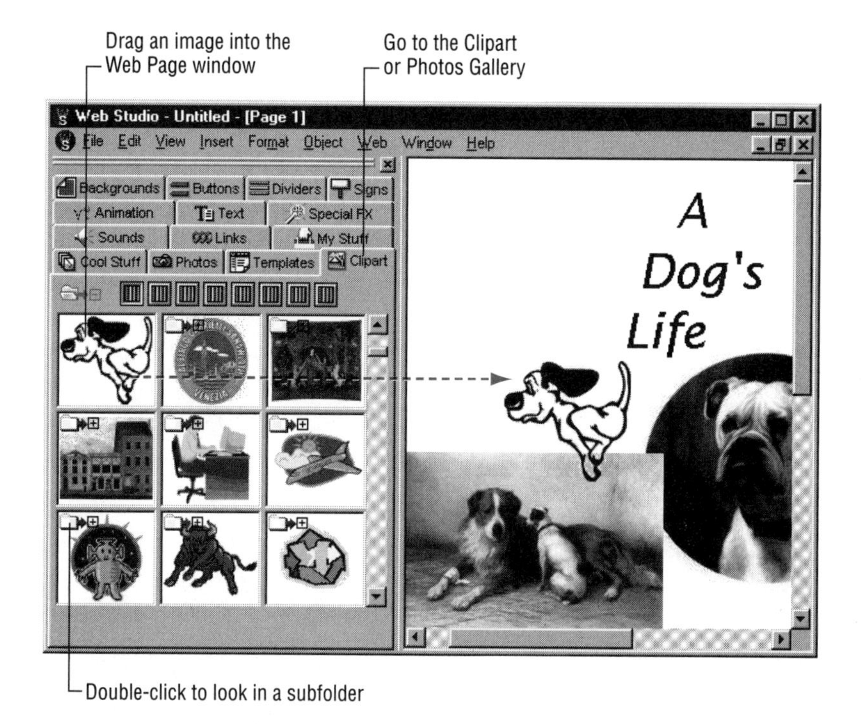

Bringing in a Photo or Graphic of Your Own

Besides images from the Photos and Clipart Gallery, you can place your own images on Web pages. Perhaps you want to proudly exhibit photographs of a child. Perhaps a Web page that publicizes your company needs a picture of the company logo.

Follow these steps to place a graphic image that is stored on your computer or computer network on a Web page:

1. Choose Insert ➢ Picture from File. The Open dialog box appears.
2. Find the folder where the graphic you want is located.
3. Click the Details button, which is located in the upper-right corner of the dialog box, to see the size of files and the file type. Now you can find the JPEG and GIF files.

At the end of this chapter, "Keeping Your Favorite Images in the My Stuff Gallery" explains how to keep the images you use time and time again in the My Stuff Gallery where you can find them easily.

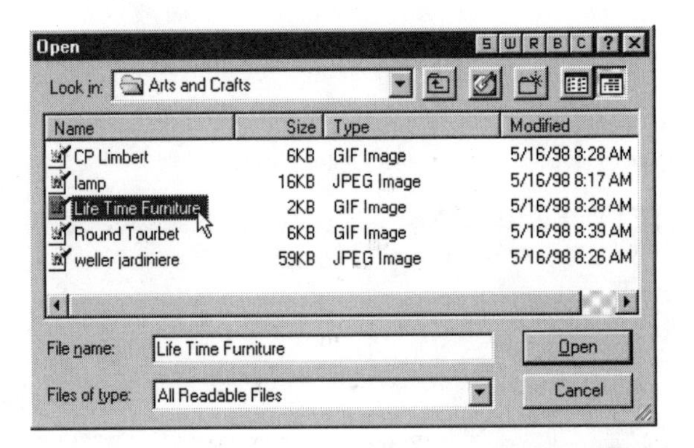

The special effects in the Special FX Gallery can be applied to a graphic you imported on your own. See "Special FX for Altering Images" later in this chapter.

4. Select the graphic you want. Ctrl+click to select more than one graphic. Ctrl+click means to hold down the Ctrl key as you select items.
5. Click the Open button.

Scanning a Graphic into a Web Page

Web Studio offers a special command for scanning an image and placing it on a Web page: the Insert ➢ Picture from Scan command. Put the photo, picture, or graphic in the scanner and follow these steps to place it on your Web page:

1. Choose Insert ➢ Picture from Scan. You see the Select Source dialog box.
2. Highlight your preferred source, be it a scanner, digital camera, or other device, and choose Select. Your scanner software opens.
3. Scan the image you want to place on a Web page.
4. When the scan is completed, click Transfer. The image is be added to your Web page.

Tip

When you scan a graphic, don't bother choosing a high resolution. As far as resolution goes, what matters is the resolution of the viewer's screen, not the resolution of the graphic itself. Choose the Screen Resolution or 72 dpi (dots per inch) setting to scan a graphic.

Getting Help from the Photo Correction Wizard

The Special FX Gallery offers a gizmo called the Photo Correction Wizard that can be very helpful for tweaking photographs and making them look better on monitor screens. By means of the Photo Correction Wizard, you can adjust a photograph's brightness, contrast, hue, and sharpness. You can even ask the Wizard to fine-tune the photograph for you, look at the result, and accept or reject the changes that the Wizard makes.

Follow these steps to test-drive the Photo Correction Wizard:

1. Click the Special FX tab in the Web Galleries.
2. Click the Photo Correction Wizard icon and drag it over the photograph that needs adjusting. The icon looks like a camera and is the first icon in the Special FX Gallery. You see the fist of several PhotoFixer dialog boxes. Watch the photograph in the dialog box. It shows what your adjustments do.

3. Click the Next button and continue to click Next after you make adjustments in the different dialog boxes. As you go along, you are invited to do the following:
   - Let the Wizard adjust the photograph (and click the Undo button if you don't like the adjustments).
   - Drag sliders to change the brightness and contrast of the photo.
   - Drag a slider to change the hue.
   - Drag a slider to change the sharpness.
4. Click the Finish button.

Copying Pictures from the Internet

Another way to get images for your Web site is to scavenge them from the Internet. Any image on the Internet can be copied. All you have to do is right-click the image and choose Copy on the shortcut menu. Here are two techniques for copying images from a Web page on the Internet:

- Copy and paste the image: In your browser, right-click an image you want and choose Copy on the shortcut menu. Then go to Web Studio, click in the Web page window, and choose Edit ➢ Paste (or press Ctrl+V).
- Drag the image into the Web Page window: Resize the browser window and Web Studio window so they are side by side onscreen. Then drag the image from the browser window to the Web Page window in Web Studio. However, if the image is a hyperlink, the hyperlink (not the image) is copied into Web Studio.

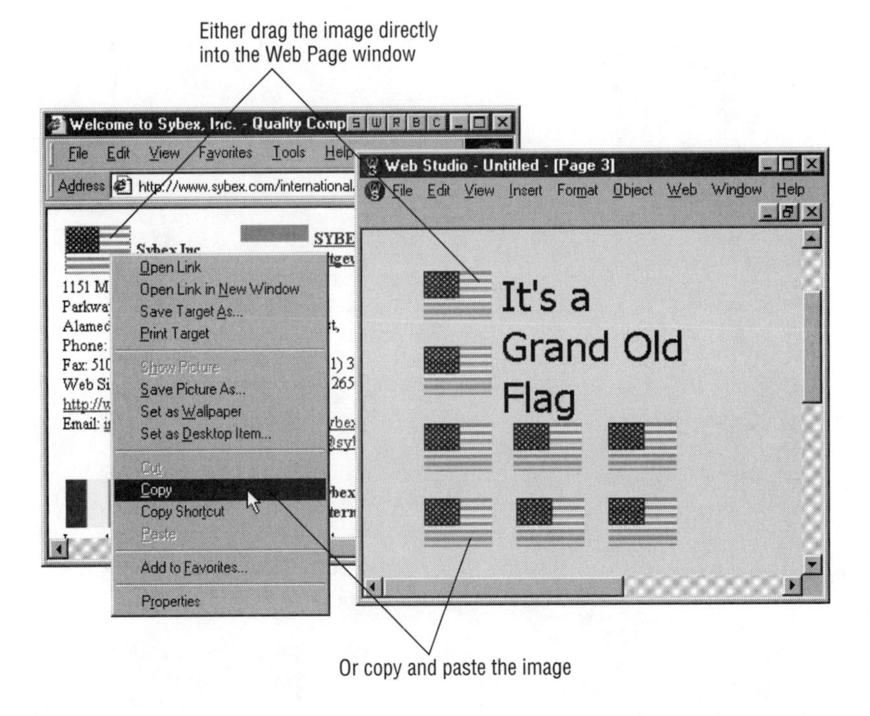

Warning

Strictly speaking, copying images from the Internet is a violation of the copyright laws. You must have permission from the owner of an image to place it on your Web site. To get permission, try e-mailing the Webmaster at the site where you propose to get the image. The Webmaster should know who owns the image, seeing as he or she must have obtained permission to use it.

Instead of copying images from the Internet one at a time into Web Studio, perhaps you want to build a library of images and then copy them into your Web pages as you need them. Follow these steps to copy an image from the Internet and save it for later use:

1. In your browser, right-click the image you want for your collection and choose Save Picture As. You see the Save Picture dialog box.

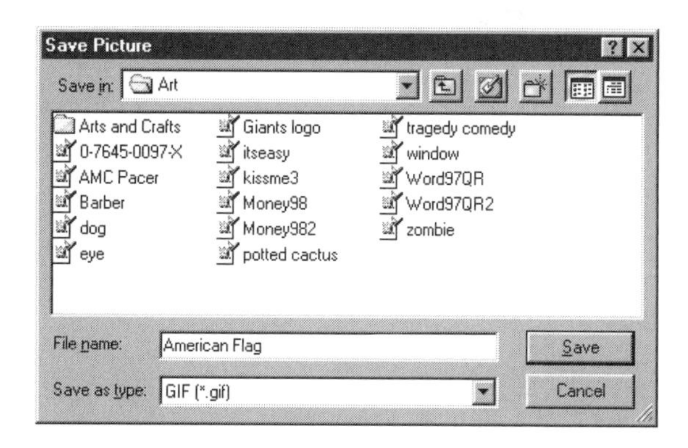

2. Locate the folder where you want to store the image.
3. Enter a descriptive name in the File Name text box if the name already given isn't descriptive enough.
4. Click the Save button.

Earlier in this chapter, "Bringing in a Photo or Graphic of Your Own" explains how to paste an image you copied from the Internet into a Web page.

Alternate Text Message
Descriptive words that appear on an image when you move the pointer over it.

Writing an "Alternate Text Message" for Images

A so-called **alternate text message** serves two purposes: it tells viewers what the image they are seeing is, and, before an image is downloaded from the Internet, it tells viewers what they are about to see. Viewers can read the alternate text message by moving the pointer over the image to which it is attached. Until an image is downloaded form the Internet, the alternate text message appears on the Web page where the image will be when it downloads. In the following

illustration, a graphic serves as a hyperlink, and the alternate text message describes what will happen if the viewer clicks the hyperlink.

Follow these steps to write an alternate text message that viewers will see when they move the pointer over an image:

1. Click the image to select it.
2. Choose Object ➢ Object Properties or right-click and choose Properties. The Object Properties dialog box appears.
3. Click the Graphic tab.

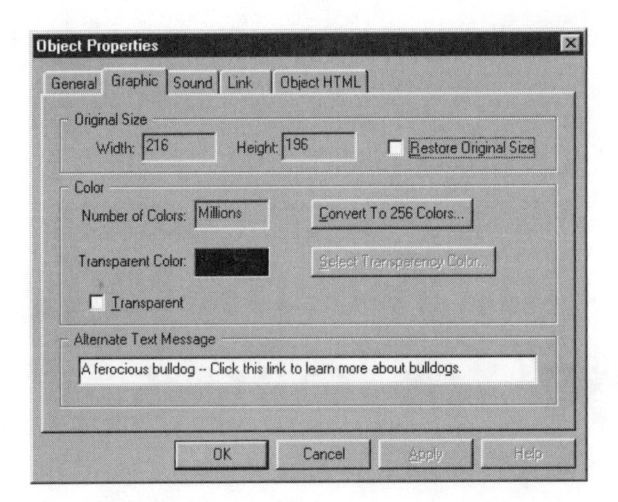

4. Enter a description in the Alternate Text Message box.
5. Click OK.

Special FX for Altering Images

If an image isn't quite right, don't despair. You can alter its appearance by means of the commands in the Special FX Gallery. Altogether, the Special FX Gallery offers 31 ways to alter an image. To alter an image starting from the Special FX Gallery, drag an icon from the gallery over the image you want to alter.

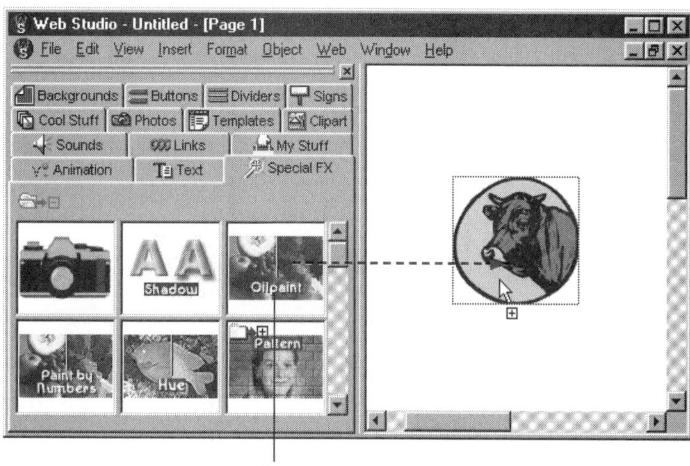

Drag a special effect icon over an object to apply a special effect

Read on to learn how to do the following:

- Change an image's orientation by rotating, reversing, or flipping it.
- Change an image's shading, tint, or color scheme by lightening, darkening, colorizing, or sharpening it, as well as changing its contrast, hue, or half-tones.
- Change an image's contours by shadowing or blurring it.
- Change an image's look by solarizing it, posterizing it, or making it look as though it were hand-painted.

Tip

Most of the special effects can be applied more than once to heighten their effect. For example, apply the Darken special effect numerous times to make an image darker, darker, and darker.

Changing an Image's Orientation

The Rotate, Reverse, and Flip special effects change an image's orientation:

- Rotate: Turns the image by 90 degrees.
- Reverse: Presents the mirror image of the image.
- Flip: Turns the image upside-down.

Changing an Image's Shading, Tint, or Color Scheme

The Special FX Gallery offers numerous special effects for changing an image's shading, tint, or color scheme. In a nutshell, here they are:

- Hue: Changes the image's tint. Choosing the Hue special effect is the same as clicking a Hue button in the Web Gallery.
- Lighten and Darken: Make the image lighter or darker on the page.

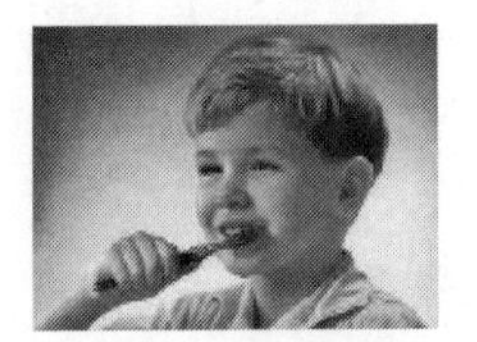
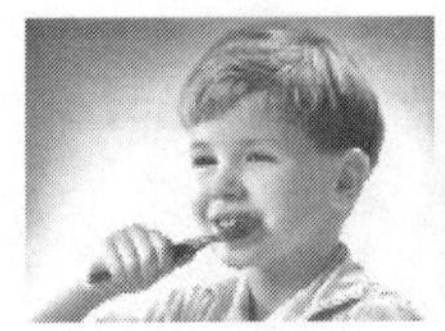
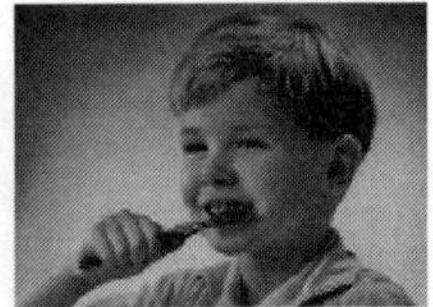

- Add Contrast, Contrast, and Sharpen: Increases or decreases the contrast between light and dark colors, or sharpens the clarity of the image. Use these special effects to give an image more or less luster.

- Colorize, Gray, and Invert Color: Change the image's color scheme. The Color dialog box appears when you apply the Colorize special effect so you can choose a new background color.

- Color Noise, Noise, and Halftone 1-2: Converts the image to dots to give it a grainy, coarse look similar to that of a newspaper photograph.

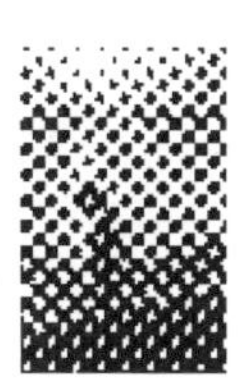

Changing an Image's Contours

The following special effects in the Special FX Gallery allow you to change the contours of an image:

- Shadow, Edges, and Enhance Edges: Alter the edges of an image. The Shadow special effect makes an image cast a shadow and thereby look three-dimensional. Open the Edges subfolder to see different types of edges, including ripped, burnt, and torn.

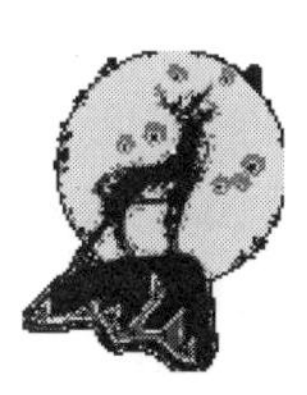

- Blur Slight, Blur Moderate, and Blur Large: Blur an image to different degrees.

- Small Mosaic, Medium Mosaic, and Large Mosaic: Pixelates the image to give the impression that it was constructed from mosaic tiles. This one is strictly for use with backgrounds, not images.

Changing an Image's Look

Finally, the following special effects in the Special FX Gallery change an image's appearance:

- Oilpaint and Paint by Numbers: Give the impression that an image was hand-painted.

- Pattern and Emboss: Change the texture of an image. Open the Pattern subfolder to choose a pattern to impose on the image—bricks, diamonds, and so on. An embossed image looks as though it was stamped out of tin.

- Solarize and Posterize 2-6: Idealize the colors to make images look more like a poster. Parts of a solarized image look normal and parts come out looking like the negative of a photograph. The Posterize 2 special effect reduces the number of colors to 2, Posterize 3 reduces the number of colors to 3, and so on.

Putting Buttons on a Page

People like clicking buttons. Most people see buttons and think, "Oh good, I get to click something and make a choice." So popular are buttons, Web Studio devotes an entire gallery to them—the Buttons Gallery.

Chapter 7 explains hyperlinks, including how to turn an object such as a button into a hyperlink.

If you want to put buttons on a Web page, remember that buttons usually come in sets and that visitors expect to go somewhere when they click a button. In other words, each button you put on a Web page should be a hyperlink. A button to which no hyperlink is attached is just a circle, square, or rectangle that occupies space on a Web page. A button without a hyperlink is a dead button.

The first seven objects in the Backgrounds Gallery are for creating three-dimensional buttons or square, coved, or rounded buttons that are or are not filled with color. Drag the 3-D object or a Square, Coved, or Rounded object into the Web Page window and the Color dialog box appears so you can choose a color for the button.

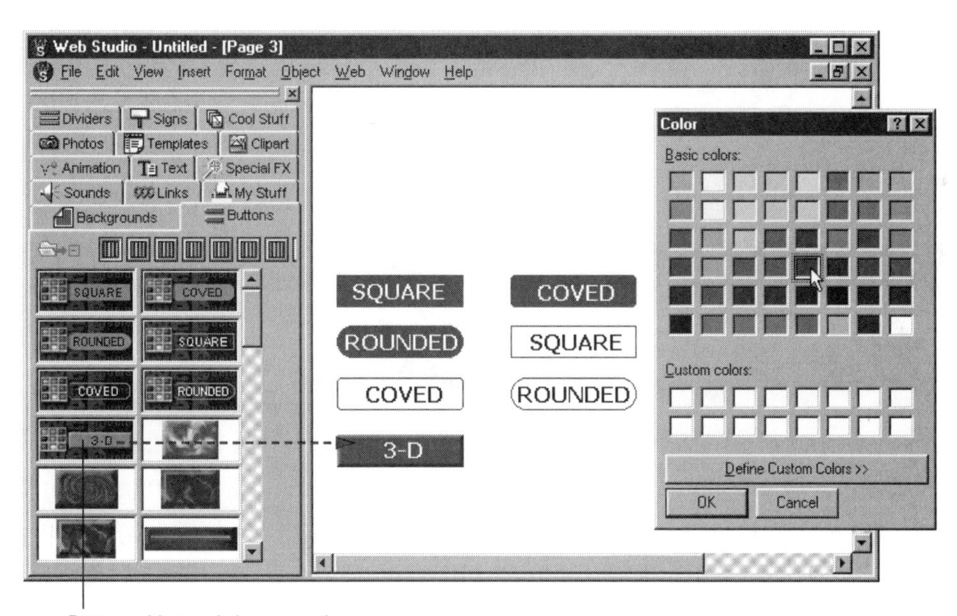

Drag an object and choose a color to create these kinds of buttons

The other buttons in the Buttons Gallery are more fanciful than the ones you get with the 3-D, Square, Coved, or Rounded objects. You will find many kinds of buttons in the gallery. Drag a button into the Web Page window when you've

found the one you like. Isn't it funny how much the buttons in the Buttons Gallery resemble cufflinks?

Chapter 4 explains how to position, merge, and align objects, including buttons.

Here are a few tips for working with buttons:

- Buttons usually come in sets. Rather than create the same button four or five times, create one and copy it by holding down the Ctrl key and dragging.
- Make use of the Object ➢ Align commands to line up buttons on the Web page.
- Make use of the Object ➢ Space Evenly Down and Object ➢ Space Evenly Across commands to spread buttons evenly across the Web page.
- If you put a text object on top of a button to give the button a label, merge the label and the button. Merging makes the button easier to move on the Web page. To merge objects, drag crosswise to draw a box around them, and then choose Object ➢ Merge Selected Objects.

Keeping Your Favorite Images in the My Stuff Gallery

For you and you only, Web Studio has reserved a special place called the My Stuff Gallery where you can keep your favorite images. Instead of resorting to the Insert ➢ Picture from File command to insert a logo or a smiling picture of yourself on a Web page, you can conveniently drag the image from the My Stuff Gallery. Photos from the Photos Gallery, clip art from the Clipart Gallery, any object in any gallery for that matter can also be stored in the My Stuff Gallery to make finding it easier.

You can keep 250 of your own images in the gallery. Read on to learn how to put graphics in the My Stuff Gallery, rearrange the items in the gallery, and remove items.

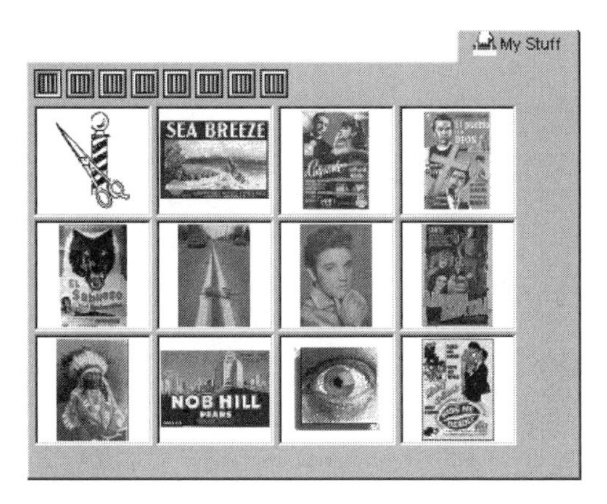

Putting an Item in the My Stuff Gallery

The makers of Web Studio have made it very easy to place items in the My Stuff Gallery. You can use commands to do it or drag the items yourself. To put graphics that are stored on your computer in the My Stuff Gallery using commands, follow these steps:

1. Choose Insert ➢ My Stuff Gallery Graphics or right-click the My Stuff Gallery and choose Add Files. The Open dialog box appears.
2. Find and select the file or files you want to keep in the My Stuff Gallery.

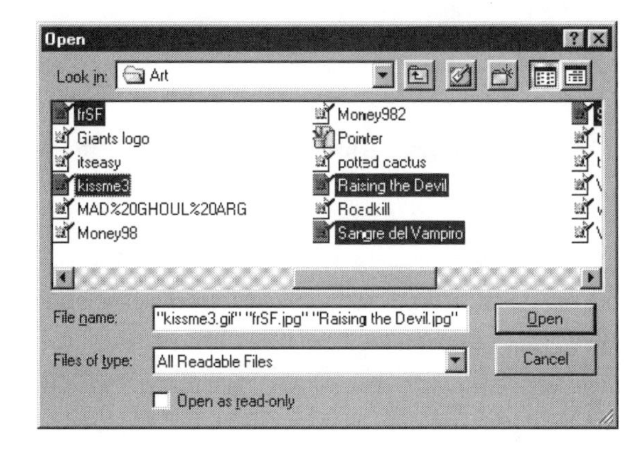

Tip

Hold down the Ctrl key and click to select more than one file. The names of files you select appear in the File Name box. To select all the files in a folder, click the first file, and, holding down the Shift key, click the last file.

3. Click the Open button.

The dragging method of putting items in the My Stuff Gallery works best when you want to place an item from another gallery or an item from a Web page on the Internet in the My Stuff Gallery. Follow these steps:

1. Display the item that you want to copy in the Page Preview window in Web Studio or in the window of your browser. Remember to press F5 or choose Web ➢ Preview Web Site to see the Page Preview window. To copy an item from the Internet, the Web Studio window and browser window must both be onscreen.
2. In Web Studio, click the My Stuff tab to see the My Stuff Gallery.
3. Drag the item into the My Stuff Gallery and release the mouse button. Do it properly and a plus sign (+) appears below the pointer when you drag over the My Stuff Gallery.

A Fully Functional My Stuff Gallery

By adding an item to the My Stuff Gallery, you merely tell Web Studio where on your computer the item is located. Next time you call upon the item in the My Stuff Gallery, Web Studio goes to the location on your computer where it thinks the item is and copies the item onto your Web page. However, if the item isn't there because you moved or deleted it, you can't insert the item. You see the Error dialog box instead. The moral of the story: Set aside a folder for storing your art files and don't move the folder or delete the files inside it without carefully considering the consequences. The My Stuff Gallery is very useful as long as you don't move or delete the files to which it refers.

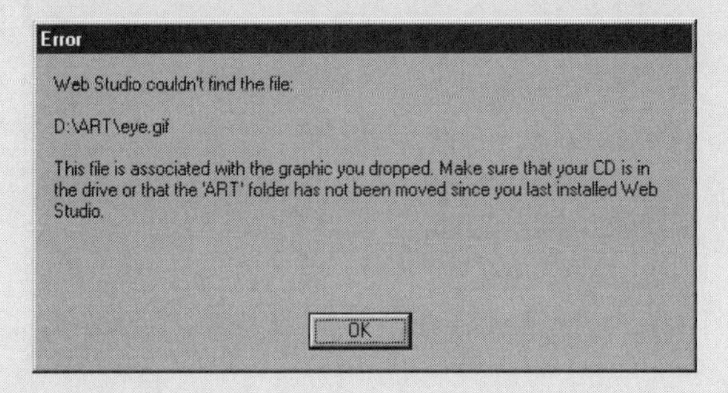

Rearranging Items in the My Stuff Gallery

To rearrange items in the My Stuff Gallery:

- Drag items to new places: Click an item, hold down the mouse button, and drag it to a new location in the My Stuff Gallery.
- Cut and paste items: Right-click an item and choose Cut on the shortcut menu. Then right-click the square where you want the item to be and choose Paste.

Removing an Item from the My Stuff Gallery

To remove an item from the My Stuff Gallery, right-click it and choose Delete on the shortcut menu. Deleting an item in no way, shape, or form deletes the item from you computer. All that happens is the reference to the item is removed from the My Stuff Gallery.

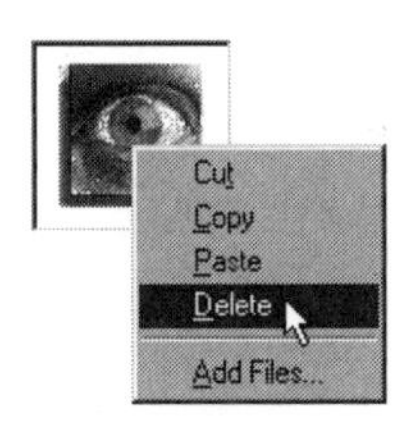

Chapter 9

Doing the Fancy Stuff—Animations, Sounds, and Slides

This chapter explains how to turn a Web site into a multimedia experience. Well, that's an exaggeration. Whether animation, sounds, and slide shows on a Web site constitute a multimedia experience is open to debate. Sometimes sounds come across as tinny, animations are annoying, and slide shows are merely a distraction, not an "experience." Still, a well-placed animation, sound, or slide show can turn a dull Web site into a lively place.

This chapter explains how to make animations, sounds, and slide shows part of a Web site.

- Decorating a Web page with animations
- Making sounds play when visitors come to a Web page
- Making sounds play when an object is clicked or brushed by the pointer
- Presenting a slideshow on a Web page

Animations to Make a Web Page Come Alive

Animation
A cartoon-like image on a Web page that moves onscreen. An animation is actually two or three images that appear quickly and give the illusion of movement.

Don't overdo it with **animations**. One, two, or, at most, three animations per Web page is the rule. By nature, the eye wants to look at anything that moves. Whether they want to or not, visitors to a Web page linger over an animation, but an animation can be distracting when you want to read text or examine a graphic.

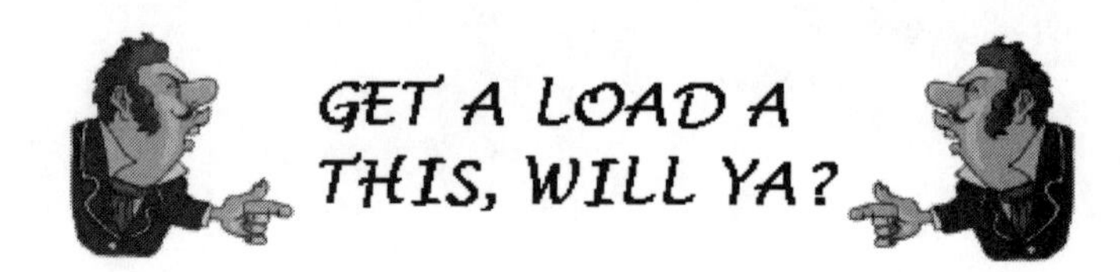

Follow these steps to drop an animation on a Web page:

1. Go to the Animation Gallery by choosing View ➢ Galleries, if necessary, and clicking the Animation tab.
2. Look in the subfolders to find a suitable animation.
3. Drag the animation into the Web Page window.

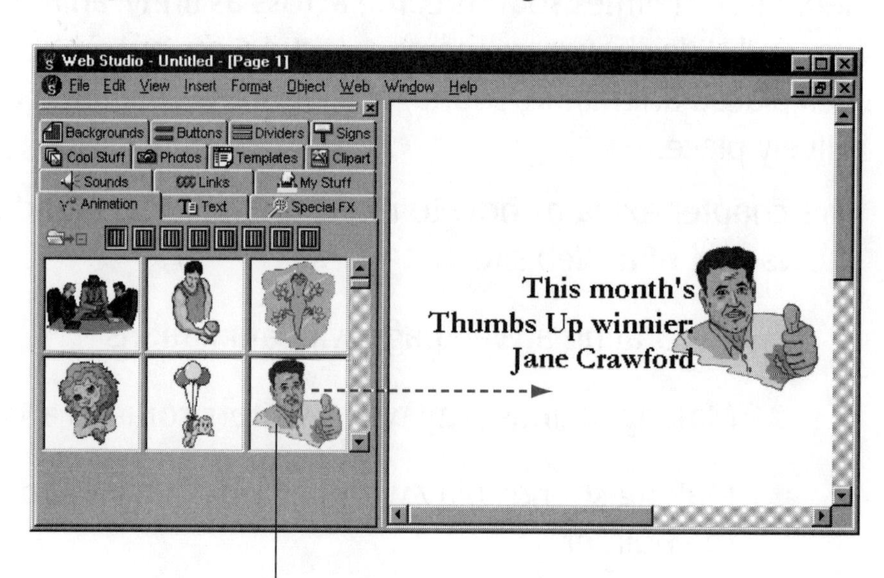

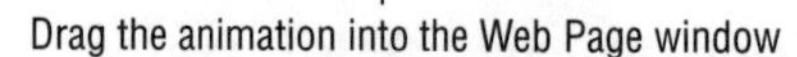
Drag the animation into the Web Page window

4. Press F5 or click the Preview Web Site button to open the Preview window, where you can see your animation do its dance.

How do you like the animation? If you don't like it, return to the Web Page window, choose Edit ➢ Undo Add From Gallery (or click the Undo button), and try again.

To Animate Once or Animate Continuously

Unless you change the settings, animations do their thing over and over and over again. In Web Studio terminology, they "animate continuously." Instead of repeating itself *ad nauseam*, however, you can make an animation repeat itself only once. Visitors to the Web page see the animation go through the motions one time only. After that, the animation stops fidgeting and looks like a graphic.

Making an animation do its thing only once is a great way to call attention to part of a Web page without overdoing it. Follow these steps to make an animation go through its dance one time and one time only:

1. Select the animation.
2. Choose Object ➢ Object Properties or right-click and choose Properties. You see the Object Properties dialog box.
3. Click the Animated Graphic tab.
4. Under How to Animate, click the Animate Once button.

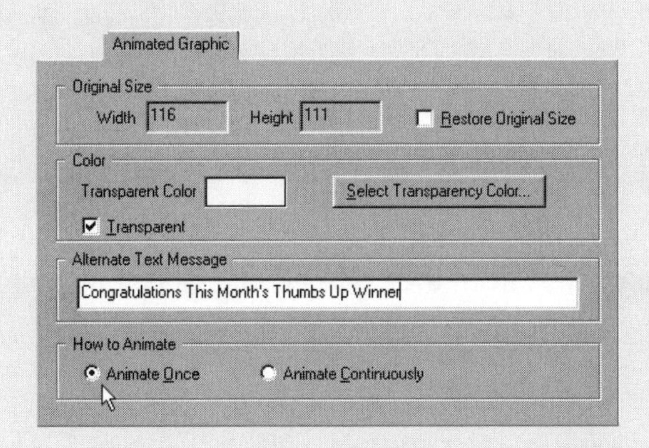

5. Click OK.

All About Sounds

These days, most computers are equipped with a sound card and can play sounds. Sounds can be part of a Web site, although, as you surely know if you have spent any time on the Internet, sounds are annoying if they are used indiscriminately. Hearing a sound when you click an object such as a hyperlink is a pleasant surprise, but a tinny rendition of a pop masterpiece played over and over on a Web site, to my mind at least, is the signal to leave in a hurry.

Web Studio offers many options for making sound part of a Web page. You can play sounds continuously or play them once when visitors arrive at a page. You can make sound part of an object so that the sound is played when the object is clicked or the pointer moves over the object. You can use sounds from the Sounds Gallery or WAV sound files of your own. And, to keep sounds from playing as you work on your Web site, you can click the Sound On/Off button. Better read on.

Warning

Sound files can take a long time to download from the Internet. Try to choose files that are under 100KB in size so your Web site doesn't take too long to download.

Getting a Sound from the Sounds Gallery

Whether you want a background sound for a Web page or a sound for an object on the page, start from the Sounds Gallery. Follow these steps to attach a sound to a Web page or to an object on the page:

1. Go to the Sounds Gallery by choosing View ➢ Galleries, if necessary, and clicking the Sounds tab.
2. Scroll to examine the different sound categories—Alarms, Animals, Annoy, and so on. There are seventeen categories in all.
3. Drag a sound into the Web page window. Where you drag the sound depends on how you want it to play:
   - Sound plays when visitors come to the Web page: Drag the sound onto a blank space on the Web page.

- Sound plays when visitors click or move the pointer over an object: Drag the sound over an object.

Scroll to find a sound

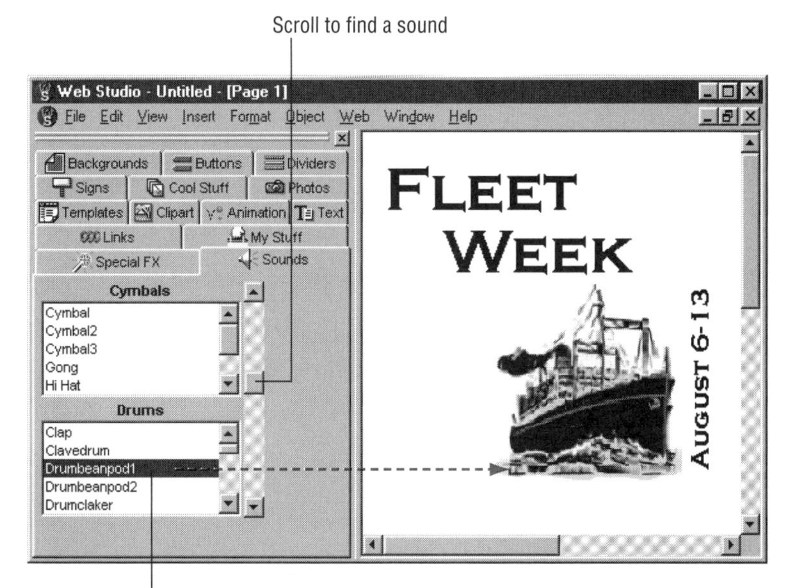

Drag the sound onto the page or over an object

Warning

You can't attach a sound to an animation. Web Studio doesn't permit it because the animation, which is actually more than one image, would cease to move.

To test your new sound, double-click the object to which you attached it. Sounds that are attached to Web pages, unless you change the settings, play continuously. You can hear a Web page sound right away.

Tip

The easiest way to find out what all the sounds in the Sounds Gallery are is to create a clip art image, open the Sounds Gallery, and drag sounds onto the image one at a time. When you are finished experimenting with sounds and know which ones you like, delete the image.

Temporarily Turning Sounds On and Off

Thankfully, the makers of Web Studio understand that hearing sounds while you are hard at work on a Web site can be a nuisance. Here are instructions for turning sounds on and off:

- Turning sounds off: Either click the Sound On/Off button and then click the Web page or object that is making the sound, or choose View ➢ Play Sounds (to remove the checkmark next to the command) and then click the Web page or object.
- Turning sounds on: Either click the Sound On/Off button and then *double-click* the Web page or object whose sound you want to hear or choose View ➢ Play Sounds and *double-click* the Web page or object.

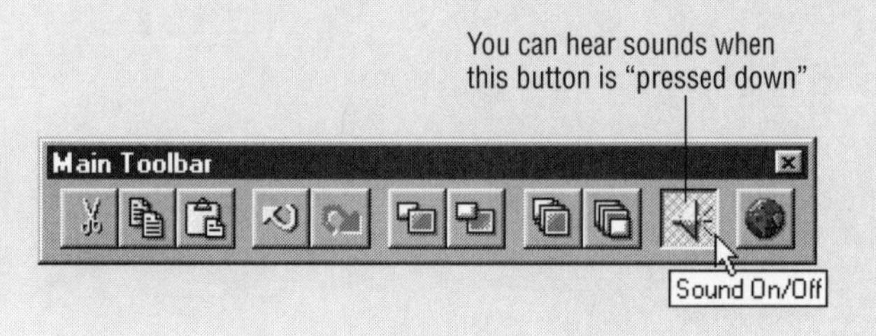

WAV
A file format under which the Windows operating system stores sounds.

Playing a Sound of Your Own

The sounds in the Sounds Gallery don't do the trick? Then use a sound of your own for a Web page or object. The sound, however, has to be a **WAV** file. Take note of where on your computer WAV files are stored and follow these steps to attach a WAV file to a Web page or object:

1. Open the Object Properties dialog box. How you open the dialog box depends on whether you are attaching a WAV file to a Web page or an object:
   - Attaching a WAV file to a Web page: Choose Object ➢ Page Properties or right-click the page and choose Page Properties.
   - Attaching a WAV file to an object: Click the object and choose Object ➢ Object Properties or right-click and choose Properties.
2. Click the Background Sound or Sound tab in the Object Properties dialog box.
3. Click the Load My Own Sound button. The Open dialog box appears.
4. Locate the folder with the sound file you want.

5. Click the Details button so you can see file sizes and file types. In the Type column, look for the words "Wave Sound." Those words identify WAV files.

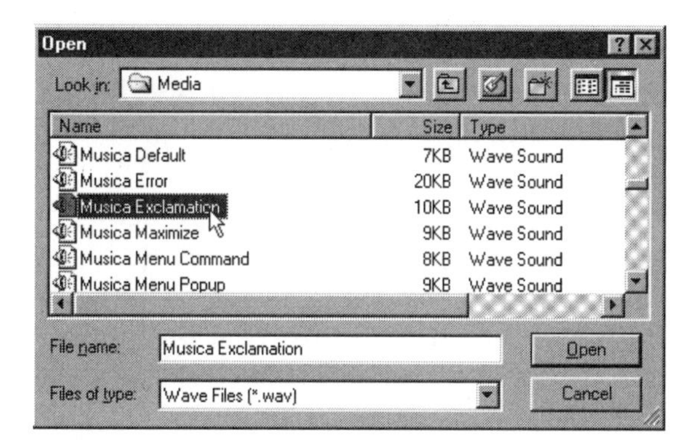

6. Select a file. Its name appears in the File Name box.
7. Click the Open button.
8. Click OK in the Object Properties dialog box.

Tip

If your computer runs on the Windows operating system, you can find many WAV files in the `C:\Windows\Media` folder. Open the folder and double-click files to hear the sounds.

Choosing How Often a Sound Is Played

Unless you change the settings, Web page sounds play continuously and sounds that are attached to objects play only once, when a visitor clicks the object. Suppose you want to change the settings? Web page and object sounds can play under these conditions:

- Web page: Sounds can play continuously or once, when the page appears onscreen.
- Object: Sounds can play when the object is clicked or when the pointer moves over the object. When the sound starts playing, it can play continuously or once only.

Follow these steps to determine how often and under which circumstances a sound is played:

1. Open the Object Properties dialog box. How you do so depends on whether you are working with a Web page or an object:
   - Web page: Choose Object ➢ Page Properties or right-click the page and choose Page Properties.
   - Object: Click the object and choose Object ➢ Object Properties or right-click and choose Properties.
2. Click the Background Sound or Sound tab in the Object Properties dialog box.

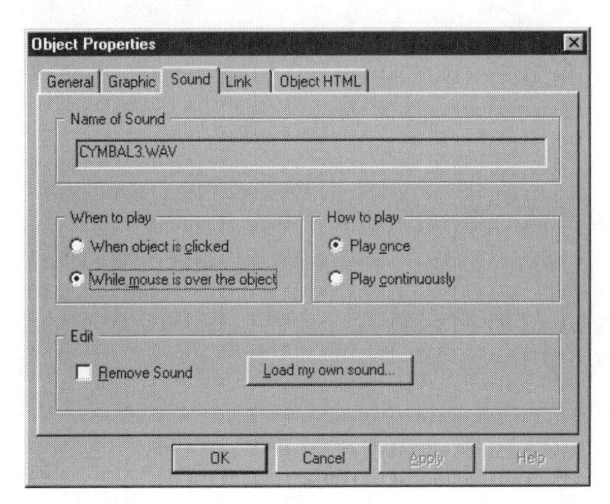

3. Choose how often to play the sound:
   - Web page: Under When to Play, choose Once When Page Loads or Continuously. Then skip to step 5.
   - Object: Under How to Play, choose Play Once or Play Continuously.
4. Under When to Play (these options only apply to objects), choose When Object Is Clicked or While Mouse Is Over Object.
5. Click OK.

Tip

On a crowded Web page with many objects, you can't tell which objects are associated with sounds. Or can you? Choose View ➢ Highlight Objects ➢ With Sounds. Each object to which a sound is attached appears in a red box.

Removing Sounds from Web Pages and Objects

If you decide that silence is golden and you want to remove the sounds from a Web page or an object, follow these instructions:

Removing Sounds from an Object Select the object and choose Object ➢ Remove Sound or right-click and choose Remove Sound. Then click the Web page.

Removing Sounds from a Web Page Choose Object ➢ Page Properties or right-click and choose Page Properties. In the Object Properties dialog box, click the Background Sound tab, check the Remove Sound check box, and click OK. Then click the Web page.

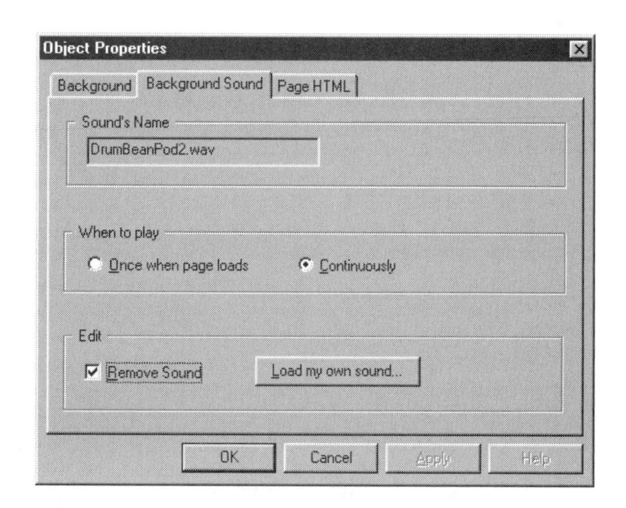

Putting a Slide Show on a Web Page

A slide show on a Web page is much like the old-fashioned living-room slide show that party guests were sometimes subjected to before the invention of the video camera. The slides—each one a graphic—are shown one after the other. Viewers politely praise the slides while secretly wishing that the show went faster. Actually, a slide show on a Web page offers a big advantage over an old-fashioned slide show: Viewers can watch it at leisure, speed it up, or go to another Web page.

Vacation photographs, children's artwork, photographs of a newborn baby, posters, and photographs of the company picnic or staff party are all candidates for a slideshow. These pages explain how to create a slideshow and how to tinker with the show after you've created it. Meanwhile, here are a few tips for putting together a top-notch slideshow:

- Use JPEG and GIF images. Graphics in other formats take too long to download.
- Choose images of roughly the same size. To make room for the slideshow, Web Studio allocates enough space on the Web page to accommodate the largest slide. If the largest slide happens to be significantly larger than the smallest, the smallest slide appears onscreen in a big, empty space—the space that Web Studio set aside for the largest slide.
- Images appear in the slideshow in alphabetical order by filename. If the order of slides is important to the presentation, rename files so that the one you want to be first is first alphabetically, the second is next alphabetically, and so on.

Warning

Files whose names contain spaces can't be used in slide shows. Rename a file, if necessary, to remove the blank spaces in its name before you include it in a slide show.

Putting Together the Slide Show

Start from the Cool Stuff Gallery to create a slide show. Choose View ➢ Galleries, if necessary, and click the Cool Stuff tab to get there. Then look for Slide Show, the first subfolder in the Cool Stuff tab, and double-click the subfolder to see the six choices for presenting your slides.

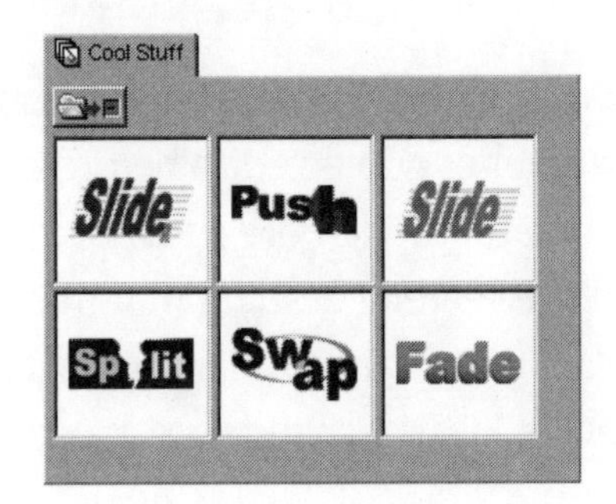

The objects in the Slide Show subfolder represent the six ways that slides can appear onscreen during the show. The choice you make now is irreversible. Drag one of these objects into the Web Page window to describe the transition of one slide to the next:

- Slide R: One slide in the show replaces the next without a transition.
- Push: The slide exits to the right while the next enters from the left.
- Slide: The slide exits to the left while the next enters from the right.
- Split: The slide splits down the middle, with one side exiting left, the other exiting right, and the next slide emerging from below the previous slide.
- Swap: The next slide appears to side-step in front of the previous slide.
- Fade: The slide fades out as the next fades in.

After you drag the object you've chosen from the Slide Show subfolder into the Web page window, the Slide Show Options dialog box appears. In this dialog box, tell Web Studio about the slideshow you want.

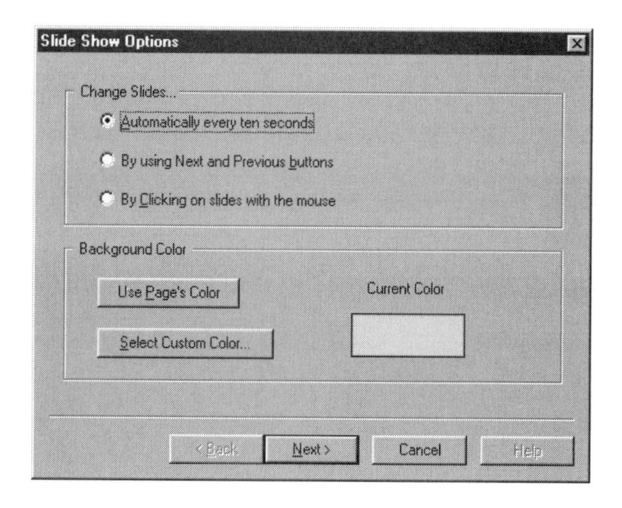

Under Change Slides, choose an option to describe when slides appear onscreen. The choice you make now can't be reversed later on.

- Automatically Every Ten Seconds: Slides appear in ten-second intervals without the viewer having a say in the matter.

- By Using Next and Previous Buttons: Viewers can click the Next or Previous button to go backward or forward in the show. Viewers also have the option of turning the sound off, if sound is part of the show.

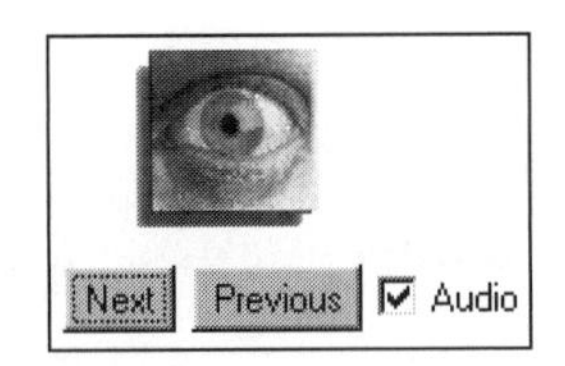

- By Clicking Slides with the Mouse: Viewers click a slide to go to the next one in the show. If you choose this option, incidentally, you have to give clicking instructions on the Web page.

Warning

Make sure the slides in your show are relatively the same size if you choose the By Using Next and Previous Buttons option. Web Studio allots enough space for the largest slide in the show and places the Next and Previous buttons below where the largest slide will be. In a show with slides of different sizes, blank space appears between small slides and the buttons, which appear further down the page to accommodate large slides.

Under Background Color, either stick with the background that is already there or choose a new color. The choice you make can't be reversed.

- Use Page's Color: The page background, whatever it happens to be, appears behind the slide. However, remember that Web studio can only fill in the background to the perimeter of the largest slide in the show. In the case of a small slide, empty space appears, as shown on the left side of the following illustration.

- Select Custom Color: Click the Select Custom Color button and choose a new background color in the Color dialog box. Again, the color you

choose will cover the page to the extent that the largest slide in the show covers the page. On the right side of the previous illustration, blue was chosen for the background color.

Click the Next button to go to the Attached Files dialog box and tell Web Studio which graphics appear in the show:

- Adding a slide to the show: Click the Add File To List button. In the Open dialog box, locate the images you want; select them by clicking, Ctrl+clicking, or Shift+clicking; and then click the Open button. The names of the files you chose, along with their folder names, appear in the Attached Files dialog box.
- Removing a slide: Click a slide and click the Delete Files From List button to remove it. You can Ctrl+click to select several slides at a time.

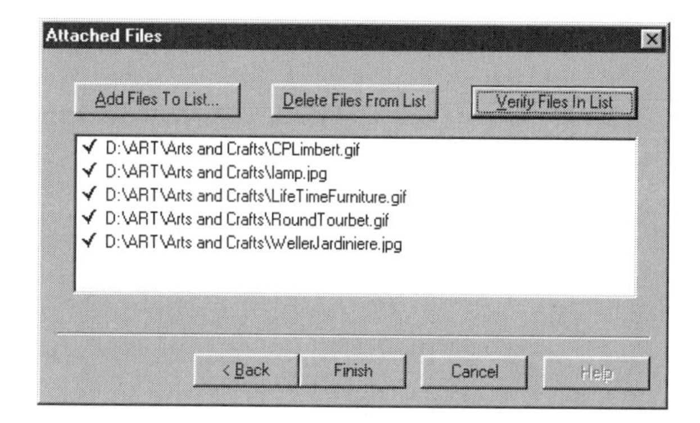

Note

The Verify Files in List button in the Attached Files dialog box is for making sure that the files in the list are where the list says they are. The button comes into play after you've created the slideshow and you need to make sure its slides are still intact.

At last, click the Finish button. An ugly graphic called SlideShow appears on the Web page. The graphic is precisely the size of the largest slide in your slideshow. Don't worry—it won't appear on your Web page. It is there only to commemorate the fact that you created a slideshow.

Press F5 (or click the Preview Web Site button) right away to go to the Page Preview window and run your slideshow. How do you like it?

Tip

If the SlideShow graphic is too much for you to bear, you can exchange it for another placeholder graphic. To do so, right-click it, choose Properties, and click the Place Holder Graphic tab in the Object Properties dialog box. Then click the Load New Place Holder Graphic button and choose a new graphic.

Revising a Slideshow

If your slideshow isn't quite what you thought it would be, you can revise it. Well, you can revise parts of it. You can remove some slides from the show and add other slides. Here's what you *can't* do:

- Change the transition between slides.
- Change when slides appear—every ten seconds, when the viewer clicks a button, or when the viewer clicks a slide.
- Change the background color of the slides.

Follow these steps to remove slides from or add slides to a slideshow:

1. In the Web Page window, select the SlideShow placeholder graphic and choose Object ➢ Object Properties (or right-click and choose Properties). The Object Properties dialog box appears.
2. Click the Attached Files tab. Does it look familiar? This tab works the same way as the Attached Files dialog box.
    - Click the Add File To List button to place a new slide in the show.
    - Select a slide and click the Delete Files From List button to remove a slide from the show.
    - Click the Verify button to find out whether files have been moved to new locations on your computer since you recruited them for the show. If a file has moved, a question mark (?) appears beside its name, as in the following illustration.

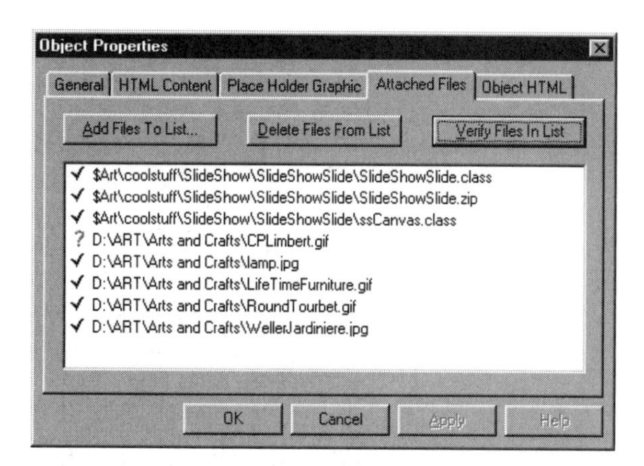

3. Click the OK button when you are finished revising your slideshow.

Chapter 10

Putting "Cool Stuff" on Your Web Pages

Who doesn't want "cool stuff" on their Web page? Clocks, calendars, and search engines keep visitors coming back for more. This chapter looks into some of the very cool devices in the Cool Stuff Gallery and shows you how to make your Web site rise above the ordinary.

- Showing visitors to your site a monthly calendar, the date, and the time
- Telling visitors when your site was last modified
- Placing a search engine on a Web page
- Including an e-mail icon on your home page so others can send you messages

Placing a Cool Stuff Object on a Web Page

Some items in the Cool Stuff Gallery—Web page links, scrolling text, the HTML object, and slideshows—are explained in other chapters.

I bet you know the routine by now: To place a Cool Stuff object on a Web page, open the Cool Stuff Gallery and drag the object into the Web Page window. Of course, you might have to choose View ➢ Galleries and click the Cool Stuff tab first.

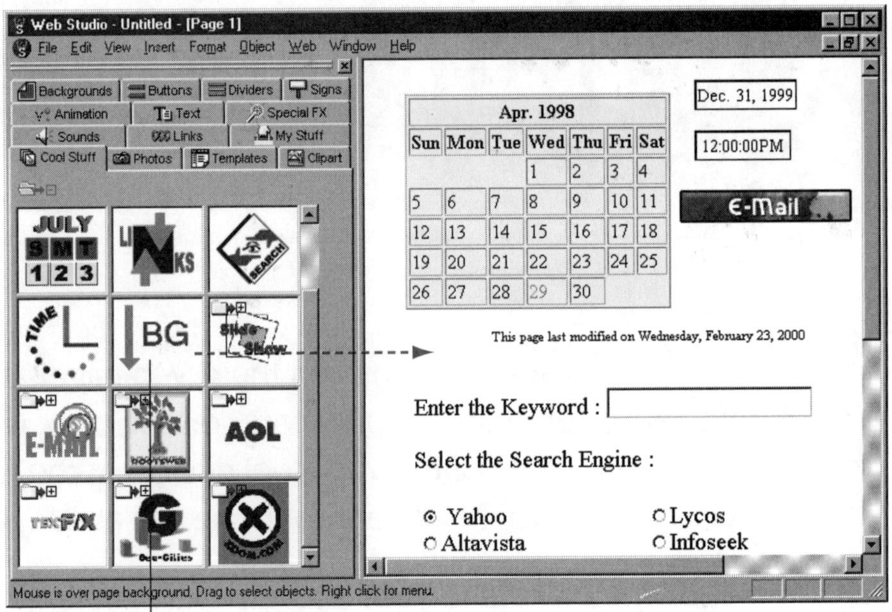

Drag the Cool Stuff object into the Web Page window

Cool Stuff objects are slightly different from other objects, but the rules for inserting and moving a Cool Stuff object are the same. Chapter 4 explains how to handle objects.

Warning

Web Studio does not permit you to change the size of these objects in the Cool Stuff Gallery: Calendar, Date, Time, and Search Engine.

Telling Your Visitors the Date and Time

Everybody needs to know the date and time. Otherwise, how will they know how behind they are, how late they are, or how far they are from meeting a deadline? Kidding aside, seeing the date and time on a Web page gives the page an air of importance.

Read on to learn how to put a calendar, the date, and the time on a Web page. You also find out how to put the "last modified date" notice on a Web page so that visitors to your site can tell whether it is up to date.

Dropping a Calendar on a Page

Drag the Calendar object in the Cool Stuff Gallery into the Web Page window to put a calendar on your Web site. The Calendar is a plain-looking affair that shows the present month and the days of the week. Today's date appears in red instead of black numbers.

Feb. 2000						
Sun	Mon	Tue	Wed	Thu	Fri	Sat
		1	2	3	4	5
6	7	8	9	10	11	12
13	14	15	16	17	18	19
20	21	22	23	24	25	26
27	28	29				

You can't change the size of the Calendar or make it transparent. Press F5 or click the Preview Web Site button to see the Calendar in the Page Preview window, and, moreover, make it display the current month and date.

Showing Your Visitors the Date

What about placing today's date on the Web page instead of a full-blown calendar? Drag the Date object in the Cool Stuff Gallery into the Web Page window to make the date appear in a small box on your Web page.

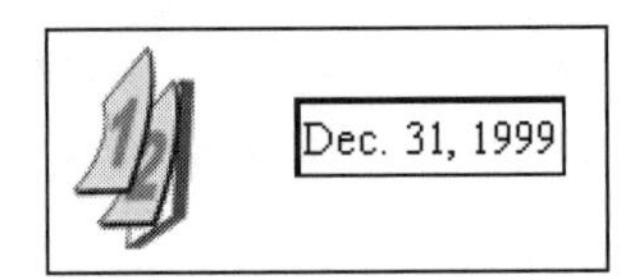

Press F5 or click the Preview Web Site button to see today's date in the Page Preview window. You can't change the size of the Date object or make it transparent. All you can do is tuck it in a corner of the Web page where visitors can see it and know instantly what today's date is.

Showing Your Visitors the Time

What time is it? Visitors to your Web site need never ask this question if you put the Clock object on a Web page. The Clock object in the Cool Stuff Gallery is the one with the word "TIME" on it. The object ticks the seconds away and includes the letters AM or PM.

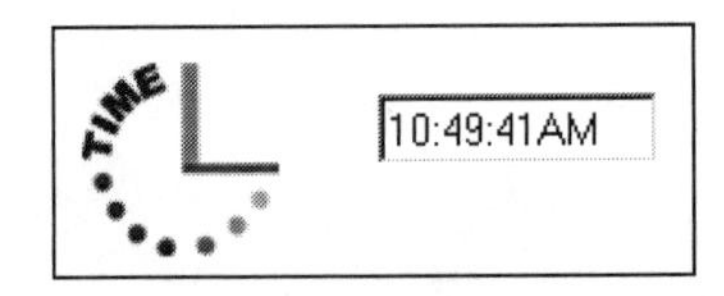

Press F5 or click the Preview Web Site button to read the time in the Page Preview window. You can't make the clock transparent or change its size. Nor can you turn the digital clock into a clock with hands.

Informing Visitors When You Last Modified Your Site

Visitors come to certain kinds of Web sites to get up-to-date information—work schedules, rosters, the latest news about this or that. Because these Web sites change from day to day, visitors need to know whether the information they are seeing is up to date. And they can tell if it's up to date if you put a Last Modified Date object on your Web page.

The Last Modified Date is simply a way for you to list the last day you worked on your Web site without having to enter the date yourself. When you are finished working on your Web site, drag the Last Modified Date object in the Cool Stuff Gallery into the Web Page window. The object enters the words "This page last modified on," the day of the week, and today's date.

You can treat a Last Modified Date object like a text object and change its size, change its background color, or change the font and font size of its characters. As long as you don't touch the day of the week or date, you can even change the words. Instead of "This page last modified on," for example, you can write, "I stayed up late into the night laboring on this site and didn't get any sleep on."

Chapter 5 explains how to handle text objects.

Including a Search Engine with Your Web Site

Search Engine
A program that searches for keywords in Web pages on the Internet and reports where the Web pages are found.

How would you like to put a **search engine** on your Web site? That sounds too good to be true, doesn't it? After all, a search engine is a very sophisticated piece of machinery. Don't you have to go to special Web sites such as Yahoo and Lycos to search the Internet?

Well, you *can* make a search engine a part of your Web site. To do so, drag the Search Engine object in the Cool Stuff Gallery into the Web page window.

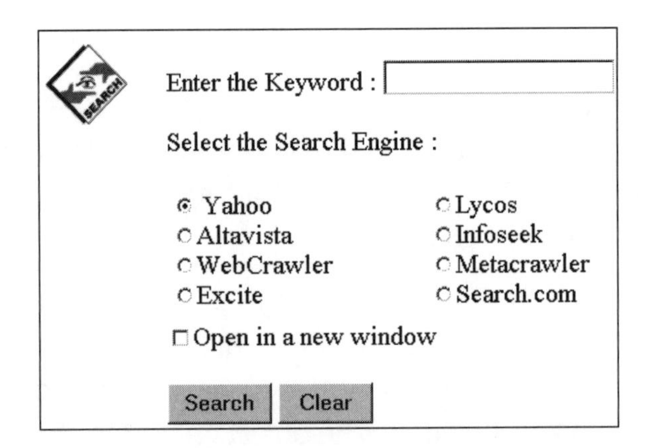

Needless to say, offering visitors to your site an opportunity to search the Internet is a mighty nice service. Press F5 or click the Preview Web Site button to open the Page Preview window and test-drive the search engine. After you enter a keyword and click the Search button, the results of the search appear in the window. Click the Back button to return to your Web site.

Tuck the search engine into a corner of your site as an extra amenity for visitors.

Inviting Others to Send E-Mail Messages

Usually, you will find the means to send an e-mail message to the Webmaster somewhere on the home page of his or her Web site. The Webmaster is the person who maintains the site. Sometimes you see the Webmaster's e-mail address, but more often you see an e-mail icon like the ones shown here. When visitors click an e-mail icon, their e-mail programs open. They see a screen for sending an e-mail message. And, to make sending it easier, the message is already addressed to the Webmaster.

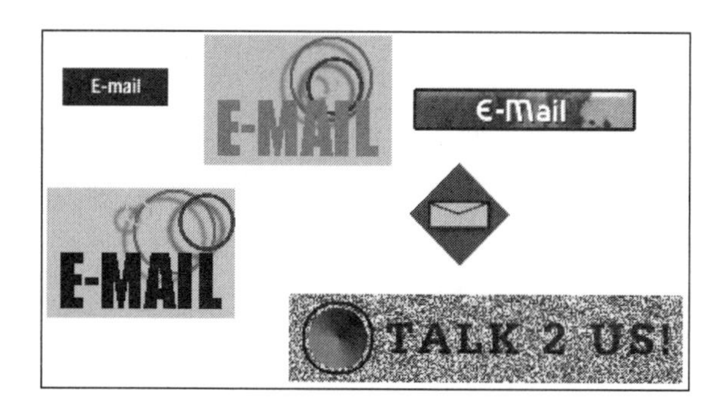

The Cool Stuff Gallery offers six e-mail icons that are ready to go. Put one on your home page, and visitors will be able to click it to send you an e-mail message right away.

Follow these steps to put an e-mail icon on your home page so that others can get in touch with you:

1. In the Cool Stuff Gallery, look for the E-MAIL subfolder and double-click to open it.
2. Choose one of the six e-mail icons and drag it into the Web Page window. You see the Enter Your Email Address dialog box.

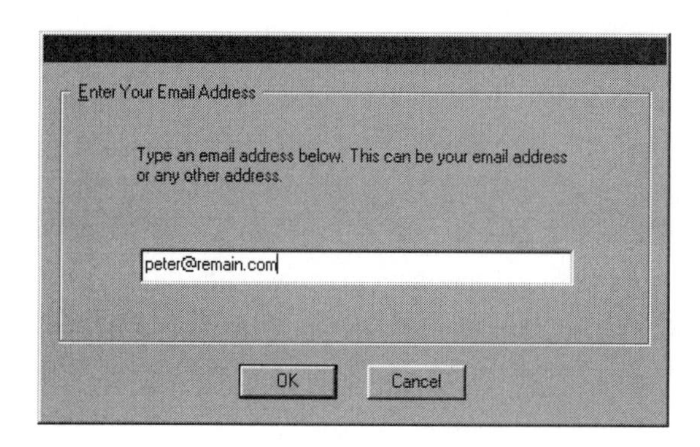

3. Enter your e-mail address in the text box. Be sure to enter it correctly. Messages that others write will go to you at the address you enter.
4. Click OK.

Press F5 or click the Preview Web Site button to go to the Page Preview window and test the e-mail icon. When you click it, your default e-mail program opens and you see a pre-addressed screen for sending messages to you!

Turning a Photo, Image, Sign, or Button into an E-mail Icon

A clip art image, photo, sign, or button from the Web Galleries can serve as an e-mail icon. Follow these steps to turn one of those objects into an e-mail icon that others can click to send you e-mail messages:

1. Click the object to select it.
2. Choose Object ➢ Object Properties or right-click and choose Properties. The Object Properties dialog box appears.
3. Click the Link tab.
4. In the Link URL box, enter **mailto:** followed by your e-mail address. For example, if your e-mail address is peter@remain.com, enter **mailto:peter@remain.com**, as shown in the following illustration.

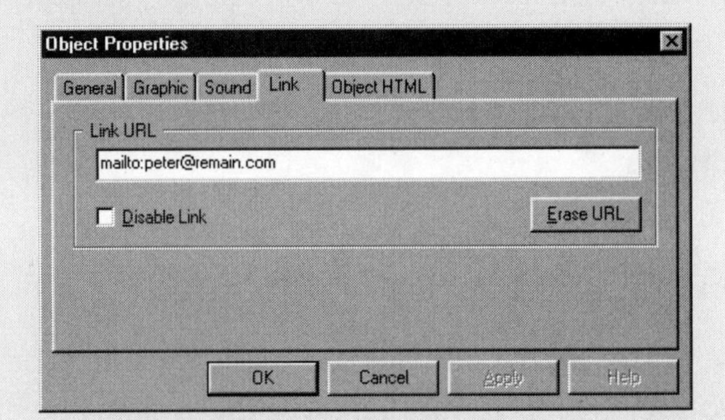

5. Click OK.

Tip

To make sure that visitors know they can e-mail you by clicking the e-mail icon, write an alternate text message for the icon: Right-click it, choose Properties, click the Graphic tab in the Object Properties dialog box, enter the message, and click OK. When visitors move the pointer over the e-mail icon, they will see the message you wrote. I suggest writing, "Click here to send me a message."

Chapter 11

Printing Your Web Pages

This short chapter is included in this book for the purposes of backward-compatibility. What does that strange term mean? In Computerese, *backward-compatibility* is when programmers add a few commands to a program solely to make it work with old, outdated software. In this chapter, you learn how to print Web pages. In other words, you learn how to pass Web pages through that ancient but venerable device, the printer.

When you need to print your Web site, perhaps to include it in a portfolio or to make proofreading it easier, turn to this chapter.

- Choosing how to print Web pages
- Saving and printing a Web page in Paint
- Telling Web Studio how to print Web pages
- Printing Web pages in Web Studio

The Two Ways to Print Web Pages

Bitmap (BMP) Graphic
A graphic composed of many tiny dots called pixels that, taken together, form an image.

Web Studio offers commands for printing Web pages, but in my experience, the best way to print them is to save them as bitmap graphics and print them in Paint, the accessory program that comes with Windows. Paint does a better job of scaling Web pages so they fit on one page, and prints the pages faster. Web Studio offers a special command, File ➢ Save Page as Graphic, for making a bitmap copy of a Web page that can then be printed in Paint.

But I should let you judge which is the best method of printing Web pages. Try them both and see which works best for you:

- "Saving and Printing a Web Page as a Bitmap Graphic" in this chapter explains how to print with Paint.
- "Printing Web Pages in Web Studio" explains how to do the job in Web Studio.

Tip

To see if Paint is loaded on your computer, click the Start button and choose Programs ➢ Accessories ➢ Paint. If Paint is on your computer and you haven't customized the menus, look for it on the Accessories menu.

Saving and Printing a Web Page as a Bitmap Graphic

So you've taken my advice and decided to print your Web pages as **bitmap graphics** in Paint. You are a wise person indeed. Printing them in Paint is easier than you might think, and the Web pages look better, too. Printing a Web page

in Paint is a two-step business. First, you save the page as a bitmap graphic in Web Studio. Then you open Paint and print the Web page there.

Follow these steps to save a Web page as a bitmap graphic:

1. In Web Studio, select the page you want to save as a graphic and print. To do so, click the page in the Page List (choose View ➢ Page List if you can't see the Page List).
2. Choose File ➢ Save Page as Graphic. The Save As dialog box appears.
3. Locate and select the folder where you will save the bitmap graphic.

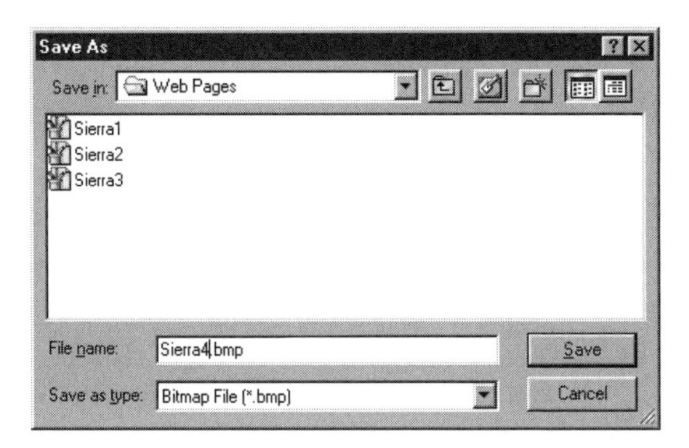

4. Enter a name for the graphic in the File Name text box. *Do not* erase the file extension, BMP, when you enter the name.
5. Click the Save button.

Now that your Web page has been saved as a bitmap graphic, you can open and print it in Paint. Follow these steps:

1. Click the Start button and choose Programs ➢ Accessories ➢ Paint to open Paint.
2. In Paint, choose File ➢ Open. The Open dialog box appears.
3. Locate the folder where you saved the Web page graphic.
4. Select the bitmap file where you saved your Web page.
5. Click the Open button. The Web page appears on the Paint screen.

At last, to print the Web page, follow these steps:

1. In Paint, choose File ➢ Print (or press Ctrl+P). You see the Print dialog box.
2. Enter a number in the Number of Copies box if you want to print more than one copy of your Web page.
3. Click the OK button.

Make one bitmap copy of every page on your Web site. That way, if you need to print Web pages in a hurry, you can do it in Paint.

Printing Web Pages in Web Studio

Very likely, you can simply choose File ➢ Print Page (or press Ctrl+P) to print Web Pages in Web Studio. But if you want to print a landscape page or print on odd-size paper, you have to visit the Print Setup dialog box and choose a paper size and printing orientation. Following are instructions for setting up your printer and printing a Web page.

Choosing a Paper Size and Orientation

Before you can print Web pages in Web Studio, you have to tell Web Studio *how* to print them. Do you want to print a portrait or **landscape page**? What size paper will you print on? Follow these steps to describe how you want to print the Web pages on your Web site:

Landscape Page
A page turned on its side so it is wider than it is tall. A portrait page, which is taller than it is wide, is the standard.

1. Choose File > Print Setup. The Print Setup dialog box appears. The settings you see are the default settings for your computer. Probably, these are the settings you want, but you can change them temporarily for the printing that you are about to do.

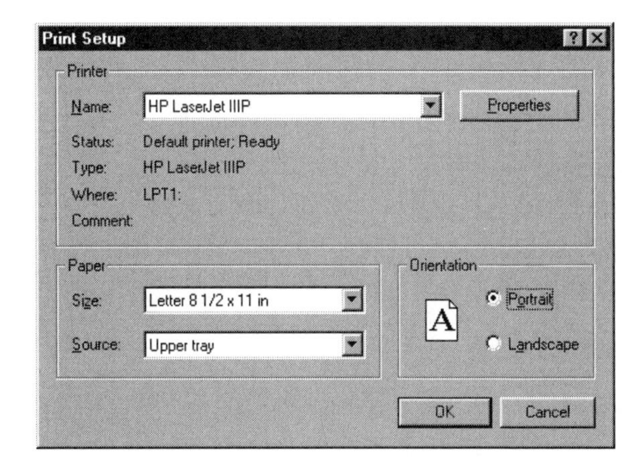

2. From the Size drop-down menu, choose the size paper you will print on, if necessary.

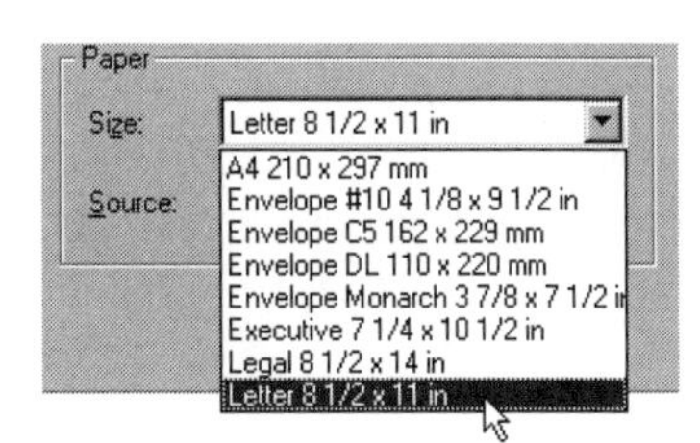

3. In the Orientation box, choose Portrait or Landscape.
4. If your computer is connected to more than one printer, open the Name drop-down menu and choose the printer on which you will print the Web page.

5. If your printer has more than one tray, choose the right tray from the Source drop-down menu.

6. Click OK.

Tip

Legal-size paper is often the best paper to print on. A large Web page can usually fit on legal-size paper, whereas letter-size or A4 paper is sometimes too small. Make sure you have legal-size paper and that your printer is capable of printing on it.

Printing the Web Page

Web pages can only be printed one at a time. Sorry—you can't tell Web Studio to print all the pages on the Web site and then go to lunch. Follow these steps to print a Web page in Web Studio:

1. Go to the Web page you want to print.

2. Choose File ➢ Print Page (or press Ctrl+P). You see the Print dialog box.

3. If you want to print more than one copy of your Web page, enter a number in the Number of Copies box.

4. Click OK.

5. Choose Scale the Web Page to Fit One Sheet of Paper and click OK in the Printing Options dialog box, if the dialog box appears (and it most likely will appear).

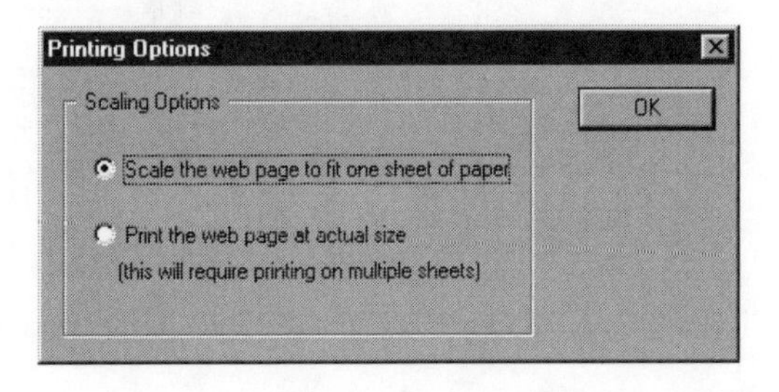

6. Click OK.

Chapter 12

Entering Your Own HTML in Web Studio

This chapter is for people who know a little bit or perhaps a lot about HTML tags and want to enter HTML tags on their own in Web Studio. And it's also for people who have been given HTML to put on their site—a banner perhaps—and need to know how to place the banner or other slice of HTML on a Web page. As I explained in Chapter 2, you don't have to know anything about HTML to create a Web site with Web Studio, but if you do know something about HTML, you can make your site a little more sophisticated by going beyond the objects and other amenities that Web Studio offers.

- Techniques for Entering HTML tags into the Object Properties dialog box
- Entering HTML with the HTML object in the Cool Stuff Gallery
- Getting HTML tags from an HTML document
- Inserting an HTML item relative to a page or relative to an object

The Three Ways to Enter HTML

Web Studio offers three ways to enter HTML:

- By way of the HTML object in the Cool Stuff Gallery: This is the best way to go, because you can choose precisely where the HTML item will appear on the Web page. See "Inserting HTML Items Where *You* Want Them to Go."
- By way of the Page HTML tab of the Object Properties dialog box: Using this technique, you enter the HTML item with respect to the page—the top of the page, near the top, or the middle. If you want to put a banner at the top of a Web page, this is the way to go. However, you can't adjust the position of the HTML item. See "Inserting HTML Items with Respect to the Page."
- By way of the Object HTML tab in the Object Properties dialog box: With this technique, the HTML item is attached to an object—a text object or graphic object, for example. Move the object and you move the HTML item as well. Go this route when the HTML item refers to an object. See "Inserting HTML Items with Respect to an Object."

The Basics of Inserting HTML in Web Studio

No matter which technique you decide to use for entering HTML, the means of entering the tags and codes is the same. You can type the tags and codes into the Object Properties dialog box yourself, click the Import button to get the tags and codes from a file, or copy and paste the HTML.

Warning

If you enter the codes by typing them, remember to type carefully. Enter a code incorrectly, for example, and the HTML items will not display correctly when others view them through their Web browsers.

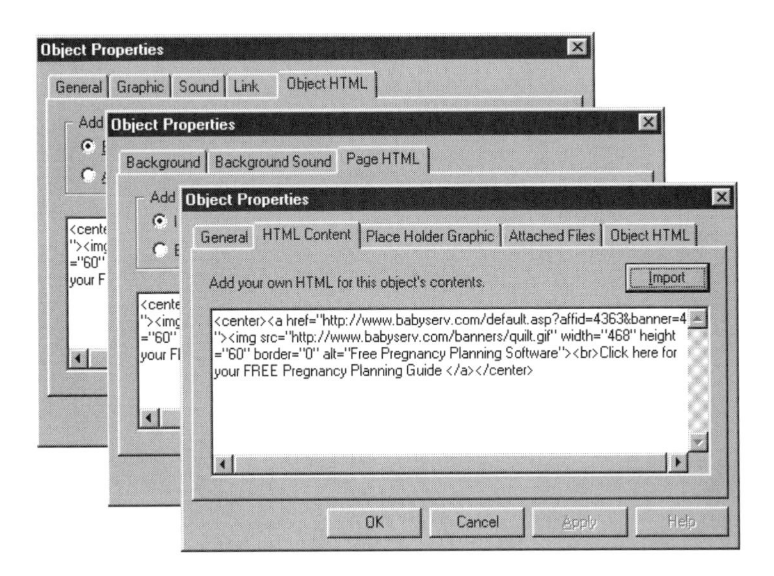

The easiest way to enter HTML tags yourself is to type them in a word processor, save them, and click the Import button to bring them into the Object properties dialog box. Remember, however, to save the HTML as a text (TXT) file or HTML (HTM or HTML) file.

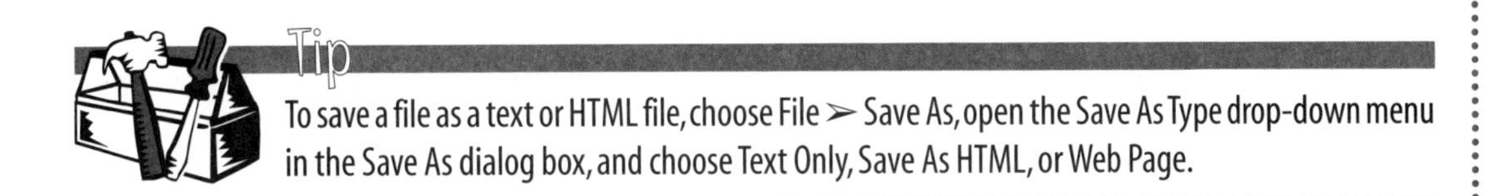

Tip

To save a file as a text or HTML file, choose File ➢ Save As, open the Save As Type drop-down menu in the Save As dialog box, and choose Text Only, Save As HTML, or Web Page.

Follow these steps to enter the codes by getting them from a file:

1. Click the Import button in the Object Properties dialog box. You see the Open dialog box.

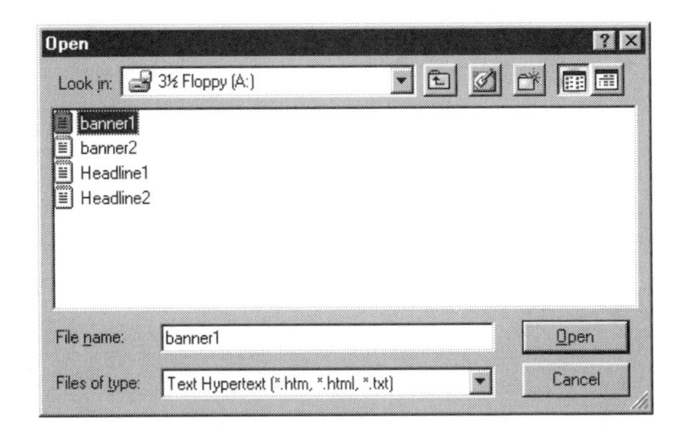

2. Locate the folder where the file you need is located.

3. Click the file to select it.
4. Click the Open button.

Tip

Another way to enter HTML in the Object Properties dialog box is to copy the tags from elsewhere, right-click in the dialog box, and choose Paste.

Inserting HTML Items Where *You* Want Them to Go

As I explained at the outset of this chapter, the best way to enter an HTML item is to make use of the HTML Object in the Cool Stuff Gallery. That way, you can drag the object on the page and decide for yourself where the HTML item goes. Follow these steps to employ an HTML Object to insert a banner or other HTML item on your Web page:

1. Go to the Cool Stuff Gallery by choosing View ➢ Galleries, if necessary, and clicking the Cool Stuff tab.
2. Drag the HTML Object, the first object in the Cool Stuff Gallery, into the Web Page window.

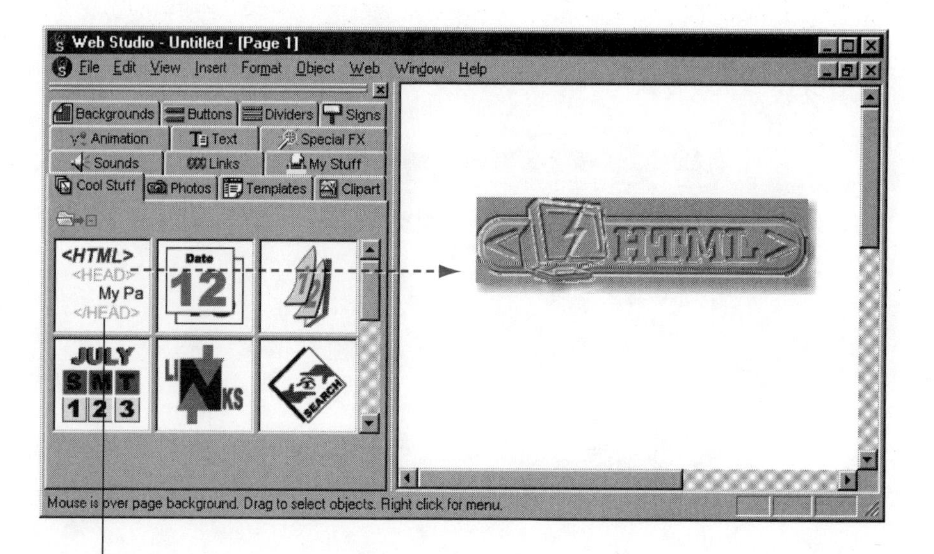

Drag the HTML Object into the Web Page window

3. Click the HTML Object to select it, and then choose Object ➢ Object Properties or right-click and choose Properties. You see the Object Properties dialog box.

4. Click HTML Content tab.

5. Enter the HTML codes in the HTML Content tab and click OK.

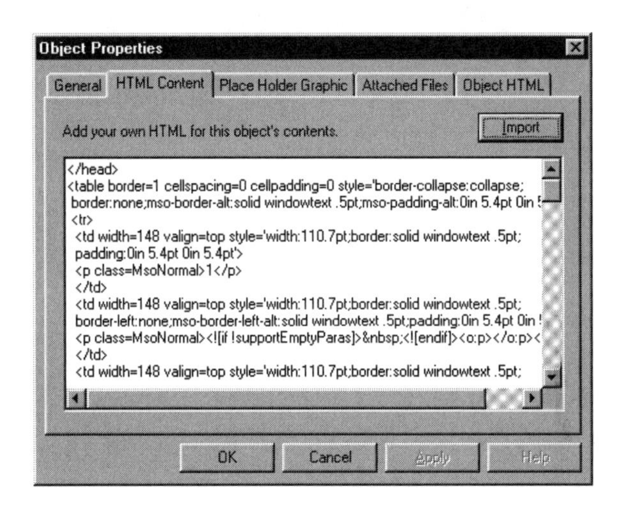

Earlier in this chapter, "The Basics of Inserting HTML in Web Studio" explains how to enter HTML in the HTML Content tab.

You can treat the HTML object like any other object and drag to move it on the Web page. Press F5 or click the Preview Web Site button to go to the Page Preview window and see what the HTML codes produce when they are viewed through a browser.

The Fast Way to Enter HTML Codes—Get them from an HTML Document

Web Studio makes entering text and graphics easy, but the program is lacking when it comes to entering tables, bulleted lists, and other fancy text formats. One way to solve this problem is to create the table, bulleted list, or what not in a word processor, save it as an HTML document, and import it into Web Studio. This way, you don't have to enter complex HTML codes yourself.

Here are instructions for putting a table on a Web page by way of Microsoft Word 97 or Microsoft Word 2000:

1. Create the table in Microsoft Word.

2. Save the table as an HTML file. To do so, choose File ➢ Save, save and name the table as you normally would in the Save As dialog box, but this time open the Save As Type drop-down menu and choose Web Page (in Word 2000) or Save As HTML (in Word 97).

3. In Web Studio, drag an HTML object onto the Web Page window and choose Object ➢ Object Properties to open the Object Properties dialog box.

4. Click the HTML Content tab.

Continued on next page

The Fast Way to Enter HTML Codes—Get them from an HTML Document (continued)

5. Click the Import button, find and select the file you saved in Step 2, and click the Open button. The codes for the table appear on the HTML Content tab.
6. Click OK.

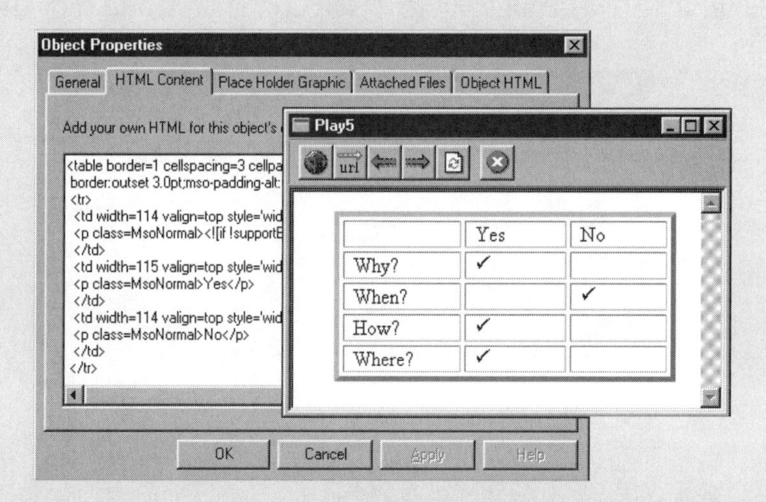

The only drawback of entering HTML this way is that much of the HTML is not essential. You don't need all of the tags. Look through the HTML in the Content tab and delete the tags that aren't necessary for displaying the table or other HTML item. In the case of a table, you can delete all tabs before the <TABLE> tag and all codes after the </TABLE> tag.

Inserting HTML Items with Respect to the Page

Inserting an HTML item with respect to the page is, as I explained at the start of this chapter, the primitive way to insert an HTML item on a Web page. You can't move the item after you insert it. If you want an HTML item, such as a banner, to appear at the top of the page, you can save a little time by inserting it with respect to the page, but that is the only advantage of inserting an item this way.

Follow these steps to insert an HTML item with respect to a Web page:

1. Choose Object ➢ Page Properties or right-click the page and choose Page Properties. The Object Properties dialog box appears.

2. Click the Page HTML tab.

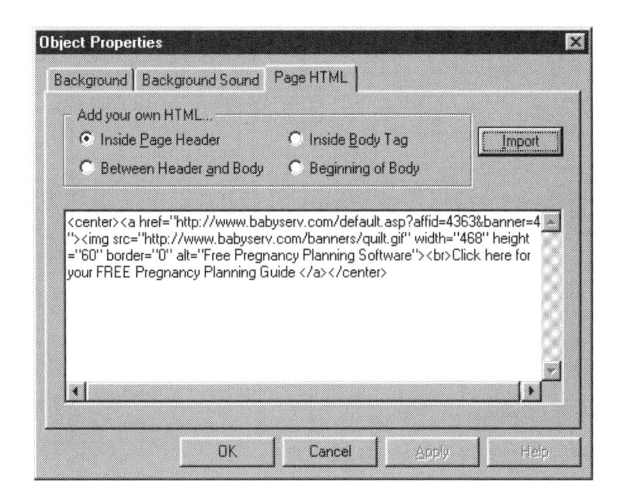

3. Click an option button to choose where on the page the HTML item will go:
   - Inside Page Header: The item is inserted at the top of the Web page, right before the </HEAD> tag. Choose this option to place a banner at the top of your Web page.
   - Between Header and Body: The item is placed lower on the page than the tags appear if you put them inside the page header. The tags are inserted right after the </HEAD> tag.
   - Inside Body Tab: The item is inserted right after the <BODY> tag.
   - Beginning of Body: The item is inserted right before the </BODY> tag.
4. Enter the HTML or click the Import button to get them from a file.
5. Click OK.

Earlier in this chapter, "The Basics of Inserting HTML in Web Studio" explains how to enter HTML in the Page HTML tab.

Inserting HTML Items with Respect to an Object

Another way to insert an HTML item is to do it with respect to an object. In effect, the item is attached to the object. When you move the object, the HTML

item moves along with it. Use this technique for inserting HTML items to save yourself the trouble of moving two items at once.

Follow these steps to insert an HTML item with respect to an object:

1. Click the object to select it.
2. Either choose Object ➢ Object Properties or right-click and choose Properties. The Object Properties dialog box appears.
3. Click the Object HTML tab.

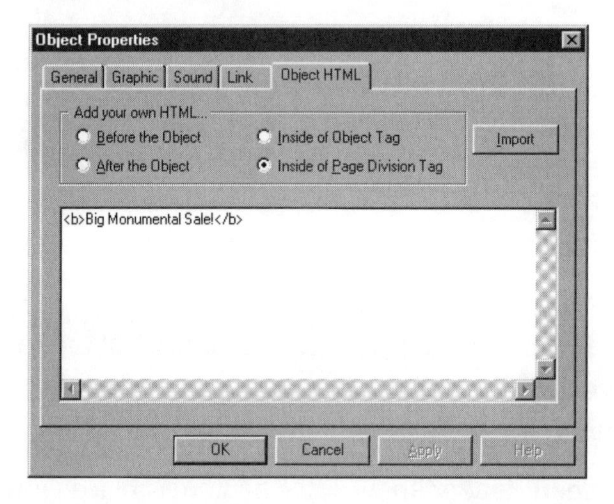

4. Click an option button to choose where the HTML item will go relative to the object:
   - Before the Object: The item appears directly above the object.
   - After the Object: The item appears directly below the object.
   - Inside of Object Tag: The item is inserted before the </DIV> tag and it appears below the object.
   - Inside of Page Division Tag: The item is inserted right after the <DIV> tag and it appears above the object.

Earlier in this chapter, "The Basics of Inserting HTML in Web Studio" explains how to enter HTML in the Object HTML tab.

Warning

If you generate your Web site with HTML 3.2, you won't see the <DIV> tags. Suffice it to say, the HTML will appear right above or right below the object.

5. Enter the HTML or click the Import button to get them from a file.
6. Click OK.

Part 4

Launching Your Web Site on the Internet

Part 4 explains how to launch your Web site on the Internet so that others can see and enjoy it. It offers tips for making your Web site easier to find on the Internet, shows how to upload your Web site to an ISP, and examines techniques for making sure your Web site functions properly.

Launching Your Web Site on the Internet

Chapter 13 • Putting on the Finishing Touches 171

Chapter 14 • Uploading Your Web Site to Your Internet Service Provider. 177

Chapter 15 • Making Sure Your Web Site Is All It Should Be 187

Chapter 13

Putting on the Finishing Touches

This short chapter describes a few details you have to attend to before you upload your Web site to the Internet (the subject of the next chapter). Read on to learn how to help search engines find your Web site and choose which kind of HTML to use.

- Entering meta information to help search engines index your Web site
- Choosing keywords that describe your site
- Deciding whether to upload Web pages in HTML 3.2, HTML 4.0, or both

Describing Your Site So That Others Can Find It on the Internet

Meta Information
Found in the <META> HTML tag of a Web page, the program in which the Web page was made, the name of the author, keywords that describe the page, and a short description.

Search engines—Yahoo, Lycos, Excite, and the rest of them—are always scouring the Internet and recording information about Web pages. The search engines work a little differently in that some record information about every word on a Web page and some only look at titles and headings. The search engines store this information in giant databases. When you conduct a search of the Internet, you are really searching a database that the search engine you are using maintains.

All search engines, when they record information about a Web site, record the meta information. The **meta information** lists the author of the Web site and keywords that describe the Web site. The meta information also lists a short description of the site and the name of the program with which it was made. Search engines give extra weight to meta information. Search the Internet with the keyword *Madagascar,* for example, and Web sites with the word *Madagascar* in their meta information will appear in the search results at the top of the list.

Search engines also give high priority to Web page names. See "Changing the Name of a Web Page" in Chapter 3 to learn how to give a descriptive name to a Web page and help search engines find it.

Viewers of a Web page can't see the meta information (unless they choose View ➢ Source in their browsers). The information is strictly for use by search engines. To help others find your Web site when they search the Internet, Web studio gives you the opportunity to enter meta information.

Follow these steps to enter meta information that will help others find your site on the Internet:

1. Choose File ➢ Web Site Properties or click the Site Properties button above the Page List. The Web Site Properties dialog box appears.
2. Click the Web Search Information tab. The information you enter on this tab will form the meta information for your Web site.

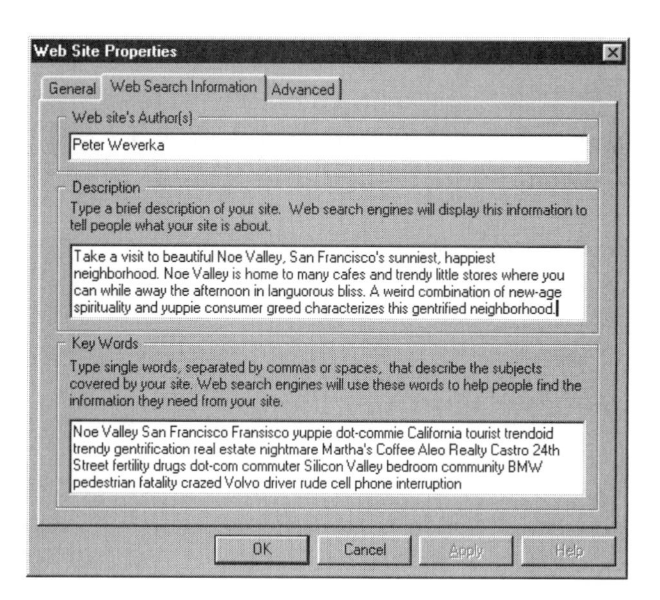

3. In the Web Site's Author(s) box, enter your name or the name of the author of the Web site. If someone does a search for the name you enter here, your Web site will turn up in the search results.

4. In the Description box, describe your Web site. Some search engines display the description you enter, word for word, in the results of an Internet search, so enter the description carefully.

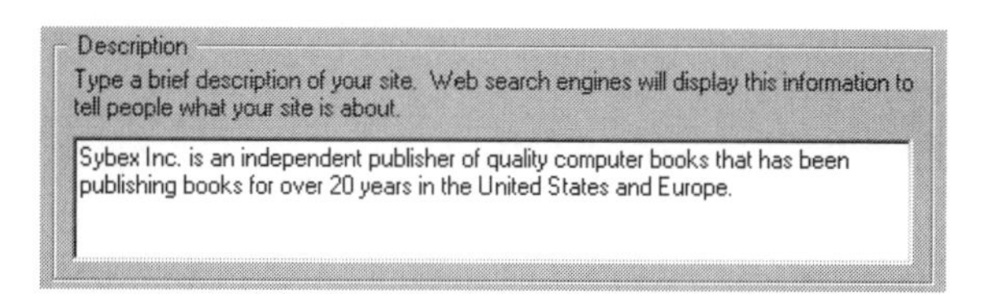

1. Welcome to **Sybex**, Inc. - Quality Computer Books - **Sybex** Inc. is an independent publisher of quality computer books that has been publishing books for over 20 years in the United States and Europe.
http://www.sybex.com/

Tip

You can't check for spelling errors in the Web Search Information tab. And the tab isn't a comfortable place to type words and descriptions. Instead of entering text in the Web Search Information tab, enter it in a word processor. Then select the text, choose Edit ➢ Copy, right-click in the Web Search Information tab, and choose Paste to enter the text.

5. Put yourself in the place of someone searching the Internet and enter all the keywords in the Key Words box that people searching for a Web site like yours might enter when conducting a search. When someone enters a keyword that matches a keyword you enter, your site will appear in the search results.

Key Words

Type single words, separated by commas or spaces, that describe the subjects covered by your site. Web search engines will use these words to help people find the information they need from your site.

Sybex computer book publisher, computer books, books, book, publishers, computer, computers, computing, how-to books, how to books, reference books, certification Cybex

Tip

People often make spelling errors when they enter keywords. To help your site get found, enter misspelled words as well as correctly spelled words in the Key Words box. Ask yourself how someone searching for your Web site might misspell a keyword, and enter the misspelling.

6. Click OK to close the Web Site Properties dialog box.

If you would like to see what meta information looks like, press F5 or click the Preview Web Site button to see your Web page in the Page Preview window. Then right-click in the window and choose View Source. Notepad opens so you can read the HTML codes, including the meta information. You will find it near the top of the page after the <META> tag.

Choosing Which Kind of HTML to Use on Your Web Pages

In 1998, a new set of HTML codes came out called HTML 4.0. The codes were an improvement over HTML 3.2, the previous set of HTML codes. As a user of Web Studio and one who doesn't have to be concerned with HTML codes, the only thing you need to know about HTML 3.2 and 4.0 is that Web Studio posts two sets of Web pages on the Internet, one for browsers that can only read HTML 3.2 codes and one for browsers that can read HTML 4.0 codes.

When someone with an older browser goes to your site, his or her browser opens the HTML 3.2 Web pages. Everyone else sees the HTML 4.0 pages.

However, posting two sets of Web pages on the Internet presents the following drawbacks:

- Because there are two sets of pages, the pages take longer to upload to your ISP.
- The pages occupy twice as much space on your ISP's server. Most people have to pay extra if the their Web pages exceed a certain number of megabytes, in which case posting two sets of Web pages can be costly.

What's more, HTML 3.2 isn't as sophisticated as HTML 4.0. If you opt for HTML 3.2 pages only, be aware of these limitations:

- Graphics that overlap are merged into a single graphic. This increases download times.
- Where graphics and text overlap, the graphics and text are merged to form a single graphic object. As a graphic object, search engines can no longer recognize the text and index it.

Rather than post both sets of Web pages to the Internet, you can post the HTML 4.0 pages. For that matter, you can post only the HTML 3.2 pages, but that would be self-defeating because the majority of browsers would read your Web pages incorrectly. Follow these steps to choose which set of HTML pages to post:

1. Click the Site Properties button above the Page List or choose File ➢ Web Site Properties. You see the Web Site Properties dialog box.
2. Click the Advanced tab.

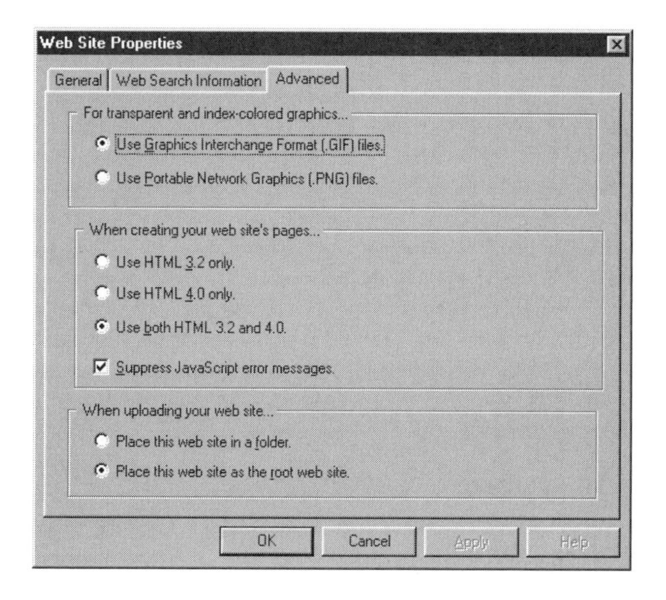

3. Under When Creating Your Web Site's Page, choose one of the following options:
   - Use HTML 3.2 Only: uploads the HTML 3.2 pages
   - Use HTML 4.0 Only: uploads the HTML 4.0 pages
   - Use Both HTML 3.2 and 4.0: uploads both sets of pages
4. Click OK.

Chapter 14

Uploading Your Web Site to Your Internet Service Provider

At last, the moment of truth has arrived. The work on your Web site is done. You have put together a little masterpiece. Now is the time to post it on the Internet. This chapter explains how to upload a Web site to an ISP or Web-hosting service for the first time. It describes the information you need to upload and tells you what to do if you fail to upload your site to the Internet.

- Getting the information you need from your ISP
- Entering ISP information so you can upload your Web site
- Uploading a Web site for the first and subsequent times
- What to do if you can't upload your Web site
- Uploading a Web site to a company network

What You Need to Know Before You Begin

In Chapter 2, "Selecting an Internet Service Provider (ISP) to Host Your Web Site" offers tips for choosing an ISP or Web-hosting service.

ftp site
A Web site that can receive Web pages for display on the Internet.

Before you can upload your Web site, you need to speak to a representative of the Internet service provider (ISP) or Web-hosting service that will host your Web site. Without the following information, you can't upload your Web pages. Call or e-mail your ISP and get or supply the following information:

A Username The ISP will know you by your username. The name helps identify you. You usually select this name yourself. Ask your ISP if the name is case-sensitive—if you need to enter upper- and lowercase letters or if you can enter all lowercase letters without regard to capitalization.

A Password For security reasons, you present a password when you upload pages to your ISP. You select the password. Again, ask your ISP if the password is case-sensitive and if you need to enter upper- and lowercase letters correctly.

An ftp site Address The Internet address to which you will send the Web pages. Here is an example of an ftp site address: *ftp.myisp.com*.

A Directory Path (or a Host Directory) The place on the ISP's computers where you will load your Web site. Not everyone needs this piece of information to upload a Web site. Find out if you need it, and, if you do, be sure to write it down correctly. Make sure the upper- and lowercase letters are recorded correctly, that slashes are in the right places, and that you have written down the entire thing.

World Wide Web Address of Your Home Page The address where you will be able to view your Web site on the Internet after you have uploaded it. You will be given an Internet address. When the time comes, you can type the address in the Address bar of your browser to see your pages online. You can also click a Preview button in Web Studio to see your Web site after you have uploaded it.

Uploading a Web Site for the First Time

The first time you upload a Web site to your ISP, you need to answer a bunch of different questions about where to upload the site. You tell Web Studio your username and password, your ISP's ftp address, the directory address (if necessary), and the World Wide Web address of your Web site. Don't worry, however, because you only have to enter this information once. Next time you upload your Web Site, all you have to do is click the Upload button.

Tip

Web Studio offers advice for uploading Web pages to Xoom, Geocities, Fortune City, AOL, and Talk City at this Web page: www.sierra.com/sierrahome/web/titles/webstudio/post.

Follow these steps to provide Web Studio with the information it needs to upload your Web site and then upload your Web site for the first time:

1. Choose File ➢ Save Web Site to Internet. You see the first Create/Edit a Destination dialog box, which explains what you need to upload your Web site.
2. Click the Next button. The Name Your Destination dialog box appears.

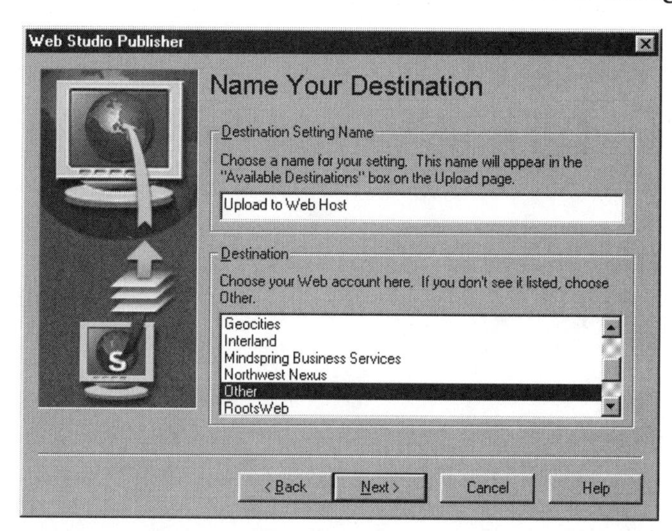

3. In the Destination Setting Name box, enter a name that describes the ISP to which you will upload your Web site. The name you enter is for

your own use. Later, when you upload your Web site, you will be able to choose this name in the Upload dialog box and bypass many of the choices you have to make the first time you upload.

4. In the Destination drop-down menu, choose the name of your ISP or Web-hosting service. If your ISP or service isn't on the list, choose Other.
5. Click the Next button. You see the Identification dialog box.

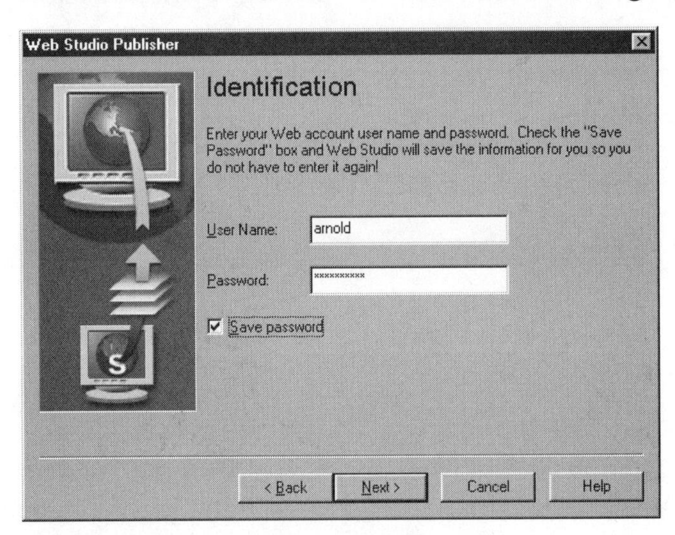

6. In the User Name box, enter your username.
7. In the Password box, enter your password.
8. Click the Save Password check box so that you don't have to enter your password the next time you upload your Web site.
9. Click the Next button. You see the Destination Address dialog box.

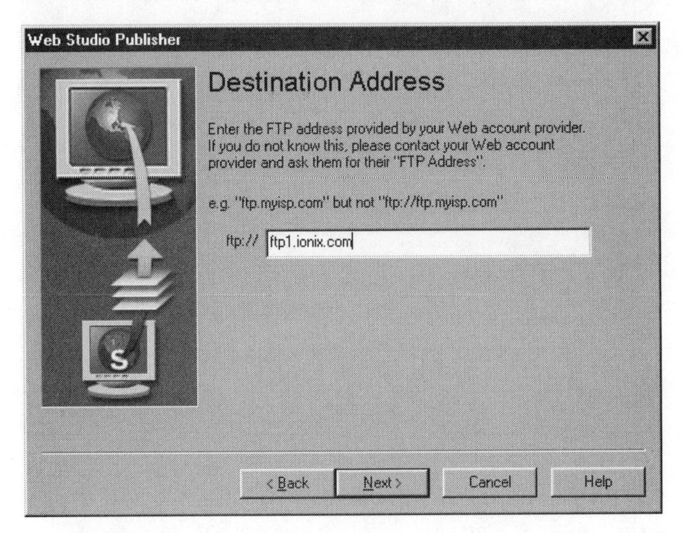

10. Enter your ftp site address.

11. Click the Next button. The Directory Path dialog box appears.

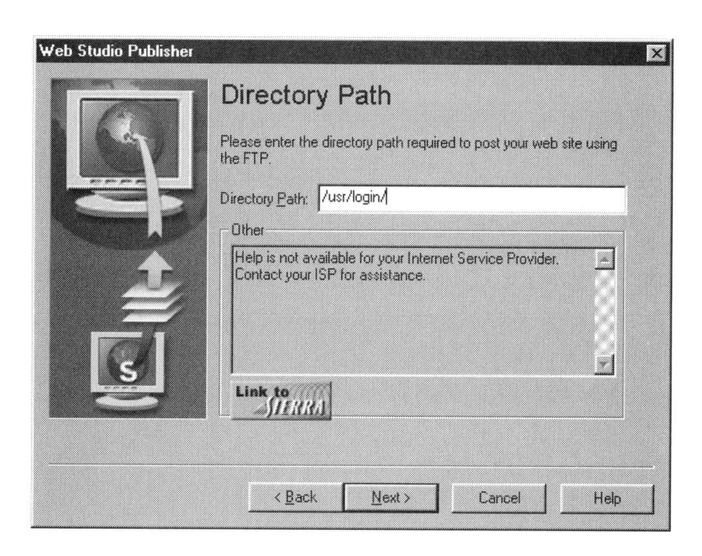

12. Enter the directory path where your Web site will be loaded on your ISP's computers. Not everyone has to enter this information.

13. Click the Next button. You see the Home Page dialog box.

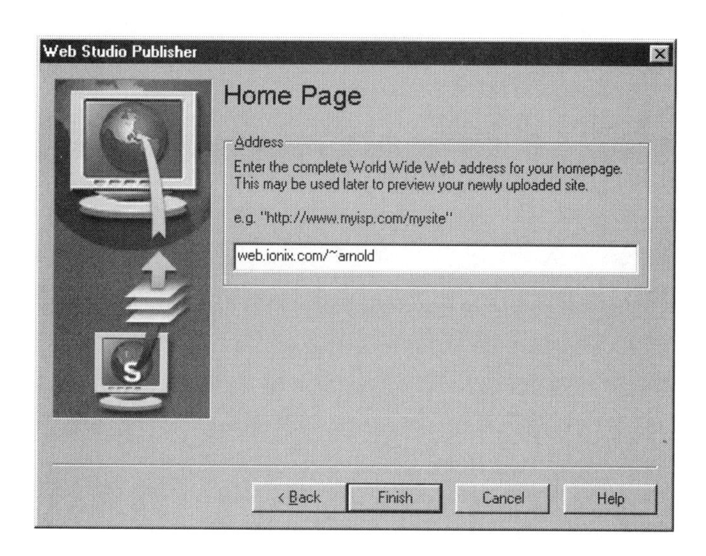

14. Enter the World Wide Web address of your home page. By doing so, you will be able to click a button and visit your Web site after it is finished uploading.

15. Click the Finish button. You see the Upload message box.

16. Make sure the destination name you entered in Step 3 is selected, and, if it's not, select it.

17. Click the Upload button.

18. If you are not already connected to the Internet, click the Connect button (or whatever it's called in your software) to connect to the Internet now. The Upload Progress dialog box appears as your Web site is sent to a computer at your ISP or Web-hosting service. Then you see the Complete dialog box.

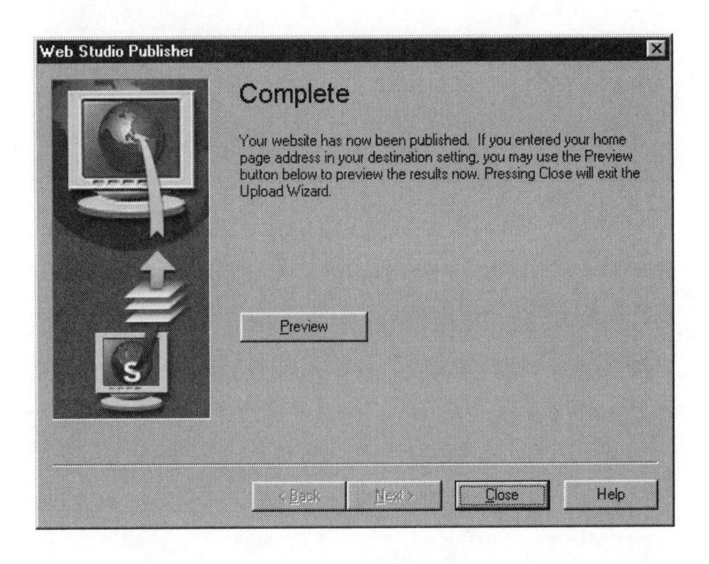

Appendix C explains how to bookmark a Web page.

19. Click the Preview button. Internet Explorer opens and you see the home page of your Web site.

In Appendix B, "Visiting and Posting Messages on the Web Publishing Message Board" explains how to get help—including help with uploading a Web site—from the Web Studio message board.

How do you like your Web site? Click a few hyperlinks and have a look around. If I were you, I would bookmark your Web site. That way, you can quickly have a look at it whenever you are surfing the Internet.

What to Do if the Upload Fails

Suppose the upload fails and you can't get your Web site onto the Internet. Don't worry, and don't panic. Not being able to upload a Web site the first time is the single biggest problem that novices have. All you have to do is enter one letter or number incorrectly in the Create/Edit a Destination dialog box, and

uploading a Web site fails every time. In most cases, you see a message box like the one shown here when an upload fails. Take note of what the message box says so you can fix the problem.

Try these techniques to fix a problem so you can upload your Web site:

Review and Change the Destination Information It's possible that the upload failed because destination information was entered incorrectly. Choose File ➢ Save Web Site to Internet, select a destination in the Upload dialog box (if more than one is listed), and click the Edit button. You see the Create/Edit a Destination dialog box—the same dialog box in which you entered your username, password, and so on.

Start clicking the Next button and reviewing the information you entered. If you entered your username, password, ftp site address, directory path, or Web address incorrectly, enter it correctly this time and try to upload the site again.

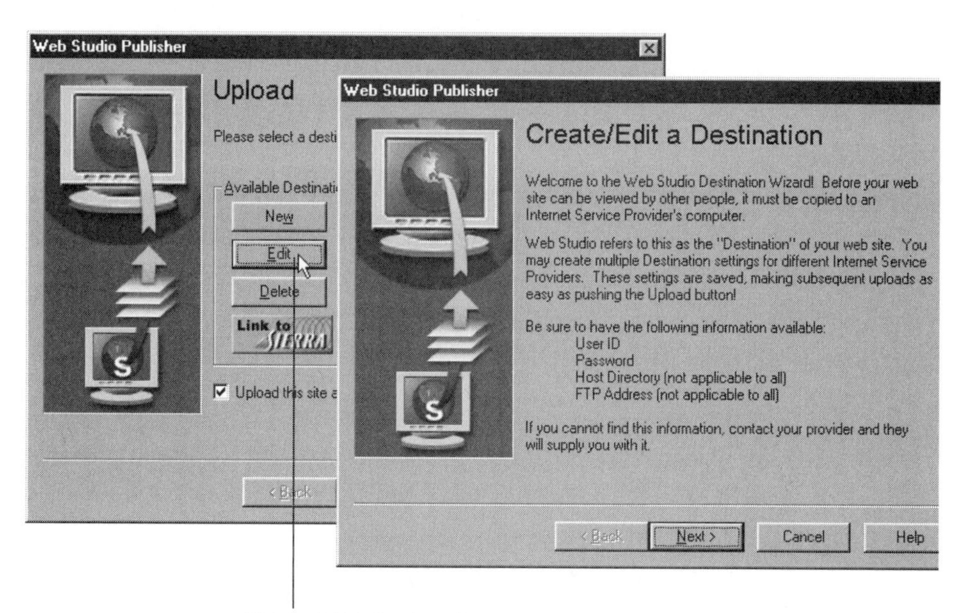

Click the Edit button to review and change destination information

Tip

Usually, an error in entering destination information can be traced to an incorrectly entered letter. Make sure you entered your username, password, ftp site address, and directory path correctly with the right combination of upper- and lowercase letters.

Call Your ISP or Web-Hosting Service If you reviewed the destination information and discovered that you entered it correctly, your ISP or Web-hosting service may have given you the wrong information to enter. Call your ISP or Web-hosting service to discuss the problem.

Tip

Nine times out of ten, the problem is caused in the directory path. Make sure your ISP gave you the right directory path. If your ISP told you that a directory path isn't needed, confirm this information with another technician. Perhaps a directory path *is* needed.

Uploading a Web Site

Uploading a Web site is easy after you have done it the first time. Now Web Studio knows your username, your password, your ISP's ftp address, and your directory path. Follow these steps to upload a Web site:

1. Choose File ➢ Save Web Site to Internet. The Upload dialog box appears.

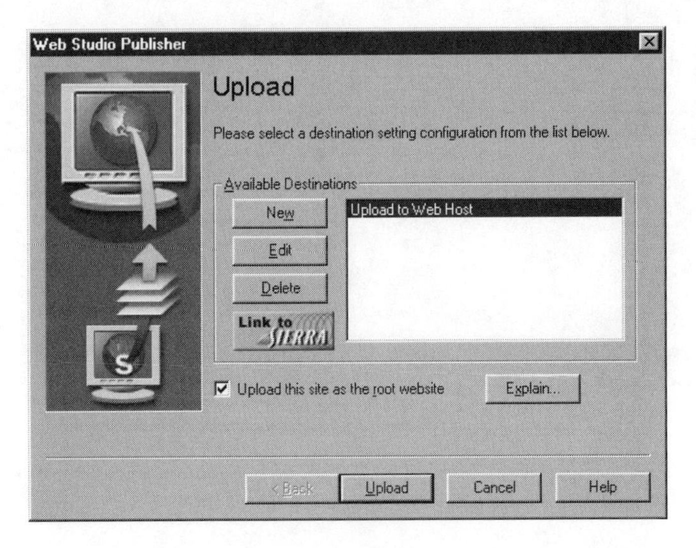

2. In the Available Destinations box, choose the correct destination (if more than one destination is listed because you upload to more than one ISP).
3. Click the Upload button. The Upload Progress dialog box appears as the Web pages are sent to your ISP. Soon you see the Complete dialog box.
4. Click the Preview button to open Internet Explorer and view your Web site there.

Other FTP Programs for Uploading Web Sites

Web Studio isn't the only ftp program that offers a means of uploading a Web site to the Internet. Very likely, one such program—Web Publishing Wizard—is already loaded on your computer. And you can download ftp programs from the Internet as well.

Web Publishing Wizard is part of the Windows 98 operating system, although it is not installed as part of a standard installation of Windows 98. If your computer runs on Windows 98, you can upload with the Web Publishing Wizard. To install it, you probably need to reinstall Windows, and when you reinstall, go to the Internet Tools category and select Web Publishing Wizard. Click the Start button and choose Programs ➢ Accessories ➢ Internet Tools ➢ Web Publishing Wizard to run the program.

CuteFTP, a shareware program, and WS_FTP, a freeware program, are the most popular ftp programs for uploading Web sites. If you want to try them out, go to Download.com (`www.download.com`), a Web site that offers computer programs, and download them to your computer. (At Download.com, click the Internet hyperlink and then the FTP hyperlink to see the list of ftp programs.)

Like Web Studio, other ftp programs ask for your username, your password, your ISP's ftp address, and your directory path in order to upload Web sites. However, other ftp programs ask for another thing—the folder on your computer that you want to publish on the Internet. In Web Studio, that folder is `C:\Sierra\Web Studio 2\Upload\`*`Your Web site name`*. In the following illustration, for example, my Web Site is called "Dogshow." To upload my Web site using Web Publishing Wizard, I select the `C:\Sierra\Web Studio 2\Upload\Dogshow` folder.

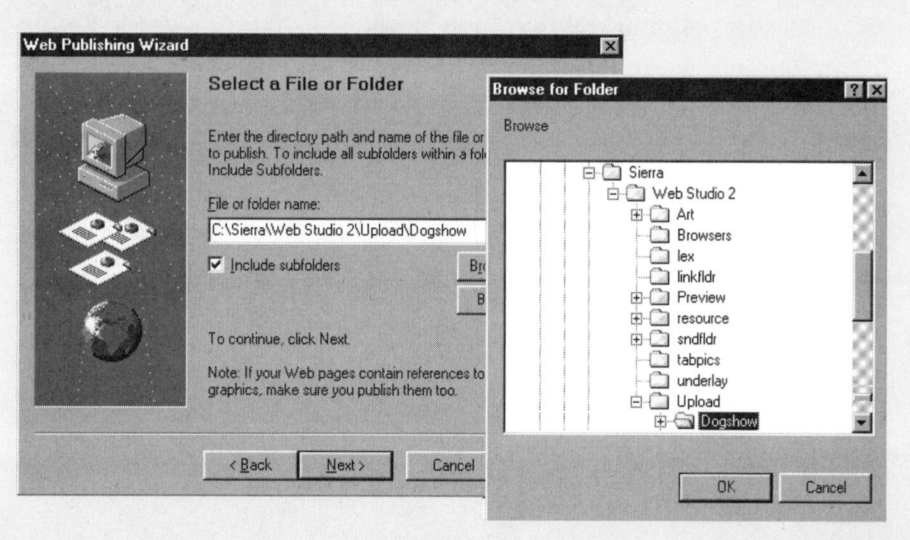

Whether you upload your Web site with Web Studio or another ftp program, you still have to choose File ➢ Save Web Site to Internet. By doing that, you place a copy of your Web site in the `C:\Sierra\Web Studio 2\Upload\`*`Your Web site name`* folder—the one that gets uploaded to your ISP or Web-hosting service when you post a Web site on the Internet.

Uploading Your Web Site to a Place on the Company Network

If all you want to do is place your Web site on the company network, you've got it made. Uploading a Web site to a network address is easy. Speak to your network administrator about where to place the Web site. And speak to your co-workers, too, to tell them where they can find the Web site on the company network.

Follow these steps to upload your Web site to a place on the network for the first time:

1. Choose File ➢ Save Web Site to Hard Drive. You see the Save Web Site to Hard drive dialog box.
2. Locate the address and folder on the network where you will place the Web site.
3. Enter a name for the folder where you will keep the Web site.
4. Check the Test the Web Site After Saving check box to view the Web site in Internet Explorer after you have placed it on the network.
5. Click the Save button.
6. Click the Yes button when Web Studio asks if you want to create the new folder for the Web site.

Subsequently, follow these steps to place an up-to-date copy of your Web site on the network:

1. Choose File ➢ Save Web Site to Hard Drive.
2. Locate and select the network address and folder where you keep the Web site.
3. Click the Open button.

Chapter 15

Making Sure Your Site Is All It Should Be

A Web site is like a finicky English sports car. Unless you tune it now and then, unless you inspect it to make sure it is running well, it will break down. This chapter explains how to make sure your Web site is working properly. And you also find out how to register a domain name and promote your Web site so it doesn't get lost in the shuffle.

- Finding out how long your Web site takes to appear onscreen
- Making sure the hyperlinks work
- Viewing your Web site through different browsers and at different resolutions
- Establishing a domain name for your Web site
- Promoting your Web site

Seeing How Long the Pages Take to Download

Modem

The hardware device by which computers can transmit data over the telephone lines.

"It takes too long to appear onscreen" is the biggest complaint that most people have about a Web site. What these people are really complaining about is download times. When you visit a Web page, all the files that make up the Web page—the HTML documents, the graphics, the sound files—are downloaded from a Web server to your computer. Your first task after you put your Web site on the Internet is to find out how long it takes your Web site to download. And if it takes too long, your next task is to jettison a few of the items that make downloading go so slowly—photos, sounds, and animations.

Professionals find out how long their Web sites take to download by testing download speeds on different **modems**. You probably don't have the luxury of testing download speeds that way. You can test download speeds only on the modem that is attached to your computer. What's more, after you have downloaded your Web site the first time, you can't realistically find out how long the download time is because all the images, sound files, and HTML documents on your site have already been downloaded to your computer. The second time you visit a Web page, your browser simply gets the images, sound files, and HTML documents from your computer. The second time you visit a Web page, the Web page isn't really downloaded. It is reassembled from items that were downloaded previously.

How do you find out how long your Web site takes to appear onscreen? The best way is to visit it from others' computers. Next time you are at a friend's house, a library with a computer, or a cyber-café, visit your Web site and note how long it takes to appear onscreen.

You can also go to your Web site and click the Refresh button in your browser. This way, your browser will think that you have never visited your Web site before. It will start afresh and download your Web site as if you were a first-time visitor. You will see how long it takes a new visitor whose modem operates at the same speed as yours to download your Web site.

Making Sure the Links Work

If you've spent any time on the Internet, you know that Web pages get taken down after a while. Quite often, when you click a hyperlink, your browser hiccups and a notice informs you that "The page cannot be found."

The page cannot be found

The page you are looking for might have been removed, had its name changed, or is temporarily unavailable.

Besides testing the hyperlinks that lead to places in your Web site, test the hyperlinks that go outside your Web site. Periodically make sure that the Web pages to which your hyperlinks go are still on the Internet. The easiest way to test hyperlinks is to click them and see what happens. Dead hyperlinks are like warts on a Web site. Remove them immediately.

Tip

To find out precisely where hyperlinks are on your Web pages, choose View ➢ Highlight Objects ➢ With Links.

If phone numbers and addresses are found on your Web site, periodically make sure that they are up to date as well.

Viewing Your Web Site through More Than One Browser

Viewing a Web site that you created with Web Studio in the Internet Explorer browser is easy. After all, Web Studio and Internet Explorer work hand in hand. A copy of Internet Explorer is already loaded on your computer.

However, in case you didn't know it already, a little under half of the people who surf the Internet do so with a browser called Netscape Navigator. If you want to be especially serious about making sure others see your Web pages properly, you need to look at them in Netscape Navigator as well as Internet Explorer. You need to see what users of Netscape Navigator see when they view your Web site.

Resolution
For video displays, the number of pixels displayed vertically and horizontally.

Netscape Navigator is free. You can download a copy from the Netscape Netcenter Web site by following these steps:

1. Type the following address in the Address bar of Internet Explorer and press Enter: **www.netscape.com**. Soon, you arrive at the Netscape Netcenter Web site.
2. Click the Download hyperlink. You come to a Web page with instructions for downloading Netscape Navigator.

3. Follow the instructions for downloading Netscape Navigator.

As far as displaying Web pages, the differences between Internet Explorer and Netscape Navigator are not very great, but they are worth looking into if you want to be a serious Web site developer.

Viewing Your Web Pages at Different Resolutions

Web pages look different at different **resolutions**. As "Changing the Size of Web Pages" explains in Chapter 3, the Web pages you create in Web Studio are, by default, 576 pixels wide by 720 pixels high. Web pages are set to that default size so that people whose monitors are set to the 640-by-480 pixel resolution

can view the pages without scrolling. In the following illustration, which shows a Web page at the 640-by-480 pixel resolution, viewers have to scroll left to right to read the page.

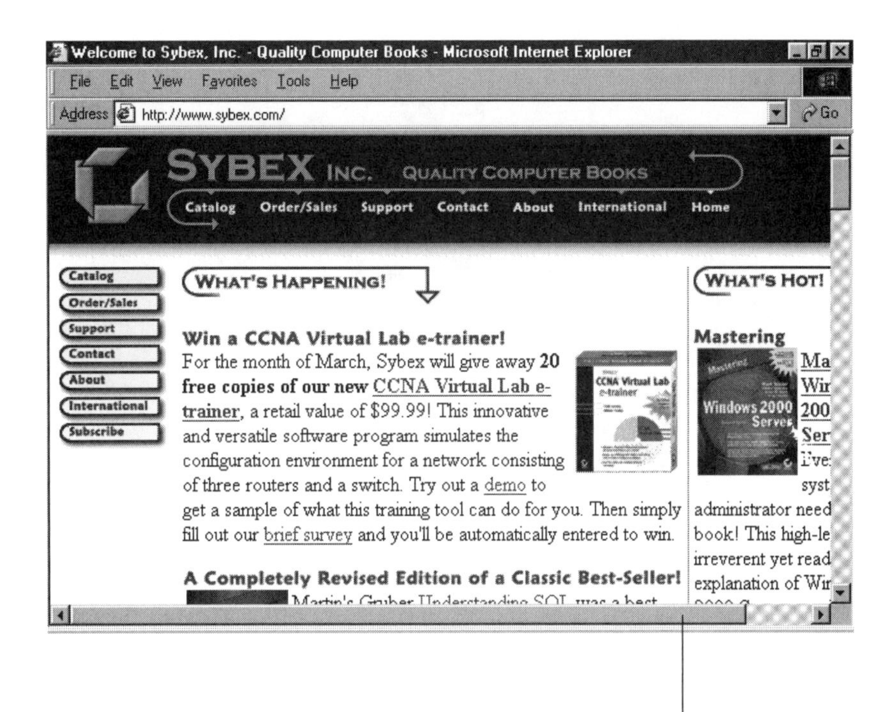

Viewers have to scroll to read this page

Especially if your monitor is set to the more common 800-by-600 pixel resolution, you need to see what your Web pages look like to people who view them in a resolution that is different from yours. Follow these steps to change the monitor resolution on your system momentarily and look at your Web pages at a different monitor resolution:

1. On the Windows desktop, right-click and choose Properties. You see the Display Properties dialog box.
2. Click the Settings tab.
3. Under "Screen Area," drag the slider to 640 by 480 pixels, 800 by 600 pixels, or 1024 by 768 pixels.

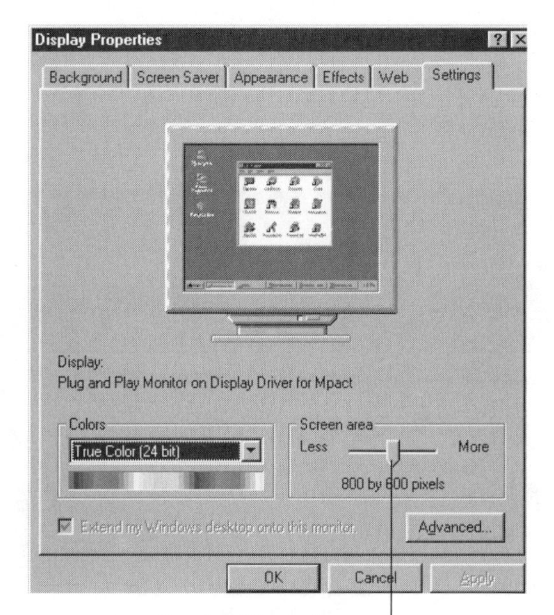

Drag the slider to change screen resolutions

Domain Name
The familiar, easy-to-remember name of the computer on the World Wide Web where a Web site is hosted. For example, sierra.com is the domain name of Sierra, the company that makes Web Studio.

4. Click OK.
5. Click OK in the confirmation box. Your screen changes resolution.
6. Click Yes in the Monitor Settings dialog box.

After you have examined your Web pages at different resolutions, return to the resolution that you favor the most.

Registering a Domain Name for Your Web Site

When you signed up to put a Web site on the Internet, your ISP or Web-hosting service gave you the address of the computer where your Web site is hosted. To view your Web site, you go to the address you were given. Others can also go to the address to view your Web site.

More than likely, however, you would prefer your Web site to be known by a **domain name**. Domain names are easier to remember and easier to type into the Address bar of a Web browser. Instead of *http://web.ionix.com/~arnold* as the address of a Web site about petunias, you could use a domain name such as

www.petunia.com. A domain name is a convenient way for others to find the computer where your Web site is hosted on the Internet.

Before you can claim a domain name as your own, you have to register it. After you register, anyone who types your domain name into the Address bar of a browser will go to your Web site. Registering entails paying a fee to a *registrar,* which is a company that handles domain name registrations. The company determines whether the name you chose has already been registered, and, if the name hasn't been claimed yet, the registrar enters your name with InterNIC (Internet Network Information Center), the organization that is responsible for mapping computer addresses to domain names. A domain name registration is good for two years, after which it must be renewed.

Go to the InterNIC Web site at `http://rs.internic.net` to learn about registering a domain name for your Web site. The InterNIC Web site offers a list of registrars where you can register your Web site, a FAQ about registering domain names, and a search engine so you can find out whether the name you want has been claimed.

After you have been given a domain name, follow these steps to make it the place you go after you upload your Web site to the Internet.

1. Choose File ➢ Save Web Site to Internet. You see the Upload dialog box.
2. In the Available Destinations box, choose the correct destination (if more than one destination is listed because you upload to more than one ISP).
3. Click the Edit button. The Create/Edit a Destination dialog box appears.
4. Click the Next button five times to go to the Home Page dialog box.

5. Enter your domain name in the text box.
6. Click Finish to upload your Web site.
7. Click the Preview button. This time when you go to your Web site, your domain name (*not* the address of a computer at your ISP or Web-hosting service) appears in the Address bar.

Promoting Your Web Site

Without further ado, here is a list of ways to promote your Web site:

In Chapter 13, "Describing Your Site So That Others Can Find It on the Internet" explains another way to promote your Web site—by including meta information that encourages search engines to find your site.

Submit Your Web Site to Popular Search Engines Most search engines give you the opportunity to submit your Web site. After it is reviewed, your Web site turns up in Internet searches. Following are the addresses of popular search engines where you can submit your Web site. Go to these Web pages and look, usually at the bottom of the page, for a link called "Add Your Site," "Suggest a Site," "Submit URL," or something similar, and follow the link to offer your Web site for consideration.

Search Engine	Address
Alta Vista	`www.altavista.com`
Galaxy	`www.galaxy.com`
Go.com	`www.go.com`
Hotbot	`www.hotbot.com`
Lycos	`www.lycos.com`
NorthernLight.com	`www.northernlight.com`
Starting Point	`www.stpt.com`
WebCrawler	`www.webcrawler.com`
Yahoo	`www.yahoo.com`
Yellow Pages	`http://theyellowpages.com`

Post Your Web Site on Newsgroups Place a notice about your Web page on newsgroups where members might be interested in a Web site like yours.

Link Your Site to Other Sites—and Hope They Reciprocate Include a "Links" Web page on your site where hyperlinks to sites similar to yours are listed. Then send an e-mail message to the Webmaster at each Web site to which your Web site is linked and hope that the Webmaster reciprocates. Maybe the Webmaster will link his or her site to yours.

Submit Your Site to "Cool Site of the Day" Web Sites You must have noticed them—the "Cool Site of the Day" awards that sometimes appear on Web pages. Get your Web site mentioned as the "Cool Site of the Day" and you are guaranteed more visitors. To get a list of Cool Sites of the Day, go to Yahoo (`www.yahoo.com`), enter **cool site of the day** in the Search text box, and click the Search button.

List Your Web Site Address at the Bottom of Your E-Mail Messages Casually, at the bottom of the e-mail messages you send, enter a link to your Web site. Doing so encourages more people to visit your site.

Appendix A

Installing Web Studio and Internet Explorer 5

This appendix explains how to install Web Studio and what to do before you install the program. Don't worry—installing the program is easy. Depending on how you install Web Studio, the installation takes five to fifteen minutes. The Web Studio software is on the CD that comes with this book.

You will also find instructions here for installing Internet Explorer 5. The Internet Explorer 5 software is also on the CD. To run Web Studio, Internet Explorer 5 must be installed on your computer.

As you will discover after installation, Web Studio comes with numerous clip art images, buttons, dividers, and other items for decorating Web pages. As part of the installation procedure, you decide how many of these items to load on your computer. You can load all of them, some of them, or none of them. If you load some or none of them, you can still use the decorative items on your Web pages, but to do so, you have to keep the Web Studio CD in your computer as you do your work in Web Studio.

Also in this appendix are instructions for uninstalling Web Studio, in case the program isn't for you.

Getting Ready to Install Web Studio

Before you install Web Studio, close any programs that are running on your computer. Installing a new program on a computer is a delicate business. Unless you close all programs before you install a new one, you could install the new program incorrectly.

Your computer must meet these requirements to run Web Studio:

Operating System Windows 95, Window 98, Windows NT, or Windows 2000.

Disk Space 160MB for a recommended installation (you need 560MB to run Web Studio without keeping the Web Studio CD in your computer).

Processor A Pentium 100 or higher processor.

Memory At least 16MB of RAM (32MB is recommended).

CD-ROM A CD-ROM drive is required.

Internet Explorer 5 You need the Internet Explorer 5 browser. Later, this appendix explains how to install it from the Web Studio CD.

To find out how much disk space is unoccupied on your computer, double-click the My Computer icon on the Windows desktop. The My Computer window appears. In the window, right-click the C drive icon and choose Properties on the shortcut menu. You see the Properties dialog box, which shows how much used and free space is on your computer.

Tip

Want to find out which processor and how much RAM (random access memory) your computer has? Right-click the My Computer icon on the Windows desktop and choose Properties on the shortcut menu. The System Properties dialog box appears. Under the word "Computer" on the General tab, you can see the processor's name and how much RAM is on your computer.

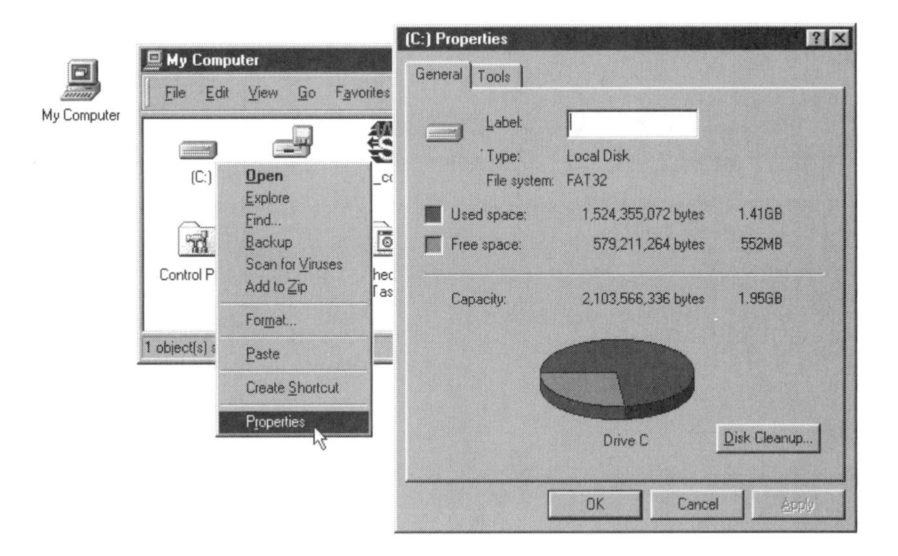

Installing Web Studio

To install Web Studio, start by putting the Web Studio CD in the CD-ROM drive on your computer. What happens next depends on whether your computer has the AutoPlay feature.

Your Computer Has AutoPlay If your computer has the AutoPlay feature, installation begins right away. Soon you see the Welcome to Web Studio dialog box shown on the left side of this illustration. Click the Install Web Studio button.

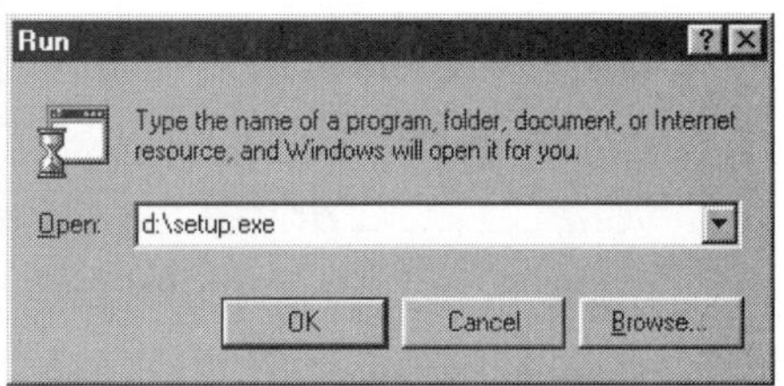

Your Computer Doesn't Have AutoPlay If your computer doesn't have the AutoPlay feature, you have to install Web Studio the old-fashioned way: Click the Start button and choose Run. Then, in the Run dialog box, type **d:\setup.exe** and click OK, as shown in the previous illustration. (If *D* is not the drive letter of your CD-ROM, substitute the correct letter.)

After a moment, you see the first of several Installation dialog boxes. Keep clicking the Next, Yes, or Finish button until the installation is complete. You will make several choices along the way. Keep reading to find out what they are.

Selecting a Setup Type

As I mentioned at the start of this appendix, Web Studio comes with numerous clip art images, buttons, dividers, and other items for decorating Web pages. The Select a Setup Type dialog box asks how you want to handle these decorative items. Loading them all on your computer requires a lot of disk space. You can put them all on your hard disk, put a few on, or put none on:

Minimum (50MB) Only the program files are installed—not the clip art, buttons, dividers, and other decorative items. In order to use Web Studio, the Web Studio CD has to be in the computer's CD-ROM drive. When you put a decorative item on your Web page, Web Studio grabs it from the CD.

Standard (160MB) The program files as well as a few decorative items are installed on your computer. To be specific, buttons, dividers, backgrounds, and signs are installed. Under this setup, you still need to keep the Web Studio CD in the CD-ROM drive for those occasions when you put clip art and sounds on a Web page.

Complete (560MB) All program files as well as decorative items are installed on your computer. The Web Studio CD doesn't have to be in your CD-ROM drive when you create Web pages because all the decorative items are available on your computer. Only choose this setup option if your computer has a lot of disk space to spare.

Tip

The makers of Web Studio recommend choosing the Standard (160MB) installation.

Choosing a Destination Folder

Unless you choose a different folder, Web Studio is installed by default on the `C:\Sierra\Web Studio 2` folder on your computer. The installation program creates the folder for you. You can click the Browse button and choose a different folder in the Choose Folder dialog box, but only if you know what you're doing and have a good reason for keeping the files in a folder other than the default folder.

Warning

Keep the Web Studio files in the `C:\Sierra\Web Studio` folder. The program looks for the files it needs in that folder, so if you load the files elsewhere, the program may not be able to find them.

Selecting a Program Folder

Although you might not know it, the Select Program Folder dialog box really asks which menu commands you want to choose to start Web Studio. Unless you change the settings in the dialog box, you start Web Studio by clicking the Start button and choosing Programs ➢ Sierra ➢ Web Studio 2.0 ➢ Web Studio.

Simply click the Next button in the Select Program Folder dialog box to accept the default recommendations.

After you make choices in the dialog boxes, the installation program copies the Web Studio program files (and decorative items) to your computer.

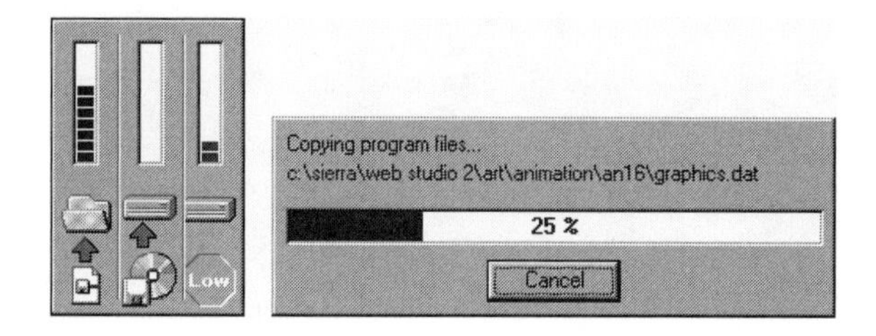

Odds and Ends

After the Web Studio files have been copied to your computer, you are asked whether you want to register your copy of Web Studio. Click OK and register

either over the Internet or by printing a registration form. Or click the Register Later button to save that task for another day.

Tip

You can register at any time by clicking the Start button and choosing Programs ➢ Sierra ➢ Web Studio 2.0 ➢ Product Registration.

You are also asked if you want to create a shortcut icon for Web Studio. If you click Yes in the dialog box, a Web Studio 2.0 shortcut icon appears on your desktop. Double-clicking the shortcut icon is the fastest way to start Web Studio, so you may as well click the Yes button.

Next, the installation program asks if you want to have a look at the Read Me file. This file includes last-minute information about Web Studio that didn't get included in the Help files. You can always look at the Read Me file later by clicking the Start button and choosing Sierra ➢ Web Studio 2.0 ➢ Web Studio Readme.

At last, the installation is complete, and the Setup Complete dialog box invites you to click the Finish button to restart your computer. Go ahead—click the Finish button and be done with it.

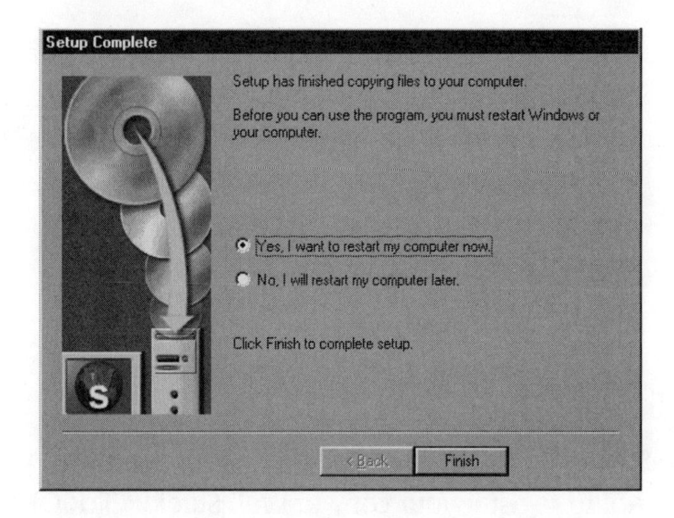

Warning

Be sure to restart your computer after you finish installing Web Studio. Key files that Web Studio needs to operate won't be available until you restart. Do it right away.

Warning

When you load new programs on you computer, those programs sometimes overwrite files that Web Studio needs, and Web Studio stops working. If that happens, reinstall Web Studio.

Installing Internet Explorer 5

Web Studio offers special commands for viewing Web pages in the Internet Explorer 5 browser. To take advantage of these commands, however, Internet Explorer 5 has to be installed on your computer. Fortunately, you can install it from the Web Studio installation CD.

To install Internet Explorer 5, start by removing the installation CD from the CD-ROM drive (if you left it there after you installed Web Studio). Next, put the CD back in the CD-ROM drive. What happens next depends on whether your computer has the AutoPlay feature.

Your Computer Has AutoPlay If your computer has the AutoPlay feature, you soon see the Welcome to Web Studio dialog box. Click the Install Microsoft Internet Explorer 5.0 button.

Your Computer Doesn't Have AutoPlay If your computer doesn't have AutoPlay, click the Start button, choose Run, wait for the Run dialog box to appear, and type the following in the Open text box: **d:\ie\ins\win32\en\ie5setup.exe** (substitute the correct letter if *D* is not the drive letter of your CD-ROM). Click OK or press Enter when you are done typing.

A series of dialog boxes appears. Keep clicking Next, Yes, or Finish until Internet Explorer has been installed on your computer.

Uninstalling Web Studio

If Web Studio isn't for you and you decide to uninstall the program, do so by clicking the Start button and choosing Programs ➢ Sierra ➢ Web Studio 2.0 ➢ Uninstall Web Studio. Then click the Yes button in the Confirm File Deletion dialog box.

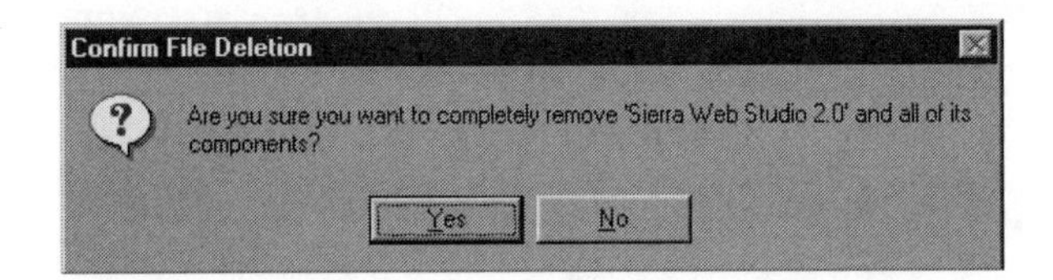

The Remove Programs From Your Computer dialog box appears as the program files and folders are removed from your computer. When the bottom of the dialog box reads, "Uninstall successfully completed," click OK and be done with it.

Web Studio does not remove any Web sites or files that you placed on your hard drive, including the Web Studio folder itself. You have to manually delete those files.

Warning

The Remove Shared File? dialog box may appear when you uninstall the program. The dialog box appears if a file being removed might be needed by another program on your computer. Click the No to All button to keep the file and all other shared files from being removed.

Appendix B

Getting the Help You Need

This appendix describes how to seek help with Web Studio apart from the help you can get with this book. You can seek help from the Web Studio Help program or go on the Internet for help.

- Searching the Web Studio Help program for instructions and information
- Playing the Web Studio video
- Getting help from the Web Studio homepage
- Visiting the Web Studio message board

Getting Help from the Web Studio Help Program

When you installed Web Studio, you also installed the Help program. Web Studio's Help program is a Windows-style program with three tabs: Contents, Index, and Search. You're on familiar ground if you've used a Help program like this before, because the Web Studio Help program works exactly like other Windows-style Help programs.

Follow these instructions to open the Help program:

- Choose Help ➢ Web Studio Help. The Help program opens to the Contents tab.
- Choose Help ➢ Web Studio Feature Guide. The Help program opens to the Feature Guide, where Web Studio features are described.

The three tabs in the Help program—Contents, Index, Search—offer three different ways of getting help. Help instructions appear on the right side of the window.

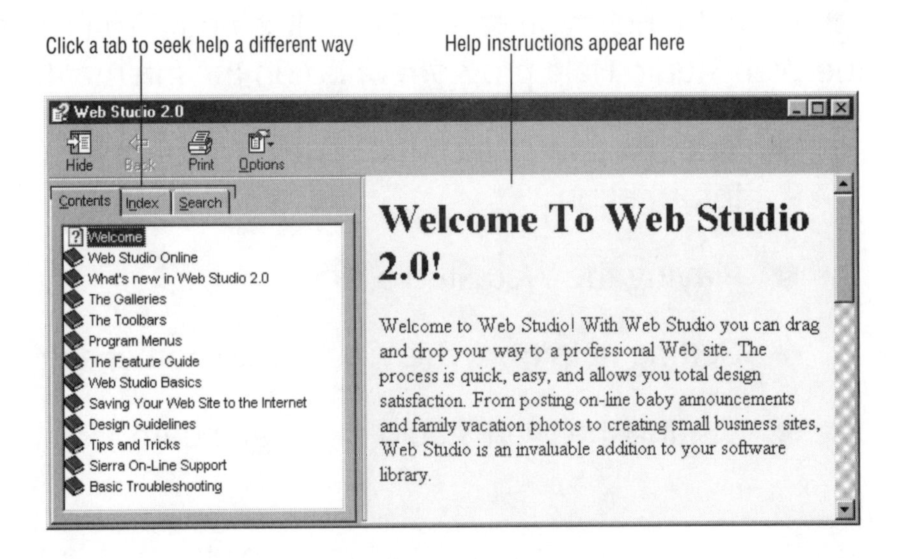

Tip

The Help program is like any other computer program. A Help program button appears on the taskbar when you open the Web Studio Help program. By clicking the Help program button and the Web Studio button on the taskbar, you can go back and forth from Web Studio to Help as you build Web pages.

Follow these directions for seeking help on the three tabs:

Contents Tab Presents general topics, much like a table of contents. Double-click a book icon to see a list of subtopics, each with a question mark beside its name. Click the name of a subtopic that interests you and you get instructions or information that pertains to the topic.

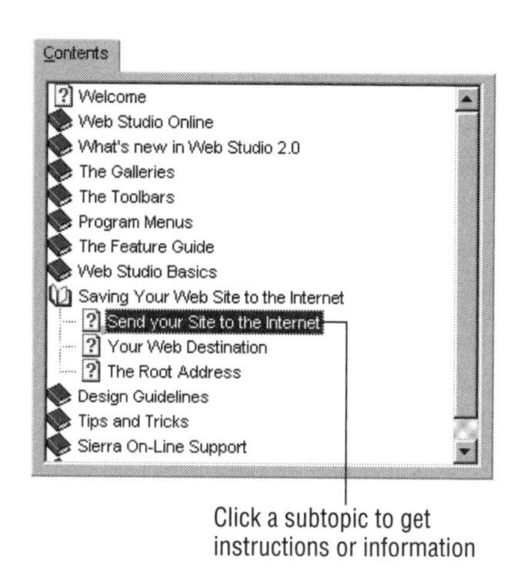

Click a subtopic to get instructions or information

Index Tab Presents topics in alphabetical order, much like a book index. Either scroll down the list and select a topic or type a few letters that describe a topic to move down the list. Double-click a topic to learn about it.

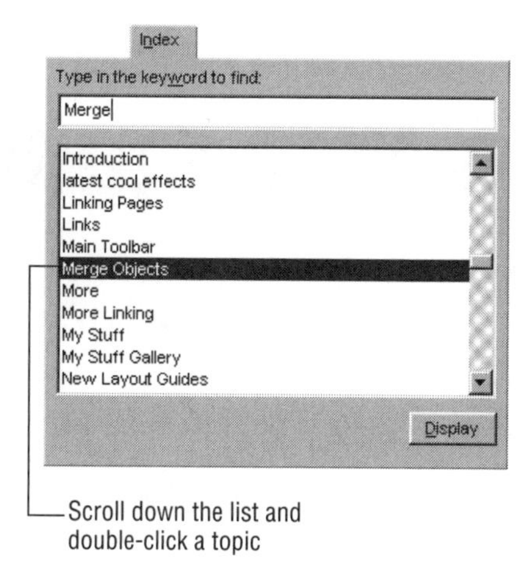

Scroll down the list and double-click a topic

Search Tab Permits you to search the help files with a keyword, much like searching the Internet. Type a keyword in the text box and

click the List Topics button. A list of help topics that include the keyword appears. Double-click a topic to learn about it.

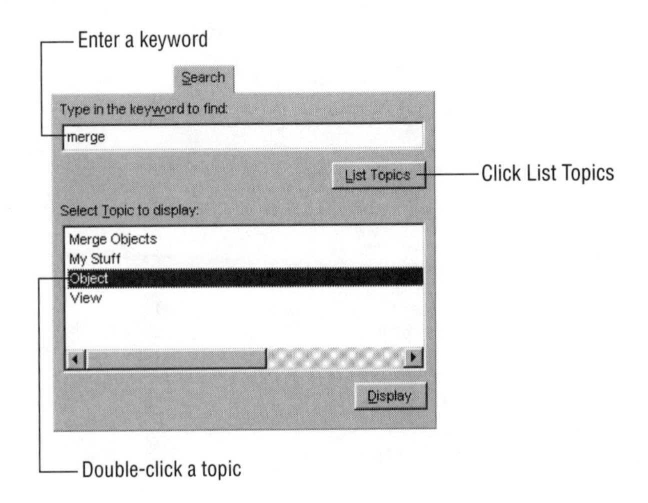

Click the Print button to print a set of instructions and always have them on hand. Then click OK in the Print dialog box.

Tip

The Help program keeps track of all the Help screens you visit in the course of a search for help. Click the Back button to return to a Help screen you saw before. Click the Options button and choose Forward to return to a Help screen you retreated from.

Playing the Web Studio Video

As long as your computer is capable of playing sound and video, you can pretend you are at a drive-in movie theater and watch a video about using Web Studio. To play the video, make sure that the Web Studio CD is in your computer's CD-ROM drive, start Web Studio, and choose Help ➢ Getting Started.

The video offers a quick overview of Web Studio. It lasts five minutes.

Tip

To play the video, your monitor must be set to 800 by 600 pixels and High Color (16-bit). To change monitor settings, right-click the Windows desktop and choose Properties. Then click the Settings tab in the Display Properties dialog box and change the Colors and Screen Area settings.

Getting Help on the Internet

The next batch of commands on the Help menu takes you to the Internet, where you can get instructions for using Web Studio. Connect to the Internet and choose one of these commands to search in cyberspace for help with creating Web pages:

- Help ➢ Official Web Studio Web Site: Goes to the Sierra Home Web Publishing page (`www.sierra.com/sierrahome/web`), where you can read articles about and get tips for using Web Studio.
- Help ➢ Web Site Services: Goes to a Web page where you can read about Internet Service Providers that host Web pages.
- Help ➢ Web Studio FAQ: Goes to the Web Studio Troubleshooting Guide, where you can seek solutions for problems that other Web Studio users have encountered with the software.
- Help ➢ Sierra On-Line Support: Goes to the Web Studio Technical Support page, where you can search The Knowledge Base database for the answer to a question.

> Chapter 1 explains how to handle the Tip of the Day, which you can read by choosing Help ➢ Tip of the Day.

Posting Messages on the Web Publishing Message Board

If you can't find the answer to a question in this book or in the Help program, you can always try the Web Publishing Message Board. Sierra On-Line, the makers of Web Studio, maintains the message board so that users of Web Studio can submit questions about using the program. With a little luck, another user of Web Studio or a technical support person will answer your question. Maybe the answer to your question has already been posted on the message board.

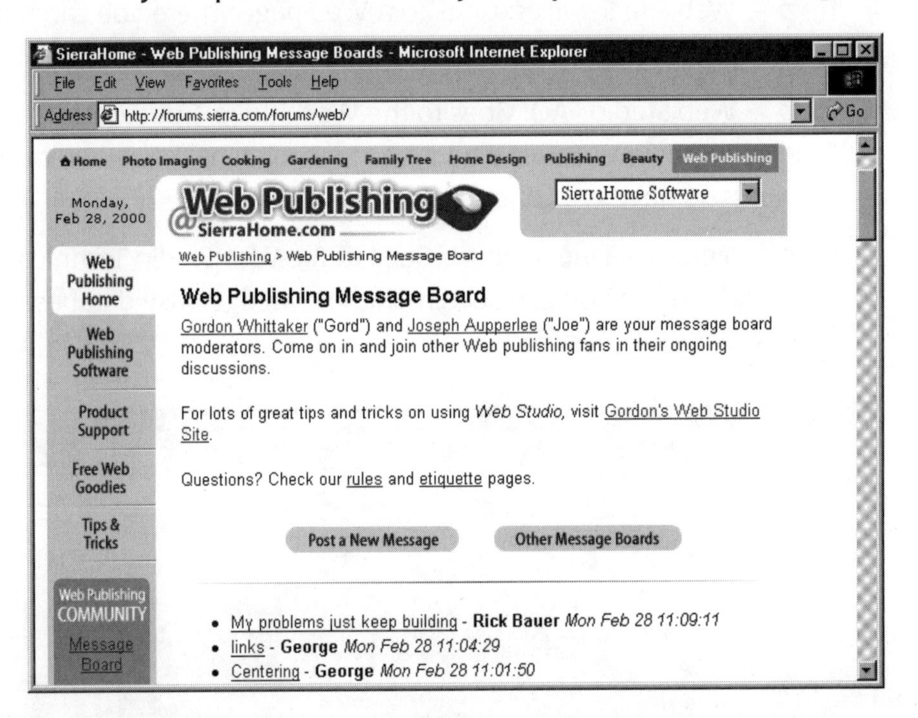

Follow these steps to visit the Web Publishing Message Board and submit a question:

1. Either choose Help ➢ Official Web Studio Web Site and click the Message Board hyperlink on the Web Studio homepage, or go to the message board by entering its address in your browser: **http://forums.sierra.com/forums/web**.
2. Scroll through the list of questions and see if the one you want to submit is already there. If it is, double-click it to read the post.
3. To submit a question, click the Post a New Message hyperlink, fill out the Post a New Message form, and click the Post Message button.

Appendix C

The Ins and Outs of Internet Explorer 5

When you install Web Studio, you get the chance to install Internet Explorer 5, the latest edition of Internet Explorer. Internet Explorer is a Web browser, a computer program that connects to Web sites and displays Web pages. As Appendix A explains, you need Internet Explorer to see what your Web pages look like in a browser.

Of course, you can do more than preview Web pages with Internet Explorer. You can do a lot more. This appendix describes how to make Internet Explorer 5 your companion when you visit Web sites and search the Internet.

- Going to a Web page whose address you know
- Searching the Internet
- Backtracking to visit sites you've visited before
- Bookmarking sites so you can visit them quickly
- Going to a site that you bookmarked

Surfing the World Wide Wed with Internet Explorer

Address Bar
The place in Internet Explorer where the address of the Web site you are visiting is listed. You can type addresses in the Address bar.

Internet Explorer offers many tools for getting around quickly on the Internet. These pages explain how to visit a Web page when you know its address and how to search the Internet for news, views, and information. You also discover how to backtrack and visit Web pages you've visited before.

Visiting a Web Site Whose Address You Know

Next time you go on the Internet, look in the **Address bar** of Internet Explorer (choose View ➢ Toolbars ➢ Address bar if the Address bar isn't displayed). You will see the address of the Web site you are visiting. Every Web page on the Internet has an address.

If you know the address of a Web site you want to visit, you can get there by typing the address in the Address bar. Follow these steps:

1. Click in the Address bar to highlight the address that is currently there.

2. Type the address. The letters you enter replace the ones that were there.

3. Press the Enter key. Soon you arrive at the Web site whose address you entered.

Internet Explorer remembers the addresses of Web sites you have visited. Sometimes you type the first few letters, and a menu appears with the addresses of Web sites that are similar to the address you are typing. In that case, you can click an address on the menu to enter an address without having to type the whole thing.

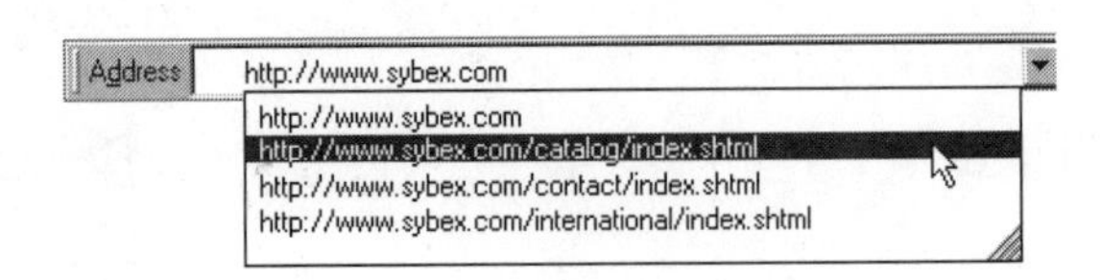

Searching the Internet

Starting from Internet Explorer 5, you can search with these seven search engines simultaneously: Alta Vista, GoTo.com, Infoseek, Lycos, MSN Search, Northern Light, and Yahoo. Follow these steps to search the Internet:

Explorer Bar
A panel that appears on the left side of the Internet Explorer screen when you click the Search, Favorites, or History button.

1. Click the Search button (if you don't see the Search button, choose View ➢ Toolbars ➢ Standard Buttons). The **Explorer bar** appears on the left side of the screen.
2. In the Find a Web Page Containing box, enter a keyword or keywords to describe what you are looking for.

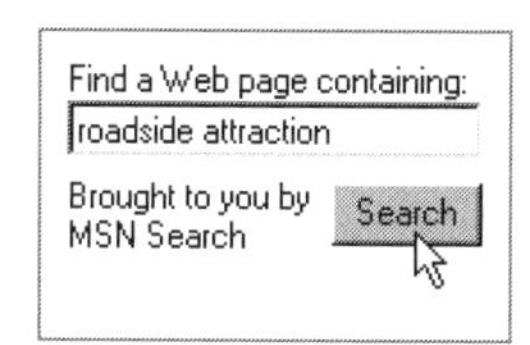

3. Click the Search button. A list of Web site names appears below the button.
4. Gently move the pointer over Web site names and read the descriptions. This way, you can make an informed decision when choosing which Web site to visit. Scroll to the bottom of the list and click the Next button if none of the Web pages interests you.

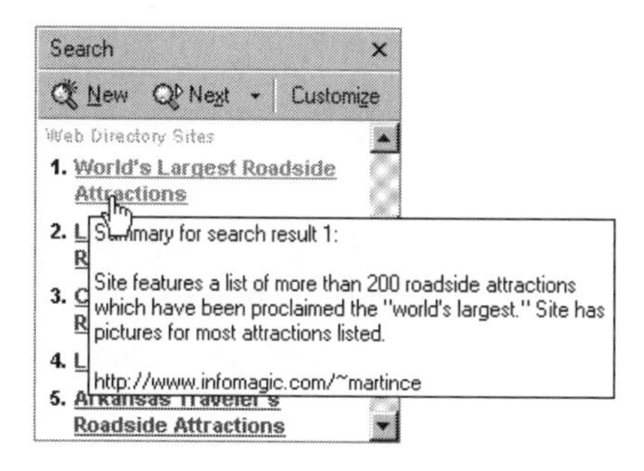

5. Click the name of the Web site you want to visit. It appears on the right side of the Internet Explorer screen.
6. Click the Search button again to close the Explorer bar and view the Web page better.

To resume searching the Internet, click the Search button again. The list of sites you found earlier reappears. Click the New button in the Explorer bar to start a new search.

Starting from the Homepage of a Search Engine

Another way to search the Internet is to start from the homepage of a search engine. By starting there, you can try out advanced search commands. All search engines are different. Experiment with a few until you find the one you like best. Eventually, you will learn a search engine's ins and outs and become an expert at using its commands to search the Internet.

Here are the names and addresses of popular search engines:

- Excite: `www.excite.com`
- Google: `www.google.com`
- HotBot: `www.hotbot.com`
- Infoseek: `www.infoseek.com`
- Lycos: `www.lycos.com`
- Northern Light: `www.northernlight.com`
- WebCrawler: `www.webcrawler.com`
- Yahoo: `www.yahoo.com`

Revisiting Web Sites

Because many Web surfers venture too far and wish to return to a Web page that they visited earlier, Internet Explorer offers many ways to backtrack. Follow these instructions to revisit Web pages you visited in the course of an Internet adventure:

Later in this appendix, "Bookmarking a Site So You Can Visit It Again" explains another way to revisit Web sites—by bookmarking them.

Clicking the Back and Forward Buttons Click the Back button to return to the last Web page you visited; click the Forward button to move ahead to the page from which you retreated. What's more, you can click the down-arrows beside the Back and Forward buttons to leap forward or backward by several Web pages.

Clicking the History Button Click the History button to revisit a Web page you visited in the past 20 days. In the Explorer bar, click the time period in which you visited the page (Two Weeks Ago, Last Week, or a day of the week), click the name of a Web site, and the click the name of a Web page.

Bookmark
To place a shortcut to a Web page in the Favorites folder so you can revisit the page quickly.

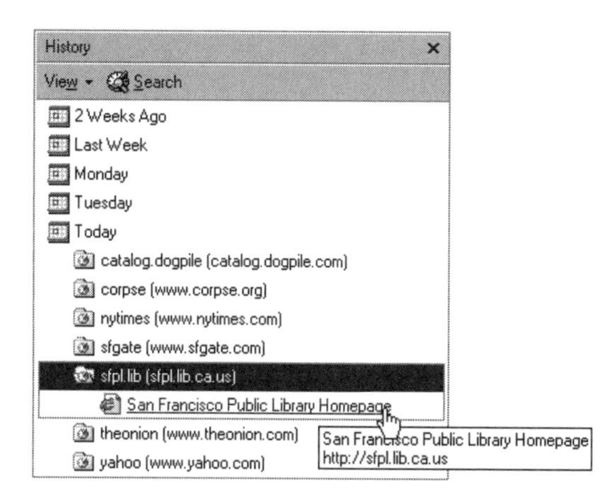

Tip

To keep the boss from finding out which Web sites you have been visiting, click the History button, find the site you want to remove from the list, right-click it, and choose Delete. To remove all of the Web sites on the list, choose Tools ➢ Internet Options and click the Clear History button on the General tab of the Internet Options dialog box.

Bookmarking a Site So You Can Visit It Again

If you have the slightest interest in returning to a Web page, **bookmark** it. The Internet is vast and the number of Web pages is growing by the millions. Unless you bookmark a Web page, finding it again is difficult. Besides, "unbookmarking" a Web page is easy. Read on to learn how to bookmark a Web page, visit a Web page you bookmarked, and manage your bookmarks.

Bookmarking a Favorite Web Site

Bookmark the Web pages that you will return to later on. That way, you don't have to type Web page addresses or conduct an Internet search to find a Web site you want to visit. Follow these steps to bookmark a Web site and be able to revisit it quickly:

Later in this appendix, "Renaming, Deleting, and Managing Bookmarks" explains how to "unbookmark" a Web page.

1. Go to the Web page that you want to bookmark.
2. Choose Favorites ➢ Add to Favorites. You see the Add to Favorite dialog box.
3. Double-click the Links folder icon to open the Links folder. The Links folder is where bookmarks are stored.

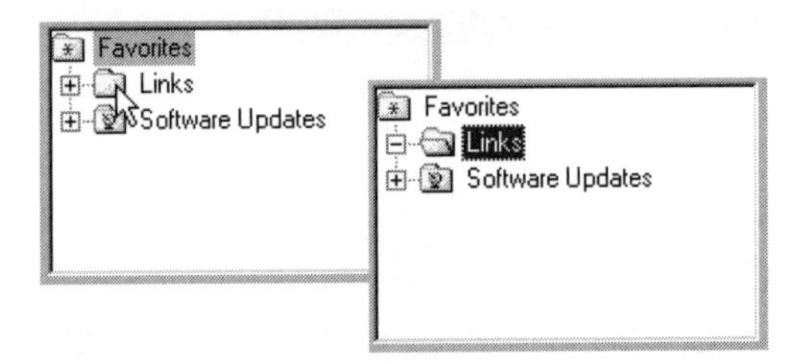

Warning

Be sure to double-click the Links folder and place the bookmark there. If you put the bookmark in the Favorites folder, you run the risk of crowding your Favorites folder with bookmarks. The Favorites folder is the same folder that appears when you click the Favorites button in the Open or Save dialog box. Shortcuts to often-used files and folders are kept in the Favorites folder. If you crowd it with bookmarks, you will have a hard time opening your favorite files and folders.

4. In the Name text box, enter a descriptive name for the bookmark if the name that is already there isn't descriptive enough for you.
5. Click the OK button.

Preventing Overcrowding in the Links Folder

Bookmarking Web pages is addictive. The Links folder can quickly fill with bookmarks. Besides deleting the bookmarks you no longer need, you can get around the problem of overcrowding in the Links folder by creating subfolders in the Links folder. In the following illustration, I have created seven subfolders for storing different kinds of bookmarks.

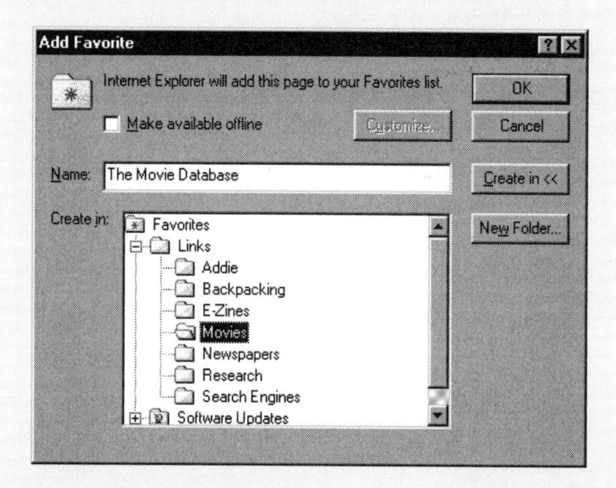

Follow these steps to create a subfolder in the Links folder:

1. Choose Favorites ➢ Add to Favorites to open the Add to Favorite dialog box.
2. Double-click the Links folder icon to open the Links folder.
3. Click the New Folder button. You see the Create New Folder dialog box.

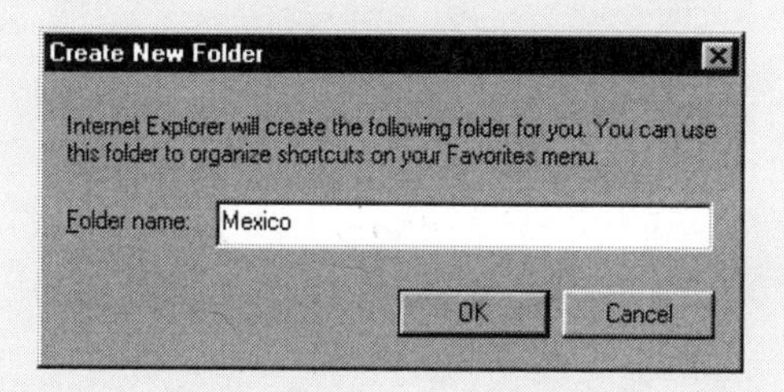

4. Enter a descriptive name for the subfolder.
5. Click OK twice.

To store a bookmark in a subfolder, choose Favorites ➢ Add to Favorites and double-click the Links folder as you normally do. However, after you double-click the Links folder, double-click the subfolder where you want to store your new bookmark.

Visiting a Site that You Bookmarked

Visiting a Web site that you have bookmarked is as easy as falling off a log. Internet Explorer offers two ways of doing it:

- Click the Favorites button, click the Links folder in the Explorer bar (and click a subfolder name, as well, if you keep bookmarks in subfolders), and click the name of the bookmark.

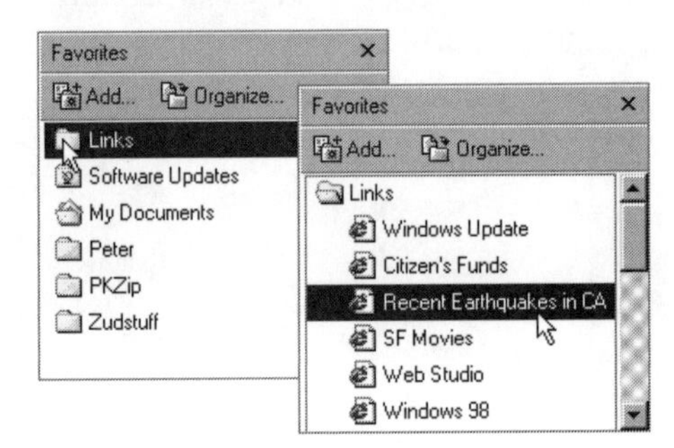

- Choose Favorites ➢ Links (as well as a subfolder name if you keep bookmarks in subfolders) and click the name of the bookmark.

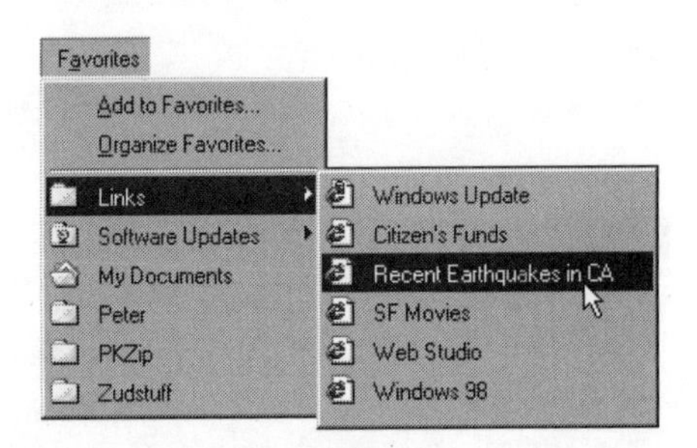

Renaming, Deleting, and Managing Bookmarks

Occasionally, bookmarks need to be renamed, deleted, moved to a different place, or moved to a different folder. Follow these steps to manage your bookmark:

1. Choose Favorites ➢ Organize Favorites. The Organize Favorites dialog box appears.

2. Double-click the Links folder (and double-click a subfolder, as well, if you want to manage its bookmarks).

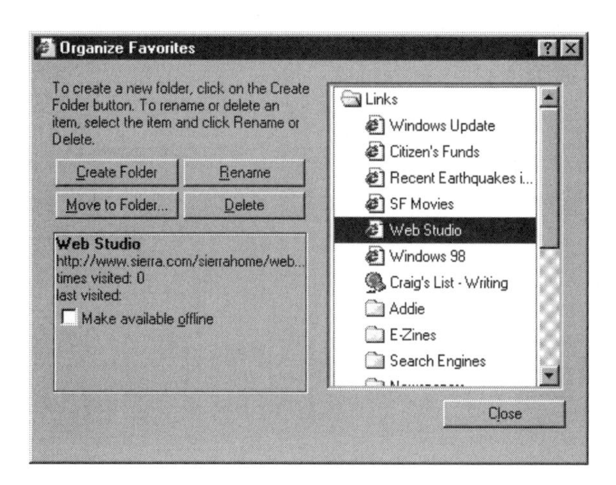

3. Click the name of the bookmark that needs deleting, renaming, or moving.
4. Delete, rename, or move the bookmark:
   - Deleting a bookmark: Click the Delete button and then click Yes in the confirmation box.
   - Renaming a bookmark: Click the Rename button and type a new name.
   - Moving a bookmark to a different folder: Click the Move to Folder button and select another folder in the Browse for Folder dialog box.

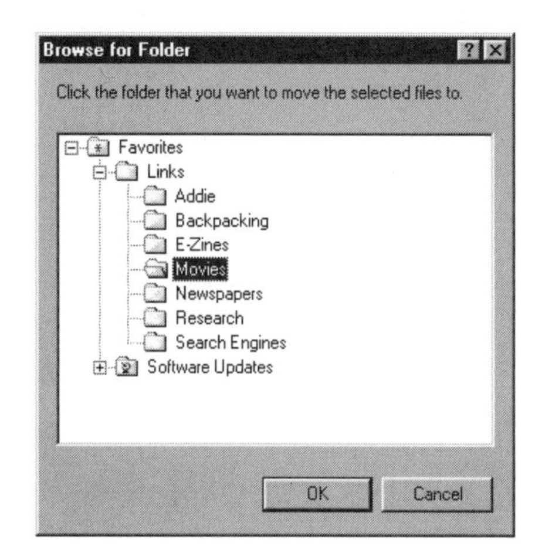

- Move a bookmark up or down in the list: Drag a Web site name up or down the dialog box to move it up or down on the Explorer bar and Favorites ➢ Links menu.

Tip

A faster way to handle bookmarks is to open Windows Explorer, go to the `C:\Windows\Favorites\Links` folder, and rename, delete, or move the bookmarks there.

Appendix D

Speed Techniques for Working with Web Studio

This short appendix explains a few tried-and-true techniques for working fast. These techniques are mentioned in passing elsewhere in this book, but they have been assembled here to help you become a speedy user of Web Studio. This appendix describes techniques that I have found especially useful. A quick reading of this appendix can save you a lot of time and trouble down the road.

- Quickly fixing errors
- Selecting several objects at a time
- Merging and copying objects
- Aligning and distributing objects on a Web page
- Storing your favorite graphics in the My Stuff Gallery

Undoing (and Redoing) Errors

Everybody makes errors, and the fastest way to correct them in Web Studio is to reach for the Edit ➢ Undo command (or press Ctrl+Z). Choosing Edit ➢ Undo reverses your most recent action. Choosing it a second time reverses the action you took before that. And choosing it a third time reverses the action before that. As the following illustration shows, the Edit menu lists the command that will be undone when you choose Edit ➢ Undo—in this case inserting a text object, inserting an object from a Web Gallery, or inserting a hyperlink.

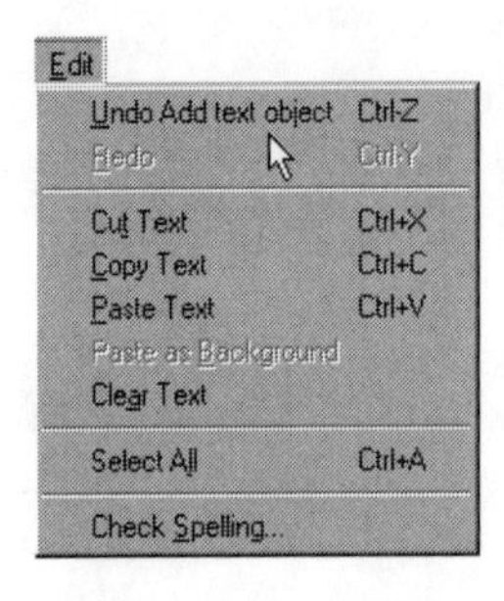

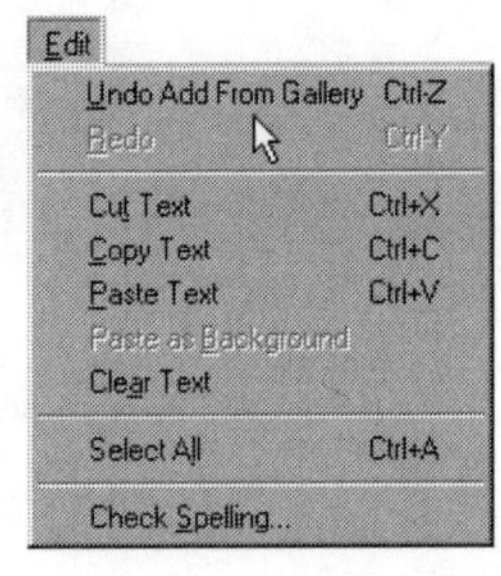

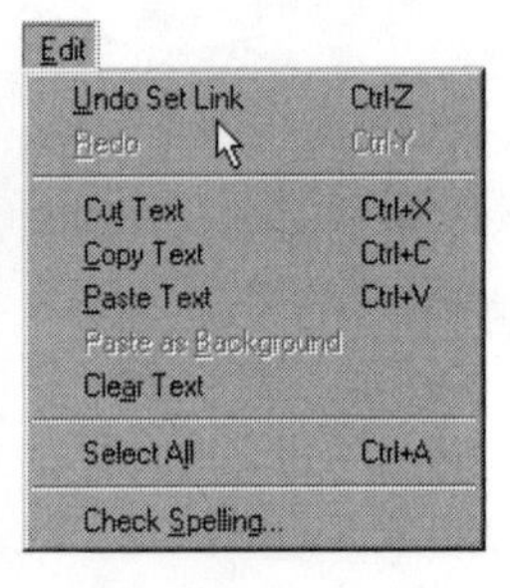

Web Studio keeps track of all the commands you choose, objects you move, Web pages you create, and so on. When you notice an error, either correct it yourself or choose Edit ➢ Undo as many times as necessary to make Web Studio correct it. If you made the error recently and you don't mind reversing your last several actions to reach into the past and fix the error, choosing Edit ➢ Undo is the way to go. But if digging into the past to fix an error also means undoing tedious or complicated work that you did since you made the error, fix the error yourself.

Warning

When you choose File ➢ Save to save a file, you prevent yourself from taking advantage of the Edit ➢ Undo command. Web Studio clears the dock when you save files. All records of the commands you made and actions you took are erased. Make it a habit to save files only after you have reached a point where you don't have to reverse any errors with the Edit ➢ Undo command.

What if you reverse an error with the Edit ➢ Undo command but discover that it wasn't an error after all? In that case, choose Edit ➢ Redo (or press Ctrl+Y).

Choosing Edit ➢ Redo reverses the Undo command. The Edit menu also lists the command that will be reversed when you choose Edit ➢ Redo.

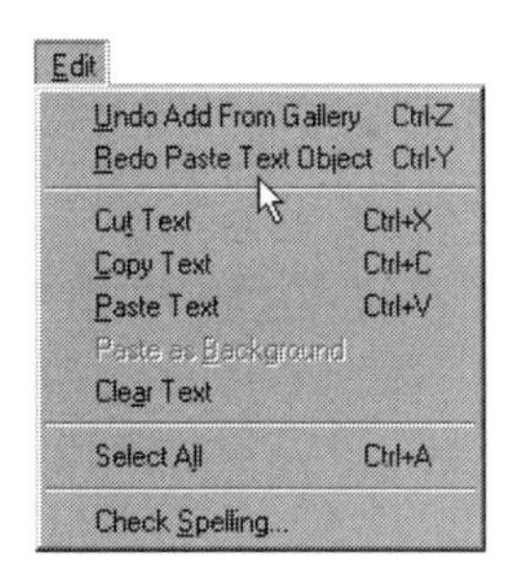

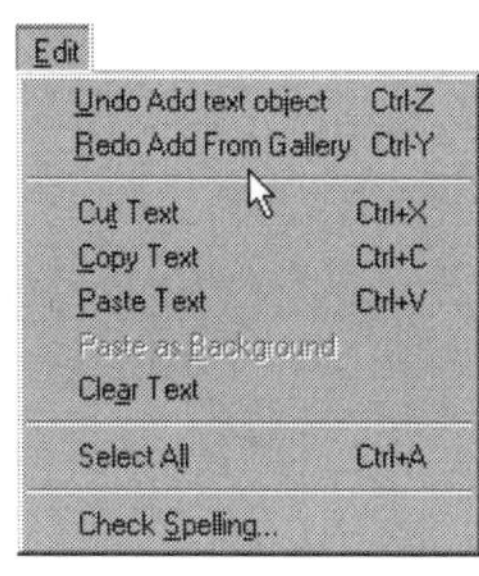

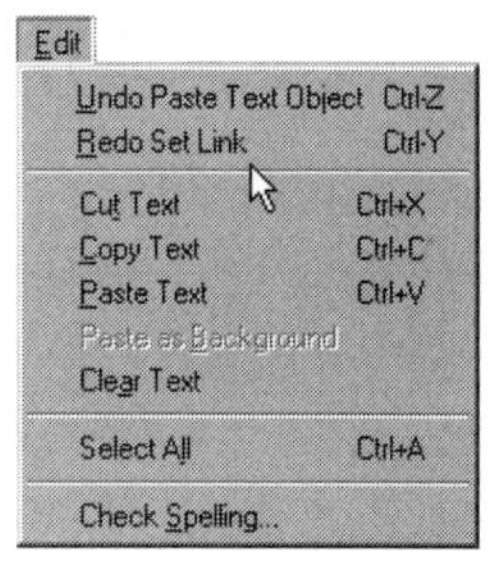

Context Menu

The menu that appears when you right-click. Also called a shortcut menu.

Making Use of the Context Menus

You can usually tell who the fast computer users are—they are the ones who right-click instead of choosing commands from the menu bar. Right-clicking an object in the Web Page window brings up a **context menu** and list of commands that pertain to the kind of object you right-clicked.

You can save a lot of time by right-clicking objects instead of searching menus or scouring toolbars for the right command or button. Context menus offer an abridged set of commands, one of which is very likely the one you need. The following illustration shows the context menu that appears when you right-click a clip art image. Apart from moving it, everything you can do to a clip art image can be done by choosing commands on this context menu.

Selecting More Than One Object at a Time

Everybody knows that you click an object to select it. Many people, however, don't understand that you can select several objects at once and that being able to select several objects is an essential skill. After the objects are selected, repositioning, copying, moving, merging, and realigning them is that much easier.

Here are the ways to select more than one object:

- Hold down the Shift key and click each object.
- Imagine drawing a box around the objects, click a corner of the box, hold down the mouse button, and drag to the opposite corner. A box appears onscreen. When you release the mouse button, all the objects that fell inside the box are selected, as shown in the following illustration.

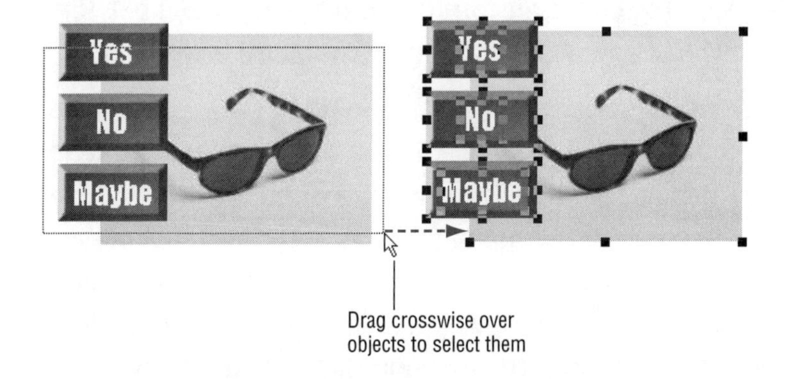

Selection handles appear on all the objects after they are selected. Now you can reposition, merge, copy, move, realign, or distribute them.

Warning

Be careful to hold down the Shift key, not the Ctrl key, to select several objects at once. Holding down the Ctrl key *copies* the object. And to make matters worse, the copy is placed under the original. You might not know it's there.

Merging Objects So You Can Work with Several at Once

As a Web page starts to take shape and is nearing completion, you owe it to yourself to merge objects. Merging objects makes them easier to work with. Objects that have been merged are easy to move, copy, enlarge, and shrink. Instead of dealing with two, three, or several different objects, you only have to deal with one.

To see the benefits of merging, consider the illustration on the left. It comprises four objects: a clip art object and three text objects. In the illustration on the right, the objects have been merged. Instead of 32 selection handles, there are only eight. Moving, copying, and changing the size of a merged object is easy because what was formerly several objects can be treated as one object.

Follow these steps to merge objects:

1. Either Shift-click to select the objects you want to merge or drag the mouse to select them.
2. Choose Object ➢ Merge Selected Objects or right-click an object you selected and choose Merge Selected Objects.

The previous section in this appendix describes how to select objects.

So much for the advantages of merging. Here are the disadvantages:

- Except for choosing Edit ➢ Undo Object Merge, you can't "unmerge" an object. Make sure you are finished tinkering with objects before you merge them. If you find a spelling or layout error in objects that have been merged, you're out of luck. You have to start all over.

- An object can be assigned only one hyperlink and one sound. Merging buttons and other objects that come in sets is tempting, but don't do it if you intend to make each button a hyperlink or make a sound play when each button is clicked.

Copying Objects by Pressing Ctrl and Dragging

Many kinds of objects—especially buttons and dividers—are presented in sets, where each object is identical to the one beside it. Rather than go to the trouble of placing these kinds of objects one at a time, place one object in the Web Page window and then copy it by pressing the Ctrl key and dragging.

As you drag, a second copy of the object emerges from the original. Drag the new object where you want it to go and release the Ctrl key.

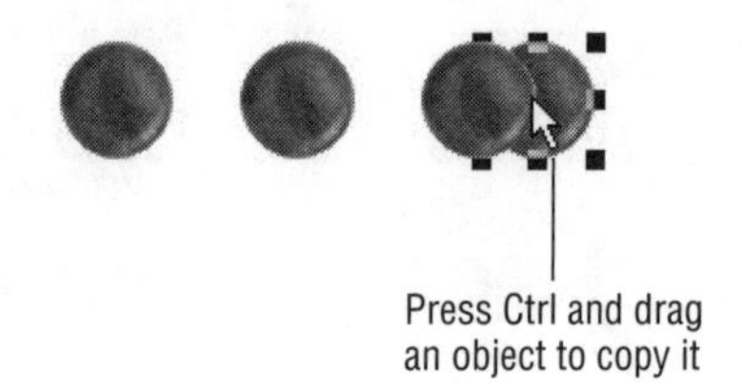

Press Ctrl and drag an object to copy it

Making Use of the Align and Space Evenly Commands

Making objects line up squarely with one another is an essential task. A row of buttons that aren't neatly lined up gives a bad impression. Similarly, buttons that lie haphazardly on the page and aren't the same distance from one another look sloppy.

Web Studio offers two sets of commands for lining up objects. Between the Object ➢ Align commands and the Object ➢ Space Evenly commands, you can make objects snap to attention and stand in orderly fashion on a Web page.

Follow these steps to align objects:

1. Select the objects by Shift+clicking or dragging the pointer crosswise over them.

2. Either choose an Object ➢ Align command or right-click and choose an Align command. Objects can be aligned on their left sides, right sides, tops, or bottoms. The objects in the following illustration are aligned on their top sides.

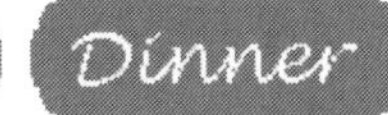

3. Either choose an Object ➢ Space Evenly command or right-click and choose a Space Evenly command. The objects in the following illustration are spaced evenly across the page.

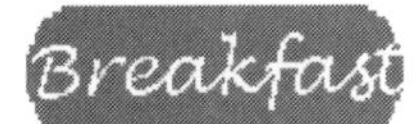

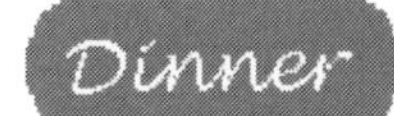

In Chapter 4, "Aligning and Spacing Objects on the Page" explains the Align and Space Evenly commands in detail.

Keeping Your Favorite Graphics on Hand in the My Stuff Gallery

Everybody has a graphic or two that they use time and time again on Web pages—a company logo, a favorite image, or an emblem of some kind. Rather than rummage in the Web Galleries or choose Insert ➢ Picture from File to find the graphic, you can keep it in the My Stuff Gallery. All you have to do to bring it into a Web page is drag it from the My Stuff Gallery to the Web Page window. What's more, you can keep the art you created inside Web Studio in the My Stuff Gallery and never have to create it all over again.

"Keeping Your Favorite Images in the My Stuff Gallery" in Chapter 8 explains the My Stuff tab in detail.

Make a note of where on your computer or network the graphic is kept, and follow these steps to make it available in the My Stuff Gallery:

1. Either choose Insert ➢ My Stuff Gallery Graphics or right-click the My Stuff Gallery and choose Add Files. The Open dialog box appears.
2. Locate and select the file or files you want to keep in the My Stuff Gallery.

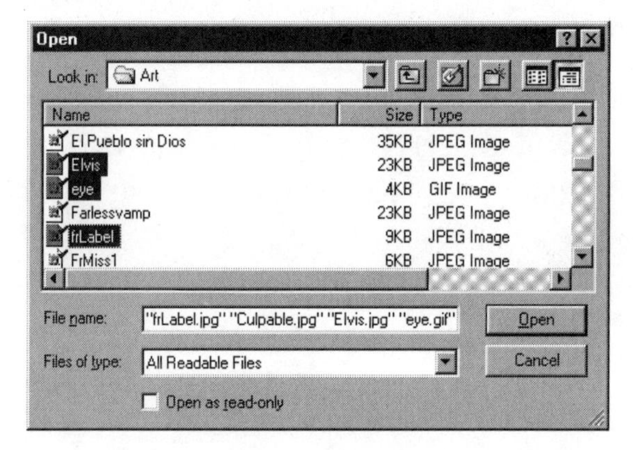

Tip

Hold down the Ctrl key and click to select more than one file. The names of files you select appear in the File Name box.

3. Click the Open button. The graphics land in the My Stuff Gallery.

To remove a graphic from the My Stuff Gallery, right-click it and choose Delete. Deleting it from the Gallery in no way removes it from your computer. The image in the My Stuff Gallery is merely a link to the folder on your computer where the graphic is kept.

Appendix E

Glossary of Internet and Web Studio Terminology

Address bar

In Internet Explorer, the place where the address of the Web site you are visiting is listed. Choose View ➢ Toolbars ➢ Address Bar if it isn't displayed.

alternate text message

Descriptive words that appear on an image when you move the pointer over it. Choose Object ➢ Object Properties and click the Graphic tab to enter the message.

anchor

For the purpose of hyperlinking two places on the same Web page in Web Studio, the target of the hyperlink. In the Links Gallery, click Add Anchor to Object and drag over an object to create an anchor.

animation

An image on a Web page that appears to move onscreen. An animation is actually two or three images that appear quickly onscreen and give the illusion of movement.

banner

A large decorative graphic found at the top or in the margin of a Web page.

bitmap (BMP) graphic

A graphic composed of many tiny dots called *pixels* that, taken together, form an image. Popular bitmap graphic formats include CompuServe Graphics Interchange Format (GIF), JPEG Interchange Format (JPEG), PC Paintbrush (PCX), and Tagged Image File Format (TIF).

bookmark

To place a shortcut to a Web page in the Favorites folder so you can revisit the page quickly. In Internet Explorer, click the Favorites button, click the Links folder, and click the name of a Web page you bookmarked to visit it.

browser

A computer program that connects to Web sites and displays Web pages. The most popular browsers are Internet Explorer and Netscape Navigator.

Clipboard

A holding tank to which you can copy or move text and graphics. Text and graphics can be pasted from the Clipboard onto a Web page.

content

The droll term that Web site developers use to describe what is presented on a Web site. The person responsible for writing the text on a site is sometimes called the "content provider."

context menu

The menu that appears when you right-click. Choosing commands from context menus is faster than choosing commands from the menu bar. Also called a "shortcut menu."

cookie

A small data file that some Web sites place automatically on visitors' hard drives. Look for cookies in the `C:\Windows\Temporary Internet Files` folder on your computer.

counter
A device that counts the number of visitors to a Web site.

dither
A graphic-editing technique whereby different colors are merged into a single color on a graphic when the graphic is shrunk or enlarged.

divider
A thick line, or bar, on a Web page that divides one part of the page from another.

domain name
The familiar, easy-to-remember name of the computer on the World Wide Web where a Web site is hosted. Visitors can enter a Web site's domain name to visit a Web site on the Internet.

download
To transfer a copy of a file or program from a site on the Internet to a personal computer. *See also* upload.

drag
To hold down the left mouse button as you slide the mouse across the screen. Among other tasks, you can drag to move objects around a Web page as you create it.

FAQ (frequently asked questions)
A page on a Web site on which common questions are answered. Rhymes with "back."

font
The catchall name for a type style and type size.

ftp (file transfer protocol)
The protocol, or rule, that governs how files are sent to an Internet Service Provider.

ftp site
A Web site that can receive Web pages for display on the Internet.

gallery
See Web Galleries.

home page
The first page, or introductory page, of a Web site. Usually the home page offers hyperlinks that you can click to go to other pages on the Web site. In the Page List, the home page is marked with a house icon. *See also* Page List.

hyperlink
An electronic link between two Web sites or different pages on the same Web site. When you click a hyperlink, you go directly to another location. You can tell when the pointer has moved over a hyperlink because the pointer changes into a gloved hand.

Hypertext Markup Language (HTML)
The tags or language that browsers read in order to display Web pages on the Internet or on an intranet.

Internet Service Provider (ISP)
A company that provides customers access to the Internet. Some ISPs also allow customers to post Web pages.

intranet
A private network, usually maintained by a company or institution, to which only employees or members have access. Web sites and Web pages can be posted on intranets as well as the Internet.

ISP
See Internet Service Provider.

justify
To align text on its left side or right side.

keyword
For the purpose of searching the Internet (or searching for instructions in a Help program), a word that describes what information is needed. If the keyword is found on a Web page, the Web page is named in the results of the search.

landscape page
A page turned on its ear so it is wider than it is tall.

margin
The empty space along the left side, right side, top, and bottom of a Web page.

meta information
Found in the <META> HTML tag of a Web page, the information includes the program in which the Web page was made, the name of the author, keywords that describe the page, and a short description.

modem
The hardware device by which computers can transmit data over telephone lines. You need a modem to travel the Internet or send e-mail messages. The term stands for "modulator-demodulator."

object
An element of a Web page—a graphic, a frame that encloses text, a divider, etc. All the items in the Web Galleries are objects. To construct a Web page, you construct it from objects.

Page List
Found on the right side of the Web Studio screen, the list of Web pages in a Web site. Click a page icon to move from page to page.

pixels
The dots from which images on a monitor screen are constructed. The term stands for "picture element." In Web Studio, you can decide, in pixels, how tall and how wide Web pages are by opening the Web Site Properties dialog box.

post

To offer a Web page for viewing on the Internet. Also to send a message to a newsgroup on the Internet.

point

A unit for measuring the height of type. One point equals $\frac{1}{72}$ of an inch.

resolution

The fineness of detail by which images are seen on a monitor or printed page. For video displays, the number of pixels displayed vertically and horizontally.

search engine

A program that searches for keywords in Web pages on the Internet and reports where the Web pages are found.

selection handles

The squares that appear on the periphery of an object when it is selected. By dragging a selection handle, you can change an object's size or shape. *See also* object.

Shift+click

To hold down the Shift key as you click to select items. By Shift+clicking, you can select several items at once.

shortcut menu

See context menu.

template

A special kind of file that is used as the basis for creating other files. You can create Web pages with templates in Web Studio and thereby save yourself the trouble of formatting the pages yourself.

upload

To send Web pages across the Internet to an Internet Service Provider so that the Web pages can be displayed on the Internet.

URL (uniform resource locator)

A site address on the Internet. Every Web page has its own URL.

WAV file

The file format under which the Windows operating system stores sounds.

Web browser

See browser.

Web Galleries

The tabs on the left side of the Web Studio screen from which you can select items for decorating a Web site. Click a Web Gallery tab to choose from backgrounds, sounds, dividers, clip art, and other items. Choose View ➢ Galleries to see the Web Galleries.

Web page

One page in a Web site. Usually, a Web site comprises several different pages. To get from page to page, you click hyperlinks. *See also* hyperlink.

Web Page window

In Web Studio, the window in which Web pages are constructed and laid out.

Web server

The computer at an ISP where Web pages are stored. When you visit a Web site on the Internet, you download it from a Web server.

Webmaster

The person responsible for maintaining a Web site. Usually, the Internet address of the Webmaster can be found on the home page of a Web site.

Index

Note to the Reader: Page numbers in **bold** indicate the principle discussion of a topic or the definition of a term. Page numbers in *italic* indicate illustrations.

A

+ (plus sign) in creating Web pages, 36, 44, 60
Add Anchor dialog box, *107*, 107
Add Contrast effect, 82, *122*, 122
Add Link dialog box, 98–99, *99*
Add Photo dialog box, *36*
Address bars, **212**, *212*, **230**
addresses, Internet. *See* URLs; Web site addresses
aligning objects, 27, **53-54**, *54*, **226–227**, *227*
alternate text messages, **113**, **119–120**, *120*, 154, **230**
anchors, **106–107**, *106–107*, **230**
Animation Gallery, 9, *132*, 132
animations, **132–133**, *132–133*, **230**
art. *See* graphics; images
Attached Files dialog box, *143*, 143, 144, *145*
audience, 22
AutoPlay feature, *199*, 199–200, 203

B

Back button, **214**, *214*
background sounds, **139**, *139*
backgrounds, **76–91**, *See also* Web pages
  adding special effects to, 80–85, *81–85*
  from Backgrounds Gallery, 9, 76–80, *77–80*
  borrowing from other Web pages, 86
  changing hues, *79*, 79, *81*, 81
  choosing, 76, 85
  design issues, *25*, 25
  importing graphics for, 85–87, *86*
  overview of, 76
  patterns as, 78–80, *79–80*
  from personal files, 85–87, *86*
  removing, *89*, 89
  scrolling, *88*, 88–89
  solid colors as, 76–78, *77–78*
  for text, coloring, 70, *71*
  text objects as, 87–88, *88*
  transparent objects and, 89–91, *90–91*
  warnings, 78, 85
  "Web Styles" as, *80*, 80
backup copies of Web sites, *18*, 18
backward-compatibility, **155**
bitmap (BMP) graphics, *See also* graphics
  defined, **156**, **230**
  printing Web pages as, 156–158, *158*
  saving Web pages as, *157*, 157
Blur effect, *84*, 84, *123*, 123
boldfacing text, 65
bookmarking Web sites, *See also* Internet Explorer
  defined, **215**, **230**
  deleting bookmarks, *219*, 219, 220
  Favorites and, *216–217*, 216–217
  Links folder and, *217*, 217
  moving bookmarks, 218–220, *219*
  renaming bookmarks, *219*, 219, 220
  and revisiting, *218*, 218
  steps in, *216*, 216
  warning, 216
browsers, *See also* Internet Explorer
  defined, **230**
  Netscape Navigator, 190
  previewing Web sites on, 20, 189–190, *190*
Building Site dialog box, *20*, 20
Buttons Gallery, 9, **125–126**, *125–126*

C

Calendar objects, **149**, *149*
clip art. *See* graphics; images
Clipart Gallery, 9, **114–115**, *115*
Clipboard, **62**, **230**
Clock objects, **150**, *150*
Color dialog box, *69*, 69, 77–78, *78*
Color Noise effect, *84*, 84, *123*, 123
color settings, monitor, 208
coloring text, *69*, 69
Colorize effect, *83*, 83, *123*, 123
consistency issues, 23
content, **41**, **230**
context menus, **223**, *223*, **230**
Contrast effect, 82, *83*, *122*, 122
converting text to graphics, *68*, 68
"Cool Sites of the Day", **195**
Cool Stuff Gallery, *See also* Web Galleries
  background scroll options, *88*, 88–89
  Calendar objects, *149*, 149
  Clock objects, *150*, 150
  Date objects, *150*, 150
  e-mail icons, 152–153, *153*
  HTML objects, 162, *164–165*, 164–165
  Last Modified Date objects, *151*, 151
  Link Wizard options, 104–105, *105*
  overview of, 9, *148*, 148
  Search Engine objects, 151–152, *152*
  Slide Show options, *140–143*, 140–143
  text scroll options, *74*, 74
  warning, 148
copying
  HTML tags, 164
  images from the Internet, *118–119*, 118–119
  Web page objects, 52–53, *226*, 226
copyright laws, images and, 118
Ctrl key, 46, 128, *226*, 226

D

Darken effect, *82*, 82, 121, 122
Date objects, **150**, *150*
deleting, *See also* removing
  bookmarks, *219*, 219, 220
  My Stuff Gallery items, 129, 228
  Web pages, *37*, 37
directory paths, 178
Display Properties dialog box, **191–192**, *192*
dither, **49**, **231**
dividers, **91–93**, *92–93*, **231**
Dividers Gallery, 9, **92**, *92*
domain names, **192–194**, *193*, **231**

download, **26**, **231**
download times, 26, 188

E

Edges effect, *82*, 82, *123*, 123
editing
with Redo command, 222–223, *223*
text, 63
with Undo command, *222*, 222
e-mail, promoting Web sites in, 195
e-mail icons, **152–153**, *153*
Emboss effect, *83*, 83, *124*, 124
Enhance Edges effect, *123*, 123
errors, fixing quickly, *222–223*, 222–223

F

Favorites, bookmarks and, **216–217**, *216–217*
first-line indents, **72**
Flip effect, 83, 122
fonts, **66**, **231**
Format toolbar, **6**, *6*, 65
formatting text, **65–70**, *67–70*
Forward button, **214**, *214*
ftp (file transfer protocol)
defined, **231**
programs, uploading Web sites to, 185
site addresses, **178**
sites, **231**

G

GIF images, 85, 140
graphics, *See also* images
as backgrounds, 85–87, *86*
bitmap graphics
defined, **156**, **230**
printing Web pages as, 156–158, *158*
saving Web pages as, *157*, 157
converting text to, *68*, 68
design issues, 26, 27
as hyperlinks, *101–102*, 101–103
placing text in front of, *70*, 70
Gray effect, 84, 123

H

Halftone effects, *85*, 85, *123*, 123
hanging indents, **72**
help, Web Studio
on Help program, *206–208*, 206–208
on the Internet, *209*, 209
on video, 208
on Web Publishing Message Board, *210*, 210
History button, **215**, *215*
home pages, **23**, 39, **231**
host directories, 178
HTML (Hypertext Markup Language)
choosing types of, 174–176, *175*
defined, **231**
overview of, 15
Preview window and, 20
tags, entering
from Cool Stuff Gallery, 162, *164–165*, 164–165
by copying/pasting, 164
by importing, 162–164, *163*, 165–166, *166*
onto objects, 162, 167–168, *168*
onto pages, 162, 166–167, *167*
overview of, 162
for tables, 165–166, *166*
by typing in manually, 162
warnings, 162, 168
viewing, 15
hue
of backgrounds, *79*, 79, *81*, 81
of objects, 45
of Web Gallery items, *10*, 10
Hue effect, *81*, 81, 122
hyperlinks, **95–109**, *See also* Links Gallery
defined, **95–96**, *96*, **231**
and deleting Web pages, 37
design issues, 24–25
finding on Web pages, 104
graphic hyperlinks, *101–102*, 101–103
from Links Gallery, 96–100, *97–100*
overview of, 100–101
reading Link Info, 104
removing, 108
testing, *189*, 189
text hyperlinks
coloring, 108–109, *109*
creating, 103–104, *104*
defined, **96**, *96*
within pages, 105–108, *106–107*
within Web sites, 104–105, *105*

I

icons, shortcut, for Web Studio, 202
images, **113–129**, *See also* graphics
alternate text messages for, 113, 119–120, *120*, 230
animations, *132–133*, 132–133, 230
buttons, *125–126*, 125–126
from Clipart Gallery, 114–115, *115*
copying from the Internet, *118–119*, 118–119
getting permission for, 118
GIF images, 85, 140
improving photos, *117*, 117
JPEG images, 85, 140
keeping favorites, 126–129, *127–129*, 227–228, *228*
overview of, 114
from personal files, 115–116, *116*
from Photos Gallery, 114–115, *115*
scanning, 116
slide shows
changing placeholder graphics, 144
overview of, 139–140
putting together, *140–143*, 140–143
revising, 144–145, *145*
warning, 142
special effects for, *121–124*, 121–124
turning into e-mail icons, *154*, 154
warning, 119
importing
graphics, 85–87, *86*
HTML tags, 162–164, *163*, 165–166, *166*
text, *61–62*, 61–62
indenting text, 72–73
installing
Internet Explorer 5, 203
Web Studio
AutoPlay and, *199*, 199–200

choosing destination folders, 201
creating shortcut icons, 202
overview of, 197
and registering, 201–202
requirements for, 198, *199*
selecting program folders, *201*, 201
selecting setup types, 200
and uninstalling, *204*, 204
viewing Read Me files, 202
warnings, 201, 203
Internet addresses. *See* URLs; Web site addresses
Internet Explorer 5
Address bar, *212*, 212, 230
bookmarking Web sites
defined, **215**
deleting bookmarks, *219*, 219, 220
Favorites and, *216–217*, 216–217
Links folder and, *217*, 217
moving bookmarks, 218–220, *219*
renaming bookmarks, *219*, 219, 220
and revisiting, *218*, 218
steps in, *216*, 216
warning, 216
defined, **211**
installing, 203
Preview window and, 20
revisiting Web sites
using Back button, *214*, 214
using bookmarks, 215–218, *216–218*
using Forward button, *214*, 214
using History button, *215*, 215
overview of, 214
using search engines, *213*, 213–214
visiting addresses you know, *212*, 212
InterNIC (Internet Network Information Center), **193**
Invert Color effect, *84*, 84, *123*, 123
ISPs (Internet Service Providers)
defined, **12**, **232**
finding, 12–13
questions to ask, 13–14
warning, 14
italicizing text, 65

J

JPEG images, 85, 140
justifying text, **71–72**, *71*, **232**

K

keywords, **174**, **232**

L

landscape pages, **159**, **232**
Large Mosaic effect, **85**, *85*, 124
Last Modified Date objects, **151**, *151*
laying out Web pages. *See* objects
Lighten effect, *82*, 82, 122
Link Wizard, **104–105**, *105*
Links folder, *216–217*, 216–217
Links Gallery, *See also* hyperlinks; Web Galleries
adding hyperlinks to, 98–99, *99*
copying hyperlinks, 99–100, *100*
creating
interpage links, 104
intrapage links, *106–107*, 106–108
object hyperlinks, *101*, 101
subfolders in, *98*, 98
text hyperlinks, *103*, 103–104
deleting hyperlinks from, *100*, 100
editing hyperlinks, *100*, 100
Links box, *97*, 97
My Links box, *97*, 97
overview of, 9, 96–97
rearranging hyperlinks, *100*, 100
Site Links box, *97*, 97, 104, *106–107*, 106–108
testing hyperlinks, 101–102
warning, 108

M

Main toolbar, **6**, *6*
margins, **41**, **232**
Medium Mosaic effect, **85**, *85*, 124
merging Web page objects, 51–52, *52*, *225*, 225–226
meta information, **172–174**, *173–174*, **232**
modems, **188**, **232**
monitor settings, changing, 39, 208
moving bookmarks, **218–220**, *219*
My Stuff Gallery, *See also* Web Galleries
adding items to, *127–128*, 127–128, 227–228, *228*
defined, **9**, **126–127**, *127*
deleting items from, 129, 228
rearranging items in, 129

N

names, domain, **192–194**, *193*, **231**
naming. *See* renaming
Netscape Navigator, **190**
Noise effect, *84*, 84, *123*, 123

O

Object Properties dialog box
Animated Graphic tab, *133*, 133
Attached Files tab, 144, *145*
Background Sound tab, *139*, 139
General tab, 47–48, *48*, *50*, 50
Graphic tab, *120*, 120
HTML Content tab, *163*, *165–166*, 165–166
Link tab, *102*, 102–103, *154*, 154
Object HTML tab, 162, 167–168, *168*
Page HTML tab, 162, 166–167, *167*
Sound tab, *138*, 138
Text tab, *68*, 68
objects on Web pages, **44–57**
aligning, 27, 53–54, *54*, 226–227, *227*
attaching HTML tags to, 162, 167–168, *168*
Calendar objects, *149*, 149
changing hue, 45
changing size/shape, 48–51, *49–51*
Clock objects, *150*, 150
copying, 52–53, *226*, 226
Date objects, *150*, 150
defined, **14**, **232**
e-mail icons, 152–153, *153*
finding, *44*, 44, *45*, 45
graphic, as hyperlinks, *101–102*, 101–103
HTML and, 15
HTML objects, 162, *164–165*, 164–165
Last Modified Date objects, *151*, 151
making same size, 50–51, *51*
merging, 51–52, *52*, *225*, 225–226

overlapping, *55–56*, 55–57
overview of, 14, *15*
placing, *44*, 44
positioning, 47–48, *48*
preventing resizing, *50*, 50
removing, 45
Search Engine objects, 151–152, *152*
selecting, 46, *224*, 224
spacing, 53, **54–55**, *55*, *227*, 227
text, as backgrounds, 87–88, *88*
transparent objects, 89–91, *90–91*
warnings, 46, 51
Oilpaint effect, *81*, 81, *124*, 124
Open dialog box, *62*, 62, 115–116, *116*, *127*, 127
Open Page Template dialog box, 32–33, *33*
Orientation print options, *159*, 159
overlapped objects, **55–57**, *55–56*

P

Page List
defined, *6*, **7**, **232**
sizing, 8, *9*
Page Preview window. *See* Preview window
Page Wizard, *36*, 36
Paint by Numbers effect, *81*, 81, *124*, 124
Paint program, printing Web pages in, **156–158**, *158*
paragraph indents, **73**
passwords, 178
pasting
HTML tags, 164
text, 62
Pattern effect, *82*, 82, *124*, 124
patterns, background, 78–80, *79–80*
permission for using images, 118
Photo Correct Wizard, **117**, *117*
photos. *See* images
Photos Gallery, 9, **114–115**, *115*
pixels, **39**, **232**
plus sign (+) in creating Web pages, 36, 44, 60
points, **67**, **233**
portrait pages, **159**
positioning Web page objects, 47–48, *48*
Posterize effect, **84**, *84*, *124*, 124
posting Web sites. *See* uploading
Preview window
minimizing, 22, *42*, 42
opening, 42
switching between Web Page and, 21
testing Web sites in, 18–21, *19–21*, 42
printing Web pages, *See also* Web pages
overview of, 156
in Paint program, 156–158, *157–158*
in Web Studio, 158–160, *159–160*
Properties dialog box, **198**, *199*
publishing Web sites. *See* uploading

R

Redo command, **222–223**, *223*
registering
domain names, **192–194**, *193*
Web Studio, 201–202
registrars, **193**
removing, *See also* deleting
backgrounds, *89*, 89
objects, 45
sounds, 139
renaming
bookmarks, *219*, 219, 220
Web pages, 37–38, *38*
resolution, **190**, **233**
Restore button, *42*, 42
Reverse effect, 83, 122
Rotate effect, *83*, 83, 122

S

saving, *See also* My Stuff Gallery
images on Internet, *119*, 119
Undo command and, 16, *222*, 222
Web pages as BMP graphics, *157*, 157
Web sites
backup copies of, *18*, 18
commands for, 16
under new names, 17, 18
warning, 16
in Web Studio, 16–17, *17*
scanning images, 116
Screen Area monitor settings, 39, 208
scrolling
backgrounds, *88*, 88–89
text, 73–74, *74*
search engines
adding to Web sites, 151–152, *152*
defined, **233**
helping to find Web sites, 172–174, *173–174*
submitting Web sites to, 194
selecting objects, 46, *224*, 224
selection handles, **46**, **63**, **233**
servers, Web, **12**, **234**
Shadow effect, *81*, 81, *123*, 123
Sharpen effect, *84*, 84, *122*, 122
Shift key, 46, 128
Shift-click, **47**, **233**
shortcut icons, Web Studio, 202
Signs Gallery, 9, *93*, 93–94
sizing
margins, 41
objects, 48–51, *49–51*
objects, preventing, *50*, 50
Web Galleries, 8, *9*
Web pages, 39–40, *40*
slide shows
changing placeholder graphics, 144
overview of, 139–140
putting together, *140–143*, 140–143
revising, 144–145, *145*
warning, 142
Small Mosaic effect, *85*, 85, 124
Solarize effect, *84*, 84, *124*, 124
sound
animation and, 135
choosing play frequency, *137*, 137–138
overview of, 134
from personal files, 136–137, *137*
removing, 139
from Sounds Gallery, 10, 134–135, *135*
turning on and off, *136*, 136
warnings, 134, 135
spacing objects, 53, **54–55**, *55*, *227*, 227
Special FX Gallery, *See also* Web Galleries
overview of, 10, 27
tweaking backgrounds with, 80–85, *81–85*
tweaking images with, *121–124*, 121–124

speed techniques, *See also* Web Studio
- aligning objects, 226–227, *227*
- copying objects, 52–53, *226*, 226
- fixing errors, *222–223*, 222–223
- merging objects, 51–52, *52*, *225*, 225–226
- using My Stuff Gallery, 227–228, *228*
- selecting objects, 46, *224*, 224
- spacing objects, 53, **54–55**, *55*, *227*, 227

spell-checking text, **63–65**
status bar, *6*, **7**, *35*, 35, 96
storing favorite images. *See* My Stuff Gallery
subfolders
- in Links Gallery, *98*, 98
- in Web Galleries, *10*, 10

T

tables, HTML tags for, 165–166, *166*
templates
- creating Web pages from, *32–33*, 32–33, *35–36*, 35–36
- defined, **10**, **32**, **233**
- pros and cons of, 33

Templates Gallery, *35–36*, 35–36
testing Web sites
- download times, 188
- hyperlinks, *189*, 189
- on multiple browsers, 189–190, *190*
- in Preview window, 18–21, *19–21*, 42

text, **60–74**
- alternate text messages, **113**, **119–120**, *120*, 154, **230**
- as background objects, 87–88, *88*
- boldfacing, 65
- choosing background colors for, 70, *71*
- choosing font style/size, 66–68, *67–68*
- coloring, *69*, 69
- converting to graphics, *68*, 68
- design issues, 26
- dragging from Text Gallery, 10, *60*, 60–61
- editing, 63
- formatting, 65–70, *67–70*
- importing from personal files, *61–62*, 61–62
- indenting, 72–73
- italicizing, 65
- justifying, *71*, 71–72, 232
- overview of, 60
- pasting via Clipboard, 62
- placing in front of graphics, *70*, 70
- scrolling, 73–74, *74*
- spell-checking, 63–65
- text hyperlinks
  - coloring, 108–109, *109*
  - creating, 103–104, *104*
  - defined, **96**, *96*
- underlining, 65–66

Text Format toolbar, **6**, *6*, 65
Tip of the Day feature, 4, **5**, *5*
toolbars
- defined, **6**, *6*
- Main toolbar, **6**, *6*
- moving, 8
- Text Format toolbar, **6**, *6*, 65
- Web toolbar buttons, **20–21**, *21*

transparent objects, **89–91**, *90–91*

U

underlining text, 65–66
Undo command, 16, **222**, *222*
Undo Object Merge command, 225
uploading Web sites
- to company networks, 186
- to ISPs
  - for first time, *179–182*, 179–182
  - if upload fails, 182–184, *183*
  - information needed for, 178
  - via other ftp programs, 185
  - on successive times, *184*, 184–185
  - via Web Publishing Wizard, *185*, 185
  - via Web Studio, *179–184*, 179–185
- upload, defined, **13**, **233**

URLs (uniform resource locators), *See also* Web site addresses
- defined, **96**, *96*, **233**
- entering, 99, 103

usernames, **178**

V

video help, Web Studio, **208**
View menu, **8**, *8*
viewing
- object hyperlinks, 37, 104, 108
- objects attached to sounds, 138
- overlapped objects, 57
- text converted to graphics, 68
- Web Gallery items, 10

W

WAV files, **135**, 136, **233**
Web browsers. *See* browsers
Web Galleries, *See also individual galleries*
- changing object hue, *10*, 10, *45*, 45
- defined, *6*, **7**, **9–10**, **233**
- finding objects in, *44–45*, 44–45
- opening subfolders in, *10*, 10, *45*, 45
- sizing, 8, *9*
- viewing items in, 10, 45

Web menu/toolbar buttons, **20–21**, *21*
Web Page window
- defined, *6*, **7**, **234**
- minimizing, 22, *42*, 42
- opening, 41
- switching between Preview and, 21

Web pages
- adding animations, *132–133*, 132–133, 230
- adding Cool Stuff objects
  - Calendars, *149*, 149
  - Clocks, *150*, 150
  - Dates, *150*, 150
  - e-mail icons, 152–153, *153*
  - Last Modified Dates, *151*, 151
  - overview of, *148*, 148
  - Search Engines, 151–152, *152*
  - warning, 148
- adding dividers, 91–93, *92–93*
- adding signs, *93*, 93–94
- adding slide shows
  - changing placeholder graphics, 144
  - overview of, 139–140
  - putting together, *140–143*, 140–143

and revising, 144–145, *145*
warning, 142
adding sound
animation and, 135
choosing play frequency, *137*, 137–138
overview of, 134
from personal files, 136–137, *137*
and removing, 139
from Sounds Gallery, 134–135, *135*
turning on and off, *136*, 136
warnings, 134, 135
backgrounds, **76–91**
from Backgrounds Gallery, 9, 76–80, *77–80*
borrowing from other Web pages, 86
changing hues, *79*, 79, *81*, 81
choosing, 76
design issues, *25*, 25
imported graphics as, 85–87, *86*
overview of, 76
patterns as, 78–80, *79–80*
from personal files, 85–87, *86*
removing, *89*, 89
scrolling, *88*, 88–89
solid colors as, 76–78, *77–78*
special effects for, 80–85, *81–85*
for text, coloring, 70, *71*
text objects as, 87–88, *88*
transparent objects and, 89–91, *90–91*
warnings, 78, 85
"Web Styles" as, *80*, 80
choosing home pages, 39
choosing HTML code, 174–176, *175*
constructing from objects, **44–57**
aligning, 27, 53–54, *54*, 226–227, *227*
changing hue, 45
changing size/shape, 48–51, *49–51*
copying, 52–53, *226*, 226
defined, **14**
finding, *44*, 44, *45*, 45
HTML and, 15
making same size, 50–51, *51*
merging, 51–52, *52*, *225*, 225–226
overlapping, *55–56*, 55–57
overview of, 14, *15*
placing, *44*, 44
positioning, 47–48, *48*
preventing resizing, *50*, 50
removing, 45
selecting, 46, *224*, 224
spacing, 53, **54–55**, *55*, *227*, 227
warnings, 46, 51
creating blank pages, 34–35, *35*
creating from templates, *32–33*, 32–33, *35–36*, 35–36
defined, **6**, **233**
deleting, *37*, 37
entering HTML tags
from Cool Stuff Gallery, 162, *164*, 164–165
by copying/pasting, 164
by importing, 162–164, *163*, 165–166, *166*
onto objects, 162, 167–168, *168*
onto pages, 162, 166–167, *167*
overview of, 162
for tables, 165–166, *166*
by typing in manually, 162
warnings, 162, 168
handling windows in, 41–42, *42*
home pages, **23**, 39, **231**
hyperlinks, **95–109**
defined, **95–96**, *96*, **231**
and deleting Web pages, 37
design issues, 24–25
finding on pages, 104
graphic objects as, *101–102*, 101–103
from Links Gallery, 96–100, *97–100*
overview of, 100–101
reading Link Info, 104
removing, 108
testing, *189*, 189
text, creating, 103–104, *104*
text , coloring, 108–109, *109*
text , defined, **96**, *96*
within pages, 105–108, *106–107*
within Web sites, 104–105, *105*
images, **113–129**
alternate text messages for, 113, 119–120, *120*, 230
buttons, *125–126*, 125–126
from Clipart Gallery, 114–115, *115*
converting text to, *68*, 68
copying from the Internet, *118–119*, 118–119
design issues, 26, 27
getting permission for, 118
GIF images, 85, 140
improving photos, *117*, 117
JPEG images, 85, 140
keeping favorites, 126–129, *127–129*, 227–228, *228*
overview of, 114
from personal files, 115–116, *116*
from Photos Gallery, 114–115, *115*
scanning, 116
special effects for, *121–124*, 121–124
warning, 119
printing
overview of, 156
in Paint program, 156–158, *157–158*
in Web Studio, 158–160, *159–160*
renaming, 37–38, *38*
resizing, 39–40, *40*
resizing margins, 41
saving as bitmap graphics, *157*, 157
text, **60–74**
as background objects, 87–88, *88*
boldfacing, 65
choosing background colors, 70, *71*
choosing font style/size, 66–68, *67–68*
coloring, *69*, 69
converting to graphics, *68*, 68
design issues, 26
dragging from Text Gallery, *60*, 60–61
editing, 63
formatting, 65–70, *67–70*
importing, *61–62*, 61–62
indenting, 72–73
italicizing, 65
justifying, *71*, 71–72, 232
overview of, 60
pasting via Clipboard, 62
placing in front of graphics, *70*, 70
scrolling, 73–74, *74*
spell-checking, 63–65
underlining, 65–66
viewing at different resolutions, 190–192, *191–192*

Web Publishing Message Board, **210**, *210*
Web Publishing Wizard, **185**, *185*
Web servers, **12**, **234**
Web site addresses, *See also* URLs
  Address bars and, *212*, 212, 230
  "Cool Sites of the Day", 195
  Download.com, 185
  of ftp sites, 178, 231
  InterNIC, 193
  Netscape Navigator, 190
  of search engines, 194, 214
  Sierra, 13, 179, *209–210*, 209–210
  visiting ones you know, *212*, 212
  Web Studio, *209*, 209
  of Web-hosting services, 13
  Yahoo, 194, 195
Web Site Properties dialog box
  Advanced tab, *175*, 175–176
  General tab, *109*, 109
  Web Search Information tab, 172–174, *173–174*
Web sites
  adding Web pages to, 34–36, *35–36*
  creating from scratch, *32*, 32
  creating from templates, *32–33*, 32–33
  deleting Web pages from, *37*, 37
  finding via search engines, *213*, 213–214
  helping search engines find, 172–174, *173–174*
  opening, *34*, 34
  previewing, 18–22, *19–21*, 42
  promoting, 194–195
  registering domain names for, 192–194, *193*
  revisiting
    using Back button, *214*, 214
    using bookmarks, 215–218, *216–218*
    using Forward button, *214*, 214
    using History button, *215*, 215
    overview of, 214
  saving
    backup copies of, *18*, 18
    commands for, 16
    under new names, 17, 18
    warning, 16
    in Web Studio, 16–17, *17*
  selecting ISP hosts for, 12–14
  ten design tips
    audience, 22
    consistency, 23
    download time, 26
    graphics, 26, 27
    home pages, 23
    hyperlinks, 24–25
    object alignment, 27
    page backgrounds, *25*, 25
    text, 26
    topical divisions, 23–24
  testing
    download times, 188
    hyperlinks, *189*, 189
    on multiple browsers, 189–190, *190*
    in Preview window, 18–21, *19–21*, 42
  uploading to company networks, 186
  uploading to ISPs
    for first time, *179–182*, 179–182
    if upload fails, 182–184, *183*
    information needed for, 178
    via other ftp programs, 185
    on successive times, *184*, 184–185
    via Web Publishing Wizard, *185*, 185
    via Web Studio, *179–184*, 179–185
Web Studio, **3–10**
  context menus, *223*, 223, 230
  help
    Help program, *206–208*, 206–208
    on the Internet, *209*, 209
    video, 208
    Web Publishing Message Board, *210*, 210
  HTML and, 15
  installing
    AutoPlay and, *199*, 199–200
    choosing destination folders, 201
    creating shortcut icons, 202
    overview of, 197
    and registering, 201–202
    requirements for, 198, *199*
    selecting program folders, *201*, 201
    selecting setup types, 200
    viewing Read Me files, 202
    warnings, 201, 203
  Publisher, *179–184*, 179–185, *193*, 193–194
  Redo command, 222–223, *223*
  speed techniques
    aligning objects, 226–227, *227*
    copying objects, 52–53, *226*, 226
    fixing errors, *222–223*, 222–223
    merging objects, 51–52, *52*, *225*, 225–226
    using My Stuff Gallery, 227–228, *228*
    selecting objects, 46, *224*, 224
    spacing objects, 53, **54–55**, *55*, *227*, 227
  starting, *4*, 4
  Tip of the Day feature, 4, *5*, 5
  Undo command, *222*, 222
  uninstalling, *204*, 204
  Web Galleries
    changing object hue, *10*, 10, *45*, 45
    defined, *6*, **7**, **9–10**, **233**
    finding objects in, *44–45*, 44–45
    opening subfolders in, *10*, 10, *45*, 45
    sizing, 8, *9*
    viewing items in, 10, 45
  Web page creation screen
    changing, 7–9, *8–9*
    opening, *5–6*, 5–6
    Page List, *6*, **7**, **232**
    status bar, *6*, **7**, *35*, 35, 96
    toolbars, *6*, 6
    Web Galleries, *6*, 7
    Web Page window, *6*, 7
  windows
    arranging, 21
    enlarging, 22, 42
    minimizing, 22, *42*, 42
    opening, 41–42
    Preview window, *19–21*, 19–21
    switching between, 21
    Web Page window, *6*, 7
Web toolbar buttons, **20–21**, *21*
Webmasters, **25**, **152**, **234**
Windows Explorer, bookmarks and, 220
word processors, importing text from, **61–62**, *61–62*
World Wide Web addresses, **178**, *See also* URLs; Web site addresses